THE ORGANIZATION FAMILY

The Organization Family

WORK AND FAMILY LINKAGES IN THE U.S. MILITARY

Edited by

Gary L. Bowen

and

Dennis K. Orthner

New York
Westport, Connecticut
London

Library of Congress Cataloging-in-Publication Data

The Organization family.

Bibliography: p.
Includes index.
1. Soldiers—United States—Family relationships.
2. Family—United States.   3. Military dependents—
United States.   4. Sociology, Military—United States.
I. Bowen, Gary L.   II. Orthner, Dennis K.
UB403.074   1989   355.1′2   88–32440
ISBN 0–275–92813–6 (alk. paper)

Library of Congress Catalog Card Number: 88–32440
ISBN: 0–275–92813–6

First published in 1989

Praeger Publishers, One Madison Avenue, New York, NY 10010
A division of Greenwood Press, Inc.

Printed in the United States of America

∞

The paper used in this book complies with the
Permanent Paper Standard issued by the National
Information Standards Organization (Z39.48–1984).

10 9 8 7 6 5 4 3 2 1

Contents

Acknowledgments   vii

Introduction   ix

Part I. Work and Family Linkages

1 The Nature of Work and Family Linkages:
   A Theoretical Perspective

   Mady Wechsler Segal   3

2 Family Factors and Member Retention:
   A Key Relationship in the Work and Family Equation

   Gary L. Bowen   37

3 Marital Quality and Job Satisfaction of Male Air Force
   Personnel: A Test of the Spillover Hypothesis

   Peter A. Neenan   59

Part II. Special Population Groups

4 Single Parents in the Workplace:
   Conserving and Increasing Human Capital

   David W. Wright   79

5 The Dual-Career Couple: Challenges and Satisfactions

   Barbara J. Janofsky   97

6 Growing Up in an Organization Family

   *Dennis K. Orthner, Martha M. Giddings,
   and William H. Quinn*   117

Part III.   The Organizational Response

7 Toward Conceptual Refinement of Operational Outcome
   Variables: The Case of Family Life Satisfaction

   Gary L. Bowen   143

8 The "Company Town" in Transition:
   Rebuilding Military Communities

   James A. Martin and Dennis K. Orthner   163

Postscript: Toward Further Research   179

General References   189

Index   193

About the Editors and Contributors   201

Acknowledgments

It has been our good fortune to have had professional associations and personal friendships with the authors of chapters in this volume. We appreciate their responsiveness to our publication schedule and to our reviews of earlier drafts of their chapters. Most importantly, we appreciate their professional insights into work and family dynamics. Our own understanding of the complexity of the work-and-family interface has been greatly expanded and enriched by our discussions with each author.

Special appreciation is expressed to our editor, Alison Bricken, who has been like a beacon on a stormy sea, providing needed encouragement, support, and patience in completing the volume. In addition, we would like to thank Dr. John B. Turner, Dean, School of Social Work, The University of North Carolina at Chapel Hill, for his continued support of our research and scholarship endeavors. A special word of appreciation also goes to our "godparents," Dr. Richard Carr, who retired as a Major General and Chief of Chaplains for the U.S. Air Force, and Dr. Ann O'Keefe, who is presently serving as Senior Policy Advisor to the Deputy Assistant Secretary of the Navy for Force Support and Families. Drs. Carr and O'Keefe inspired and sponsored our first studies of work and family life in the military community, and we continue to be both professionally and personally enriched by our relationship with them. Their continued commitment and professionalism in support of servicemembers and their families underscore the positive impact that concerned and dedicated individuals can make in the work and family lives of others.

Last, but not least, we are particularly indebted to the military families all over the world who have given generously of their time and graciously invited us into their homes and lives so that we could better understand the military culture and its influence on families. To them, and for their contribution to peace and to the defense of this nation, this book is dedicated.

Finally, we would like to thank our spouses, Donna and Barbara, who help us understand firsthand the importance of spouse support in successfully balancing work and family demands, and to our children, Christopher, Natalie, Jason, Melissa, and Kristen, who make us humble and appreciate the most important things in our lives: our families.

Introduction

In 1956 William Whyte published *The Organization Man*, which described the absorption of men into work life. Behind this absorption was the assumption of a "social" or "bureaucratic" ethic, an ethic that reified the organization, which stressed belonging as the ultimate need of the individual, and which denied potential conflict between the goals of the organization and those of the individual.

Although Whyte did not promote unrestrained self-interest, he described this "social" ethic as static, delusory, and ill-suited to the needs of modern man. He asserted that the emphasis on group at the expense of the individual and the denial of potential conflict between the organization and the individual was detrimental not only to the individual, but also to the organization. Whyte saw conflict between the organization and the individual as inevitable and normal, requiring continuous realignment on the part of both the organization and the individual, not just the individual alone.

Dramatic changes have occurred in American society since the publication of Whyte's seminal work in the mid-1950s: a substantial growth in the labor force participation of married women, especially among mothers of preschool children (16, 37); a significant increase in the number of employed women in more prestigious, higher-paying occupations (30); the emergence of dual-career couples, for whom the careers of both the husband and wife are important (35); a decline in the share of households headed by married couples and the increase in the number of families headed by a single man or woman (14, 23); a convergence on new, more egalitarian gender-role preferences among men and women (6, 24, 33); and the emergence of the "new breed" worker, who is particularly likely to question the cost of success in the workplace, especially when success compromises opportunities for a quality family life (2, 25, 29, 36, 40).

Paralleling these demographic and value shifts, employers have become increasingly interested in developing personnel policies and support programs that enable people to hold jobs and still maintain a viable family life (7, 10, 19, 29, 38). These developments parallel the growing recognition by employers of the interdependence among organizational policies and practices, personal and family well-being, employee recruitment and retention, and job satisfaction and productivity (7, 13, 18, 19, 22, 27). It is clear that work organizations have seen the benefit, heralded by William Whyte, of adjusting the organization to improve the level of fit between organizational needs and personal needs.

The expanding and dynamic interaction between work and family roles for both men and women and the increasing recognition by employing organizations of this interaction make it necessary to extend Whyte's treatise by broadening our perspective from the "organization man" to a consideration of the "organization family." From this perspective, work and family roles are seen as interdependent, and their performance is considered potentially highly salient for both men and women in families. In addition, as men and women attempt to balance work and family demands, strain is seen as inevitable because of limited individual time and energy. Continuous adjustments will be required from the individual, the family system, and the employing organization if the individual is to successfully perform in work and family roles. Assuming a spillover perspective, it is assumed that where there exists stress or conflict at the work–family nexus, an obstacle is presented to fulfilling responsibilities in either or both systems.

While the concept of the organization family is a new one in the literature, it is an old one as a way of life. Large employers, whether private or public, have tended to dominate the personal and family lives of their employees, particularly in the nineteenth and early twentieth centuries (9). These work organizations traditionally felt that by supporting the worker and his family, loyalty to the company could be ensured. History is replete with examples of organizational and family linkages that were forged around company towns and supports such as stores, housing, parks, and doctors (19).

Attempts by work organizations to support employees' families have not always been positively received. Many families balked at the controlled life style in company towns. Employers often used their influence over the family pocketbook to force women and children to take menial jobs at low wages. The threat to reduce benefits from families was sometimes used by employers to coerce workers into complying with unreasonable demands. Some employers even took the step of paying workers more if they were married and parents, thus influencing the marriage and fertility rates of their employees and enlarging their influence over the employee through the family.

Organization families today come in a variety of forms. For example, they may be represented by the family of the corporate executive or the blue-collar worker. The families may live in a small mill town or the suburb of a large city. They may also be members of the military services living any-where in the world. These families, whatever their status, are tied to an employing organization through the benefits they receive and the common organizational culture to which they subscribe. They may or may not live in company-dominated towns, but they share in the ups and downs of the work organization, derive much of their family security from it, and are expected to support the organization and its member or members who are also part of their family.

Although Whyte (39) recognized and discussed the auxiliary functions provided by the wife and family of the organization man (e.g., entertaining colleagues and clients, maintaining community relations, doing occasional secretarial work for the husband, and providing psychological nurturing), he viewed work and family roles as separate worlds, with men occupying the work role, and women responsible for the family. The Parsonian discussion of a split between instrumental (male) and expressive (female) roles (28), reinforced by later research differentiating task leadership from socio-emotional leadership (3), undergirded this traditionally dichotomous world view. With the world seen as divided into working, instrumental males and home-making, socio-emotional females, there was little impetus to study the inter-dependence between spheres (20, 26).

Recently the needs of the organization family have become of greater concern, to both work organizations and policy makers. Work organizations are finding that the traditional spouse and family roles that Whyte observed can no longer be assumed today. Spouses and children cannot be counted on to relocate wherever the company wants at a moment's notice. Employees are reporting more family resistance to company moves, irrespective of the proposed benefits (38). Many families no longer like to consider themselves "dependents" of the organization, as if they wait at the beck and call of the worker and the company.

Policy makers are also increasingly aware of the changes in the organization family. High divorce rates have forced major changes in how company and government pensions and benefits are distributed. Organizational issues such as parental leaves, flexible work schedules, child care, and health benefits are now considered open to the national debate and too important to be left to the idiosyncrasies of organizational practices. In addition, an increasing number of organizations are finding that they are indeed spawning "organization families" as people marry within the company, leaving the company with new challenges for promotions, co-relocations, shared benefits, and potentially conflicting work demands.

The organization man of William Whyte's day is just as likely today to be an organization woman. As mentioned above, nearly one-half of the labor force is now female and the majority of women who have children at home are now employed. Their work organizations are often just as important and dominating in their lives as those of men. As women increasingly make the transition from jobs to careers, we can expect work organizations to become much more competitive for the allegiance of families.

Usually, we hypothesize, one organization or another is likely to have a controlling influence in a family, but this may not always be the case. A dominating organization probably offers the greatest financial and support benefits to the family and through this influence has greater control over the life style of the family. Dominant organizations are likely to be large, are often located in smaller communities, and may require unusually great ob-ligations from their members. Military service is an obvious example of such an organization, but there are also corporations that influence their employ-ees and members of the employee's family in much the same way.

It should be noted that not all families are "organization families" as the authors define the concept. Men and women can work within organizations that have little influence over their non-work time or relationships. The ma-jority of work organizations in the United States are small businesses that provide few benefits to their employees and expect little in the way of family commitments beyond minimal support to the worker. What makes this type of organization–family interface special is the somewhat unique ties among the organization, the employed member, and the family. In this case, the alliance of the organization and the family represents a fragile bond built upon mutual support and a common ally, the working member.

This volume extends Whyte's concept of the "organization man" to focus on the "organization family" in the U.S. military. Based on the most recent and significant literature and research on work and family dynamics in the military services today, the volume includes eight chapters that examine three major aspects of work and family: (a) the nature and dynamics of the work–family interface; (b) variations in the work–family linkages across special population groups; and (c) organizational issues and challenges in respond-ing to family-level issues in the workplace. Its aim is threefold: (a) to ad-vance our understanding of the interacting worlds of work and family in the U.S. military; (b) to provide a comparative perspective between military and civilian employers and occupations; and (c) to present implications at the policy, program, and practice levels for military leadership and family life professionals who are interested in fostering a more productive partnership between the military organization and the military family in meeting their respective needs and demands. To accomplish these objectives as well as to provide continuity throughout the book, authors were asked to provide a theoretical and/or historical perspective to their topic area, to draw relevant comparisons between the military and the civilian employment sectors, and to assume an applied orientation in developing their chapters.

As the first volume to focus exclusively on work and family linkages in the military setting, it should be well suited to both undergraduate and graduate seminars in military and family sociology, contemporary family patterns and issues, and public policy and service. It should also be particularly informative to military and civilian human service administrators and practitioners who are interested in developing a coherent set of policies, practices, and programs that enhance the ability of their respective employees to successfully respond to organizational and family demands.

THE MILITARY CONTEXT

The military community provides a unique opportunity to study the interrelationships between the work and family systems. Once the bastion of single men, the majority of military members today have family responsibilities (1). Similar to their civilian counterparts, contemporary trends in marriage, divorce, single parenthood, dual-career patterns, and voluntary childlessness are all reflected in military families today (4, 11). In addition, these families also experience many of the same pressures as other American families, such as inadequate finances, contrasting husband and wife values, changing definitions of marital roles, new definitions of parental responsibilities, and lack of viable social support systems (5, 34).

Although there are perhaps more similarities than differences between military and civilian families, the military community provides an unparalleled opportunity to study work–family interdependency because of the absorption of the family system into the work life of the military member. Service in the armed forces involves more than an occupational choice; it is the selection of a life style that permeates almost every aspect of a person's life. Few civilian occupations require the high level of commitment and dedication from their employees that the military services require. Even fewer ask their employees, much less members of the employees' families, to make such a range of personal and family sacrifices to accommodate the work mission, including long work hours, high-stress assignments, required relocations, frequent family separations and reunions, remote tours of service, long-term separations from extended family and friends, residence in foreign countries, and frequent subservience of family needs to mission responsibilities (8, 17).

On the other hand, few civilian employers offer their employees the encompassing range of benefits that tie their employees as well as members of their families to the organization both economically and socially (e.g., job security, housing and housing allowances, medical and dental care, and retirement after 20 years of service). In addition, the military services today include a number of agencies and organizations that provide an impressive range of support services and programs for military members and their families (e.g., family service, and support centers, recreational, child care, and spouse employment centers.

Similar to Whyte's (39) description of the "social" or "bureaucratic" ethic, military service is billed as a "calling," where the needs of the organization are given precedence over the needs of the individual member and family. However, what distinguishes military families from their civilian counterparts is not necessarily the nature of demands they face in an occupationally centered, regimented, and hierarchical organization, but rather the number and pattern of these challenges (31, 32). There may be no other group that confronts so many demands simultaneously, and which must constantly realign work and family roles and responsibilities. In a recent analysis Segal (34) used Coser's (12) notion of the "greedy" institution to describe the great demands that the military organization places on the commitment, time, and energy of its servicemembers and their families.

In many ways the military functions as an extended family for servicemembers and their families (31). By joining this extended family, service personnel give the military considerable authority over their lives and those of their families (31). Informally, the entire family belongs to the military, and the status and privileges of the family depend on the rank and status of the member (21, 32). In return, the military offers job security, rank and status, and benefits that pervade almost every phase of life. Goffman (15) used the term "total institutions" to describe organizations that have such an encompassing influence on the lives of its members.

It is apparent that there is more reciprocity between the worlds of work and the family than has been reported in the literature to date (25). Neither the family nor work is a closed system. Changes in one impact upon the other, and it can be argued that both the work and family institutions are undergoing modifications as each attempts to accommodate to changing trends and dynamics in the other. Given this situation, there is a need to focus on the give and take between the work organization and the family as each attempts to meet its respective goals and objectives. While not unique, the military environment does provide an important context in which to extricate the nature of work and family interrelationships, and thus to critically explore the concept of the "organization family."

ORGANIZATION AND OVERVIEW

The editors of this volume have been actively involved in research on work–family linkages since the mid-1970s, especially the investigation of these linkages in the military services. Because of its unique combination of occupational demands and occupational supports, the military community has provided a provocative milieu to study the interface between work and family systems, and the influence of this interface on the individual, the family system, and the military organization. Like their civilian counterparts, the military services have struggled to adequately conceptualize the nature of the work–family interface. As a consequence the development of policies and programs in support of families has tended to lack a consistent rationale, often failing to account for structural variations in families as well as possible variations in their needs, values, and demands.

These concerns have provided the impetus for this volume. The editors envisioned a work that would provide military and civilian leaders, researchers, and practitioners with an overarching theoretical and empirical base for guiding the development of policies, programs, and practices that promote the ability of servicemembers and their families to successfully respond to the combination of organization and family demands. To accomplish this objective, a book outline was prepared and experts across varied academic disciplines were contacted by the editors to prepare the chapters.

The first three chapters each consider the nature of work and family linkages, ranging from a broad historical and theoretical perspective to an empirical examination of the spillover hypothesis between work and family life satisfaction. In Chapter 1 Mady Segal presents a historical and theoretical foundation for the volume, discussing four levels of analysis for studying the linkages between work and family in the U.S. military: (a) institutional or cultural, (b) organizational or structural, (c) interpersonal, and (d) individual. Using these four levels of analysis as an overarching framework, Segal describes salient characteristics of the military life style that may lead to spillover between work and family demands.

In Chapter 2 Gary Bowen develops an inductively derived theoretical model to identify how and under what conditions family factors have been found to impact upon the retention decision-making process of military members. Despite the conceptual and methodological issues that seriously restrict efforts at theoretical integration at this time, the model developed by Bowen should have heuristic implications for continued research in this important area of policy and program research.

Although it is increasingly assumed that satisfaction with family life has positive implications for satisfaction with work life, Peter Neenan, in Chapter 3, finds limited empirical support for the work–family spillover hypothesis. Based on a probability sample of male Air Force members married to civilian spouses, Neenan found that indicators of marital quality failed to contribute to the job satisfaction of respondents after control variables were entered into the regression equation. However, he did find a strong and positive effect on the level of reported job satisfaction from two work-related variables: (a) intrinsic job satisfaction and (b) satisfaction with management policy.

Whereas the first three chapters discuss the integration of work and family life from a general perspective, the second three chapters focus on the nature of work–family linkages for three specified population groups: (a) single parents, (b) dual-career couples, and (c) the children of military members. In Chapter 4 David Wright discusses a non-traditional family form that has become increasingly common in the military service: the single-parent family. From his review of the literature Wright concludes that single parents are quite capable individuals who can be exceptional, highly motivated employees in organizations that are sensitive to their special needs.

Barbara Janofsky, in Chapter 5, focuses on the challenges and satisfactions experienced by dual-career couples in the U.S. military, and how these factors affect their level of satisfaction with the military life style. Based on a probability sample of 151 dual-career couples in the U.S. Air Force, Janofsky notes variation in the factors that are predictive of the level of satisfaction that husbands and wives report with Air Force life. Whereas the level of satisfaction for husbands is determined more by external Air Force–related factors, the level of satisfaction for wives is affected more by marital and family considerations.

In Chapter 6 Dennis Orthner, Martha Giddings, and William Quinn examine the lives of children who are growing up in military organization families. They propose that the developmental needs of children are inextricably tied to organizational demands and that military life places unusual pressure on children. Their research points out that moving is a major stressor on these children and that girls, in particular, find that military life takes its toll on their self-worth.

The last two chapters focus on particular issues and challenges faced by the military services in the development and implementation of family and community-level supports for servicemembers and their families. In Chapter 7 Gary Bowen discusses the difficulty that the military services have had in conceptualizing the family-related outcomes to which their policy and program actions are directed, presenting the concept of "family life satisfaction" as a case in point. Anchored in social exchange theory and the empirical literature, Bowen proposes a value-based approach for defining and conceptualizing family life satisfaction. Implications of the approach are discussed from the perspective of clinical and community practice.

In Chapter 8 Jim Martin and Dennis Orthner broaden the focus from family to community by discussing the development and operation of the military community as a prototype company town. Although they emphasize the necessity of community programs and facilities, they challenge the assumption that current self-contained military communities adequately promote readiness and retention. To achieve the goals of military readiness and retention, Martin and Orthner suggest that the military must link healthy families together via relationships that develop from small unit associations.

The volume concludes with a postscript by the editors, who discuss the importance of continued theoretical development and research on the nature of work–family linkages in the military services. However, the editors stress the importance of moving beyond the study of work and family life in general to a focus on the unique successes, problems, and challenges in integrating work and family demands faced by particular groups in the military.

Although each chapter has its own set of references, a list of general references is included at the end of the volume. Partially drawn from references recommended to the editors by chapter authors as most significant to their particular topic area, these references are intended to provide a provocative source of recommended readings for those interested in further pursuing the study of work–family linkages in organization families, such as those in the U.S. military.

NOTES

1. American Forces Information Service (1988) *Defense 88' Almanac*, September/October. Washington, D.C.: U.S. Government Printing Office.

2. Bailyn, L., and Schein, E. H. (1976) Life/career conditions as indicators of quality of employment. In A. D. Biderman and T. F. Drury (eds.), *Measuring Work Quality for Social Reporting* (pp. 151–69). Beverly Hills, CA: Sage.

3. Bales, R. F., and Slater, P. (1955) Role differentiation in small decisionmaking groups. In T. Parsons and R. F. Bales (eds.), *Family, Socialization and Interaction Process* (pp. 259–306). Glencoe, IL: Free Press.

4. Bowen, G. L. (1981) Family patterns of U.S. military personnel. In J. S. Parry and K. L. Parkinson (eds.), *Proceedings of the National Association of Social Workers Pre-Conference Institute on Social Work Services for Military Families* (pp. 34–56). Springfield, VA: Military Family Resources Center.

5. Bowen, G. L. (1985) Families-in-blue: Insights from Air Force families. *Social Casework* 66: 459–66.

6. Bowen, G. L. (1987) Changing gender-role preferences and marital adjustment: Implications for clinical practice. *Family Therapy* 14: 17–33.

7. Bowen, G. L. (1988) Corporate supports for the family lives of employees: A conceptual model for program planning and evaluation. *Family Relations* 37: 183–88.

8. Bowen, G. L. and Scheirer, M. A. (1986) The development and evaluation of human service programs in the military. *Evaluation and Program Planning* 9: 193–98.

9. Brandes, S. D. (1976) *American Welfare Capitalism: 1880–1940*. Chicago, IL: University of Chicago Press.

10. Bureau of National Affairs (BNA) (1986). *Work and Family: A Changing Dynamic*. Washington, D.C.: Bureau of National Affairs.

11. Carr, R., Orthner, D., and Brown, R. (1980) Living and family patterns in the Air Force. *Air University Review* 31 (2): 75–96.

12. Coser, L., with Coser, R. L. (1974) *Greedy Institutions*. New York: Free Press.

13. Friedman, D. E. (1983) *Government Initiatives to Encourage Employer-Sponsored Child Care: The State and Local Perspective*. New York: Center for Public Advocacy Research.

14. Glick, P. C. (1984) Marriage, divorce, and living arrangements. *Journal of Family Issues* 5: 7–26.

15. Goffman, E. (1961) *Asylums* (1st edn.). Chicago, IL: Aldine.

16. Hayghe, H. (1986) Rise in mothers' labor force activity includes those with infants. *Monthly Labor Review* 109: 43–45.

17. Hunter, E. J. (1982) *Families under the Flag*. New York: Praeger.

18. Kagan, J. (1983) Work in the 1980s and 1990s. *Working Women* (September): 30–32.

19. Kamerman, S. B., and Kingston, P. W. (1982) Employer responses to the family responsibilities of employees. In S. B. Kamerman and C. D. Hayes (eds.), *Families that work*, pp. 144–208. Washington, D.C.: National Academy Press.

20. Kanter, R. M. (1977) *Work and Family in the United States: A Critical Review and Agenda for Research and Policy*. New York: Russell Sage Foundation.

21. Lagrone, D. M. (1978) The military family syndrome. *American Journal of Psychiatry* 135: 1040–43.

22. Louis Harris and Associates (1981) *Families at Work*. Minneapolis, MN: General Mills.

23. Masnick, G., and Bane, M. J. (1980) *The Nation's Families: 1960–1990*. Boston, MA: Auburn House.

24. McBroom, W. H. (1984) Changes in sex-role orientations: A Five-year longitudinal comparison. *Sex Roles* 11: 583–92.

25. Nieva, V. F. (1985) Work and family linkages. In L. Larwood, A. H. Stromberg, and B. A. Gutek (eds.), *Women and Work: An Annual Review*, Vol. 1, pp. 162–90. Beverly Hills, CA: Sage.

26. Nieva, V. F., and Gutek, B. A. (1981) *Women and Work: A Psychological Perspective*. New York: Praeger.

27. Orthner, D. K., and Pittman, J. F. (1986) Family contributions to work commitment. *Journal of Marriage and the Family* 48: 573–81.

28. Parsons, T., and Bales, R. F. (eds.) (1955) *Family Socialization and Interaction Process*. New York: Free Press.

29. Raabe, P. H., and Gessner, J. (1988) Employer family-supportive policies: Diverse variations on the theme. *Family Relations* 37: 196–202.

30. Reubens, B. G., and Reubens, E. P. (1979) Women workers, nontraditional occupations and full employment. In A. F. Cahn (ed.), *Women in the U.S. Labor Force*, pp. 103–26. New York: Praeger.

31. Ridenour, R. I. (1984) The military, service families, and the therapist. In F. W. Kaslow and R. I. Ridenour (eds.), *The Military Family*, pp. 1–17. New York: Guilford Press.

32. Rodriguez, A. R. (1984) Special treatment needs of children of military families. In F. W. Kaslow and R. I. Ridenour (eds.), *The Military Family*, pp. 46–70. New York: Guilford Press.

33. Scanzoni, J., and Fox, G. L. (1980) Sex roles, family and society: The seventies and beyond. *Journal of Marriage and the Family* 42: 743–56.

34. Segal, M. W. (1986) The military and the family as greedy institutions. *Armed Forces and Society* 13: 9–38.

35. Sekaran, U. (1986) *Dual-Career Families*. San Francisco: CA: Jossey-Bass.

36. Statuto, C. M. (1984) *Families in the Eighties: Implications for Employers and Human Services*. Washington, D.C.: Catholic University of America.

37. Teachman, J. D., Polonko, K. A., and Scanzoni, J. (1987) Demography of the family. In M. B. Sussman and S. K. Steinmetz (eds.), *Handbook of marriage and the family*, pp. 3–36. New York: Plenum Press.

38. Voydanoff, P. (1987) *Work and Family Life*. Newbury Park, CA: Sage.

39. Whyte, W. H., Jr. (1956). *The Organization Man.* New York: Simon and Schuster.

40. Yankelovich, D. (1979). Work, values and the new breed. In C. Kerr and J. Rosow (eds.), *Work in America: The Decade Ahead* pp. 3–26. New York: Van Nostrand Reinhold.

I

WORK AND FAMILY LINKAGES

1

The Nature of Work and Family Linkages: A Theoretical Perspective

Mady Wechsler Segal

There are some dramatic shifts taking place in military/family relations in the United States, against a backdrop of more general normative and structural changes in military forces, family patterns, and gender roles. Some of these shifts are occurring in work–family linkages in other occupations, but the intensity of the systemic conflict is perhaps more evident in the armed forces because of the almost unique constellation of organizational demands on service members and their families. These demands intersect with the family life cycle, creating particular points of stress.

There have been three primary perspectives in the literature on work and family (e.g., 7, 52, 76, 77, 97): the "segmented" or "no relationship" model, the "compensatory" model, and the "spillover" model. The segmented model analyzes work and family as separate domains of life, with little effect on each other. The compensatory approach still views the two domains as separate, but sees potential for individuals to compensate for disappointments in one of the domains via gratification in the other. The spillover model emphasizes the direct implications for each domain of what happens in the other. All of these models tend to conceive of the relations between work and family from the point of view of the individual.

In the literature on military families, the spillover model has been most prevalent, with particular attention to the effects of the military life style on family experiences and well-being. This chapter draws on the spillover per-

The author does not purport to reflect the position of the Department of the Army or the Department of Defense.

I am grateful to Gary L. Bowen, David R. Segal, and Joel M. Teitelbaum for their very helpful comments on an earlier draft of this chapter.

spective and military family research, but extends the usual view by focusing on more macro-level dynamics and analyzing not only the effects of work on the family, but also the impact of the family institution on the work organization.

This chapter analyzes work–family linkages in the military in five steps. First, relevant general social changes are summarized. Second, four levels of theoretical analysis are specified: institutional, organizational, interpersonal, and individual. While distinctions are made among the levels, connections are also proposed. Third, salient characteristics of the military life style are described, with references to the four levels of analysis (e.g., showing how organizational policies affect individual well-being). Fourth, specific critical points of intersection of career and family life cycles are identified. Fifth, implications for organizational policy are considered.

A CHANGING CONTEXT

The Changing Nature of the Force

Since World War II the military has moved from a small cadre peacetime force, which grows in response to mobilization for war, to a large standing peacetime armed force (47). This transformation is due to the development of atomic and nuclear weapons, the development of aerial delivery systems for these weapons, and the evolution of a bipolar world, all of which have denied the United States the luxuries of time and distance from the battlefield to mobilize for the next major war (87). A large standing military force is also necessitated by the prevalence of "low intensity" conflicts all around the globe, and the need to respond quickly to such conflicts.

The very size and nature of the standing force has implications for military families. For example, maintenance of a large and heterogeneous peacetime force has contributed, along with other factors, to a loss of a sense of community and informal networks of supportive social relationships in the military. This loss of informal community supports has necessitated the provision of formal support services, a phenomenon noted more than 20 years ago by Coates and Pellegrin (22). Further, the large size of the force means that there are now large numbers of servicemembers and family members who potentially require assistance from formal services.

Historically, the military has been the province of single men, especially among junior enlisted personnel who have generally made up the bulk of U.S. armed forces in times of mobilization. Although some officers and senior non-commissioned officers in the past were married, low-ranking enlisted men were prohibited or at least strongly discouraged from getting married while in the service. A standing force has a larger proportion of career personnel who are further along in their own life cycles than a mobilization force. Modern military technology requires higher levels of technical training of enlisted personnel than previously, which in turn requires retaining them in the force longer to realize a return from the investment in training. The longer servicemembers remain in service, the more likely they are to be married.

A majority of today's military personnel are married (62), and, at any given age, service members are more likely to be married than are their civilian counterparts (28). Although the rates of marriage are lower among junior enlisted personnel than other ranks, marriage has greater consequences for the life style of young servicepeople. For example, they do not live in the barracks nor are they eligible for family housing on base, so they live off post, which draws their lives away from the military.

The move from a conscripted to a volunteer armed force in the 1970s also has had impacts on the dynamics of military–family relationships. Under a draft system with a small selection ratio from among those eligible, exemptions for family considerations were possible. A volunteer system, especially under conditions of declining size of eligible age cohorts in the 1980s and 1990s, precludes preferential selection of single recruits. Further, the retention of trained career personnel requires attention to their family needs. If family members are dissatisfied with military life, the servicemember is more likely to return to civilian life (11, 12, 37, 67, 91).

Societal Changes in Family Patterns and Gender Roles

A number of general societal trends are affecting military families. Most notable are the diverse family configurations and changes in gender role norms and behaviors. The family pattern that has served as the most prevalent cultural ideal in the United States since the end of World War II now characterizes only a small minority of American families. The ideal family was seen by many, especially among the growing middle class, as consisting of a husband who worked outside of the home, a full-time housewife, and their children. Marriages were expected to last until the death of one of the spouses. If the husband/father needed to move to advance his career, his wife and children were expected to accompany him. The wife's identity was derived primarily from her familial role.

In the 1980s, supported by substantial movement toward egalitarian gender role attitudes (e.g., 41, 60, 61), a majority of American women, including those with husbands and children, are employed outside the home (95). A wife's sense of identity is less dependent on her family roles, and women expect to be treated as individuals in their own right. More men are taking greater interest in their family roles, including more responsibility for parenting (94).

High divorce rates and freer standards of sexual behavior have led to a variety of household configurations. There have been sharp increases over the past 15 to 20 years in the number of one-parent families with minor children (92), as well as couples living together without being married (93).

These societal trends in family patterns and gender roles have had, and are continuing to have, strong impacts on the nature of work and family life in American society and on the relationship between the work and family institutions. Indeed, these trends are largely responsible for the recent growth of research and policy attention on work–family linkages and the increasing salience of the spillover model. The segmented and compensatory views are more compatible with cultural values and structural patterns of gender specialization, with men operating primarily in the world of work outside the home and women devoted to family roles. Such segregation, which may have been common in the post–World War II American middle class, has been replaced by large numbers of people whose activities are more balanced between both spheres.

The military population reflects civilian society. Recent years have seen a substantial increase in the number and proportion of women in the military, in the number of dual-career and dual-service couples, and in the number of single parents (84). Gender role attitudes of military personnel are becoming more egalitarian (16).

Societal trends in family and gender roles may eventually have even more influence on the armed forces than on civilian work institutions. The nature of the military mission, and the way organizational policies have developed in response to that mission, have produced a pattern of demands on service members and their families that is different from the demands and life styles of non-military families. The intersection of this unique pattern of life-style demands with these general societal changes in family patterns and gender roles has increased the potential for conflict in the linkages between work and family in the military at all levels.

THEORETICAL PERSPECTIVES AND ISSUES

Theoretical perspectives for studying the relationships between work and family in the military encompass different levels of analysis. While some theories are applicable to more than one level, the research questions tend to differ as a function of the particular level. While many of the issues cut across different levels, distinguishing among the levels helps us to understand the dynamics involved. The four levels of analysis are: (1) institutional or cultural, (2) organizational or structural, (3) interpersonal, and (4) individual.

Institutional Approaches

Approaching work and family linkages at the institutional level leads us to analyze cultural definitions of work and family roles and role priorities. Of special interest is how these norms are changing and the effects of this cultural change on work and family institutions, especially in terms of mutual accommodation or conflict.

The Military Institution

Societal norms govern the degree to which it is legitimate for an employer to make claims on employees and the degree and nature of individual commitments to work organizations. Historically, employers had great control over their employees' lives, especially their time. This was a factor in feudal systems, and it also characterized pre-industrial systems of apprenticeship. With industrialization, prior to the trade union movement and legislative restrictions, factory owners controlled the working conditions of their employees; they could and did require long hours. The "company town" was distinguished by one employer controlling the work lives of residents and exercising significant control over the nonworking hours of employees. The twentieth-century trade union movement brought about guarantees of better working conditions, with both negotiated contractual and legislative restrictions on the working hours employers could exact from employees.

Today there are both normative and legal limitations on employers' demands. Occupations and work organizations vary in the extent of their demands on individuals, in terms of time, energy, and commitment. The specific demands of the U.S. military (which will be discussed in detail later) include risk of injury or death, geographic mobility, periodic separation of the servicemember from the rest of the family, long working hours and shift work, residence in foreign countries, and normative pressures controlling behavior outside of working time. In making these demands of its personnel, the military has been allowed more normative and legal latitude than is granted to civilian employers.

For each of these specific organizational requirements, there are other occupations that are similar to the military. For example, physical risks are present in many jobs and prevalent in some, such as police work and coal mining. Geographic mobility is common among corporate executives and university professors. Family separations are expected among merchant marines, corporate executives, corporate sales representatives, athletes, and anthropologists. Professions such as medicine, law, ministry, and corporate management often entail long working hours, as does operating a small business. Shift work is common in policing, nursing, and blue-collar manufacturing jobs. Normative constraints on nonwork behavior are experienced by, for example, ministers, judges, politicians, and teachers.

While there are other occupations that share specific characteristics of the military life style, the military is almost unique in its constellation of requirements. The foreign service probably has the most similar set of pressures, but generally with lower physical risk. Over the course of a military career, a servicemember and his/her family can expect to experience all the specific demands mentioned above. The military's claims are so great that it possesses many of the characteristics of what Coser (23) calls "greedy institutions":

Yet the modern world, just like the world of tradition, also continues to spawn organizations and groups which, in contradistinction to the prevailing principle, make total claims on their members and which attempt to encompass within their circle the whole personality. These might be called *greedy institutions*, insofar as they seek exclusive and undivided loyalty and they attempt to reduce the claims of competing roles and status positions on those they wish to encompass within their boundaries. Their demands on the person are omnivorous. . . . Greedy institutions are characterized by the fact that they exercise pressures on component individuals to weaken their ties, or not to form any ties, with other institutions or persons that might make claims that conflict with their own demands. (23, pp. 4–6)

Coser distinguishes between his concept of greedy institutions and Goffman's concept of "total institutions." Goffman defines a total institution as "a place of residence and work where a large number of like-situated individuals, cut off from the wider society for an appreciable period of time, together lead an enclosed, formally administered round of life" (36, p. xiii). While this description is most often associated with prisons and mental hospitals, Goffman actually differentiates several types of total institutions according to their purposes. He also uses army barracks and ships as examples of total "institutions purportedly established the better to pursue some work-like task and justifying themselves only on these instrumental grounds" (36, p. 5). In fact, many of his examples come from military situations, primarily military entry training, enlisted barracks, and ships—contexts where families are excluded.

While recognizing "evident overlaps between 'total' and 'greedy' institutions," Coser distinguishes between them. He notes that "Goffman focuses on physical arrangements separating the 'inmate' from the outside world." In contrast, Coser shows that "greedy institutions, though they may in some cases utilize the device of physical isolation, tend to rely mainly on nonphysical mechanisms to separate the insider from the outsider and to erect symbolic boundaries between them" (23, p. 6).

The military institution contains various mechanisms, both physical and symbolic, that serve to separate its members from the outside world. Sometimes families are part of that outside world from which military personnel are physically separated, as when families are prohibited or discouraged from accompanying servicemembers to specific duty assignments (including most training situations). Alternatively, family members can be included within the military confines and separated from civilian contacts, as happens when family housing and facilities and services are provided on military installations. Symbolic separations of military personnel from civilians take many forms, of which the uniform is a visible example.

An important question in analyzing the intersection of the military and family institutions is the extent to which families are normatively included within the military institution, as contrasted with being seen as competing with the military for the service member's commitment. The military–family intersection is undergoing social change because of the factors described above, including changes in the military institution, the demographics of military families, and changing gender roles.

Some of the important changes taking place within the U.S. military institution have been described by Moskos (70, 71, 72, 73) as involving a movement from an "institution" to an "occupation." In the institutional military, as described by Moskos, individual commitment and self-sacrifice are legitimated through the operation of normative values, which compel the individual to accept great demands on his/her time and energy. Further, the organization controls the demands—the individual does not get to choose when and how to comply. Role obligations are diffuse, and place of residence is not separated from place of work. In return for dedicated service, the individual receives esteem from the larger society and compensation from the military, much of it in noncash form. Among the several forms of compensation that depart from fixed salary, those that have the greatest relationship to families are job security, on-base housing, medical care, allotments by family size, subsidized on-base consumer facilities, and numerous on-base services, such as schools and recreational activities.

In contrast to the institutional military, the "occupational" military resembles other occupations in that individuals are motivated by monetary self-interest. The norms of the marketplace prevail. Work and residence locales are separated and family members are socially segregated from the military community. The organization is limited in the demands it can make on the individual and these demands are determined by contract.

Note that the description of the institutional and occupational types includes both characteristics of the organization and the individual. Moskos' conception helps us to distinguish between the institutional and the individual levels, as well as to provide a link between the two levels. Moskos' model analyzes the nature of the organization's policies, but it also deals with the nature of individual motivation.

For institutions (and groups and organizations within them) to survive in the face of competing demands on individuals, they must develop mechanisms for motivating individual participation and commitment. Coser (23, p. 4) notes that social change sometimes makes meeting competing demands more problematic when "a new normative pattern for differential allocation of time and energy has not yet been established." The current competition between the military organization and the family is occurring in a period of social change without an established normative pattern and will lead to new normative patterns for resolving the conflicts. Understanding this institutional adaptation process is helpful in analyzing the intersection of work and family in the military context, especially in identifying points of conflict and potential outcomes of the process.

In essence, the military is facing pressures associated with the institutional demands that were normatively legitimated in the past. Part of the reason for the challenges to legitimacy have to do with conflicts and stresses experienced by servicemembers and their families, which are more salient now because of the wider social changes dicussed above. (These pressures occur at the interpersonal and individual levels and will be discussed after the organizational analyses have been presented.) Changes in the family institution, especially in the social expectations regarding family member responsibilities and adaptation, are having a profound impact on military organizations.

The Family Institution

Nuclear families make different demands on different members. All members are expected to be emotionally committed to the family, to display affection toward other members, to identify with the family as a unit, and to fulfill role obligations that are diffuse relative to most other social groups. However, the family is "greedier" for some members than for others.

As discussed by Coser and Coser (24), the family has been greedy for women, but not for men. In the recent past, women have been expected to be housewives, to maintain exclusive attachment to the family, and to make sacrifices for it, including giving up occupational aspirations requiring commitments that would interfere with the fulfillment of family obligations. However, the normative legitimacy of this greed has been declining.

Conflict between family demands and occupational requirements arises when "there is a normative expectation that the family will be allocated resources of time, energy, and affect that cannot be shared with other social institutions" (24, p. 92). While this conflict is generally greater for women, it occurs for men as well, to the extent that their work interferes with their ability to provide the normatively expected resources of time, energy, and affect to the family. This happens when either the family is relatively greedy or the work itself is so greedy that it interferes with the fulfillment of relatively minimal family demands.

At certain stages, of course, the family is relatively greedy for both women *and* men. This is the case, for example, with new marriages, which require greater time and emotional adjustment than established relationships, and with children who are very young or who need fairly constant supervision. As children get older, they require less constant supervision; however, parents of adolescents often find that this stage demands more emotional energy (10). Family responsibilities may be especially salient when there is only one parent.

Moreover, while care of children and household tasks have been tradi-

and the Association of the United States Army, and later the Army itself, organized several Army Family Symposia in Washington, D.C., in the early 1980s. These meetings brought together family representatives from Army installations all over the world to discuss problems, share information on effective family support programs, and make recommendations to the Army.

Responses of the military to family concerns and pressures include the creation of the position of Deputy Assistant Secretary of Defense for Family Support, Education, and Safety. Congressional concern and funding of programs for military families have increased. The Department of Defense funded a large-scale survey of military spouses in 1985. The Navy now has a Deputy Assistant Secretary for Personnel and Family Matters.

Attention by policy makers in the Department of the Army is shown in many ways, including official support of the second and third Army Family Symposia, the establishment of a Family Liaison Office in the Office of the Deputy Chief of Staff for Personnel to represent family concerns, the development and dissemination of the Army Family White Paper (99), and the Army Family Action Plan with specific actions addressed to problem resolution (27, 29). The Army Chief of Staff declared 1984 to be the Year of the Family.

There have been many activities and new programs in support of military families at the installation and unit levels in recent years, including the burgeoning of Family Support Groups in company- and battalion-size units in the Army.

Thus, at various organizational levels, recent changes have altered the way the military, as a work organization, intersects with the families of its members. Organizational mechanisms have been established for identifying and addressing areas where policy change is desirable and possible, and voices within the military organization represent family concerns. Programs have been developed that attempt to mitigate the effects of some of the organization's demands on families. Many of the organizations, programs, and activities such as those mentioned above provide military spouses with a structural link to the organization.

Despite these organizational developments toward structural linkages between the military and families, the programs developed have not yet created major institutional changes in the demands the military makes on service members and their families. Further, neither formal programs nor organizational sensitivities to family issues have been fully institutionalized. Funding for family programs is frequently in jeopardy. The work–family linkage is still often seen to be characterized by competition between the organization and the family for the time and commitment of the service member, and family issues are frequently assigned a low priority.

The behavior of many unit commanders and policy makers reflects the relatively low priority they assign to particular family issues. Reports of such behavior emerge from research on work–family conflicts for military personnel and in media coverage. A case in point is the recent controversy created by an Air Force commander threatening his subordinates with low performance evaluations if their wives were employed (8, 35, 98). Ironically, this kind of organizational pressure on wives results from the perceived need for them to be available for volunteer work in the community, which often involves helping other military families. As a result of publicity in this particular instance, the Air Force appointed a task force to examine these issues (and later formed an official policy), and the Secretary of Defense issued a statement that spousal employment status was not to be used as a criterion in performance appraisal (69, 100).

With regard to spousal employment and other areas affecting military families, there is a disjuncture between official policy and actual practices, as is common in many organizations. The experiences of military personnel and their families are generally affected not only by official organizational policy, but also by the behavior of individuals with whom they interact, such as their supervisors as well as each other.

Interpersonal Approaches

There are two major types of interpersonal processes involved in work and family linkages: relationships within the family and relationships on the job. Each of these spheres of interpersonal interaction is affected by the other and by the organizational environment. This section discusses some of the most critical interpersonal processes for military families.

The "greediness" of the military institution has strong implications for the family relationships of its personnel. The demands of the military organization shape the participation of service members in their families. The precise nature of these effects depends on the timing and duration of work demands and how these intersect with the family life cycle. Specific types of intersections will be discussed later. This section will describe a general approach to be used as a backdrop for understanding some of the dynamics involved.

Many of the important dynamics of the intersection between work and family spheres of life take place at the interpersonal level. Most role learning occurs via interaction with role partners: interpersonal behavior communicates role expectations and expresses role conflicts. Role negotiations take place at the interpersonal level. The norms and structures of wider social groups obviously influence role definitions, but the roles are enacted in interpersonal relationships. Much social construction of reality (6) takes place within the context of interpersonal relationships. Foremost among adults' prominent social relationships are marriage and associations on the job. Processes of social construction of world views and self-perceptions are embedded in the intersections of family life-cycle stages and work demands. Marriage is a process of building social reality (5). In the beginning stage of an ideal-typical marriage, two people come together with pre-existing definitions of the world and of marriage, as well as definitions of their own personal identities. The extremely personal, day-after-day interaction between new marriage partners brings about changes in definitions, largely because each person must make adaptations to a highly significant person.

In this founding stage of marriage (generally the first few years), the partners develop their relationship and their joint construction of reality. It is in this stage that "couples report the highest levels of companionship, sex, and joint activity. . . . They must smooth conflict, establish joint habits, and develop a base of intimacy, trust, and commitment. All of this lays heavy claim on their energy and attention and, in so doing, requires a high level of face-to-face interaction" (34, p. 190). Once the couple has children, which for many couples is shortly after marriage, children's needs consume much of their attention and parental roles have to be incorporated into their patterns of interaction.

Part of the social reality that the married couple must define is the priority assigned to work and the nature of their accommodations to their own and each other's work lives. Indeed, the demands of a greedy work organization can interfere with the attention to the marriage generally desired during the founding stage. The negotiation and resolution of conflicts between work and family roles are part of the couple's social reality construction.

At the same time that married couples are interacting, communicating, and developing their definitions of their family roles and their interface with work roles, work roles are being defined via interpersonal relationships with role partners at work. Reality at work is also socially constructed. Part of that reality is the priority assigned to work and family roles, and the accommodation to family demands that work associates consider appropriate and communicate to each other.

The attitude of the supervisor is important; it is especially critical in an organization with a strict hierarchical authority structure and to employees with little control over their conditions of work. Low-ranking military personnel have little leeway to attend to family needs that conflict with work requirements unless permitted by their supervisors. Supervisory behavior, which is influenced by institutional norms, as well as organizational policies and climate, affects the ability of subordinates to balance work and family demands (57). Recent research demonstrates the impact of leaders in Army units on the family lives of soldiers in those units (33, 58). Individuals are affected by their relationships with their supervisors both directly and via the impact of supervisory attitudes and actions on family role fulfillment.

Individual Approaches

The most important concern at the individual level is with well-being and satisfaction. This concern is linked to other levels via such dynamics as the effect of institutional values, organizational supports, and interpersonal conflict and support on individual well-being and satisfaction. Organizational and family demands can serve as stressors to individuals. To the extent that they lack the individual and social resources to cope with the stress, individual functioning is impaired (43, 44, 59, 81). Role conflicts between work and family demands can be especially harmful to individual well-being.

Individual satisfaction with work, including the quality of social relationships on the job, affects individual well-being (82). Work satisfaction also affects the quality of family life primarily via the intervening effects of the individual's behavior at home.

It is important to recognize that individuals are generally not forced against their will to comply with work and family demands. Labelling an institution as greedy does not necessarily imply coercion. Rather, work and family are two primary life domains for most people. It is from marriage and family life that Americans derive the most life satisfaction (19). While people are somewhat less satisfied with their work than with their family lives, they nonetheless tend to be satisfied rather than dissatisfied, and the large majority indicate that they would work even if they did not need the money (19). Indeed, it is precisely because of the importance of family and work to most people that disruptions in either of these arenas, or conflict between the two, is likely to take a psychological toll on the individual.

Work–family linkages can also be approached at the individual level by analyzing the socialization processes in the organization and in the family, with emphasis on the internalization of norms for work and family life. We can examine individual values for work and family priorities, as well as individual mechanisms for resolving competing time and emotional demands.

Processes of socialization affect not only individuals' own priorities for work and family, but also their responses to others. Particularly significant is the socialization of supervisors around how they handle family issues among subordinates. One indicator of the degree of institutionalization of family concerns is the extent to which leadership training includes materials on families, such as guidelines on accommodations to families and information on available services and how to make them accessible to families.

Also important is the amount of control individuals have over their own work and family lives and the interaction between the two spheres. Moskos' contrasts between institutional and occupational types of individual motivation point to the relative lack of individual volition in an institutional military. The organization dictates when a servicemember will be on the job, thereby determining when attention to family roles is possible.

THE MILITARY LIFE STYLE AND ITS EFFECTS ON FAMILIES

The mission of the military institution, and the organizational policies that have evolved in response to that mission, have created demands that have profound spillover effects on families. The intersection of these organizational demands with family changes cause family dynamics to spill over into the military organization. Analyzing the characteristics of this life style is essential to understanding how changes in gender roles and military family patterns have led to heightened conflict (at all four levels previously discussed). A close look at the demands the military makes on servicemembers and their families also enables us to anticipate particular work and family junctures that are especially conflictual. The outcomes of this developing conflict can then be analyzed (now and in the future) for the extent to which the military and family systems respond to each other.

Documentation of the prevalence of the demands of the military life style is available in large-scale survey results. Smaller, more in-depth studies provide us with an understanding of the processes by which families experience these demands.

In 1985 the Department of Defense conducted major surveys of active duty personnel and their spouses (38, 39, 55, 62). The generalizable population for the service member survey consisted of those with at least four months of service as of 30 September 1984 who were still in the military when the questionnaires were completed six months later in March 1985. Thus, respondents had completed at least ten months of service.

Qualitative descriptions in this section of the various reactions of some military family members to organizational demands are derived from several sources, including literature on military families in general, observations of military family members' behavior, and research interviews conducted by the author with military families and with people who provide support services to them.

Risk of Injury or Death

The risk that military personnel will be wounded or killed in the course of their duties is an obvious aspect of the institution's demands. The legitimacy for the institution to place its members in jeopardy is perhaps the greediest aspect of all. While this risk is, of course, greatest in wartime, even peacetime military training maneuvers entail some risk of injury, and military personnel can be sent at any moment to areas of armed conflict.

The potential for danger to military personnel varies systematically as a function of location, the nature of the military unit and its mission, and the type of job performed. For example, relatively high levels of risk are found in overseas assignments and combat specialties, as well as in units expected to mobilize rapidly. There are differences among and within the military services. For example, combat risks in the Air Force is greater for officers than for enlisted personnel. In the Army the danger is especially apparent for both officers and enlisted personnel in Airborne and Special Forces units, and other components of the Rapid Deployment Force.

While the risk is to the individual servicemember, there are obvious implications for family members who worry about the safety of their loved ones. When there is a casualty, the family suffers loss and grief. The effects on military families of the potential for injury and death in both peacetime and wartime are seldom studied. Therefore, we know less about them than about the effects of other military demands on families. The potential for casualty has been shown to be a source of stress during certain kinds of separations. Studies of military families conducted during and after World War II emphasized the impact of wartime separation (42; see 45 and 67 for reviews of this literature). Similarly, research has focused on the families of American prisoners of war and those missing in action in Vietnam (64). But there is much less research on the grieving process in families of servicemen who were killed. Some recent research has shown the profound impact of accidental death associated with military missions not only on grieving families, but also on those assigned as casualty assistance officers (2, 3, 4).

Geographic Mobility

The U.S. armed forces periodically transfer their personnel to new locations for new tours of duty as well as for specific types of military training. Both frequency of mobility and length of duty tours vary among the services as a function of service policy.

The DoD survey provides information on the number of permanent changes of station (i.e., transfers for regular tours of duty rather than temporary reassignments) service personnel and their families experience throughout their military service (62, pp. 177–83). In this survey, officers reported more permanent changes of station than enlisted personnel. Sixty-five percent of officers have moved at least four times during their military careers, compared to 33 percent of enlisted members. Even higher percentages of officers and enlisted personnel at the higher pay grades (who had been in the military longer) had moved four or more times, including 97 percent of officers in pay grades O5 and above and 78 percent of enlisted personnel in pay grades E6 and above. Fifty-seven percent of these more senior officers had moved at least ten times.

Although the results of the survey showed that families of military personnel move less often than servicemembers themselves, relocation is still frequent, especially for officers' families (39). Fully 62 percent of military wives had been at their present location for two years or less, and the median number of moves reported by officers' wives was double the number reported by enlisted wives (four as compared to two).

Number of moves is a function of "shared military years," that is, years of marriage while the servicemember has been in the military. The median number of moves for wives with 15 or more shared military years was six for those married to enlisted men and nine for officers' wives. The greatest mobility is evident among Army families, where the percentage who had moved at least ten times was 26 percent for enlisted wives and 58 percent for officers' wives, as compared to the DoD comparison groups overall (18 percent and 43 percent).

While many servicemembers and their spouses view the opportunity to travel as a benefit of military service, geographic mobility is also seen as a hardship that disrupts family life and necessitates adjustments under the best of circumstances (39, 65, 83, 101). Families are likely to be geographically separated from their extended kin and other longterm sources of social support. If they manage to become integrated into new supportive networks, these relationships are severed when they are required to move to a new location, an experience that is repeated with each additional move. The United States is geographically large compared with most other countries. Therefore, moves generally involve large distances, making contact with family and friends more difficult.

Besides the social disruption moving entails, there are other adjustments to a new location. The place is unfamiliar and one must learn one's way around. For families with limited resources and/or small children, this can be especially stressful. Junior enlisted families often must make do without a car or access to public transportation. The physical environment and climate may also be quite different from what the family members are accustomed to. Whatever the type (including size) of the community, some military families will be used to another type, causing disruptions in their personal and social construction of reality. For example, people from rural areas often find large military installations intimidating and are unaccustomed to living close to neighbors. The regional dialect may also be unfamiliar to them, straining communication with others and possibly making them feel like outsiders.

Moving may be especially disruptive to spouses' employment possibilities and career continuity. Substantial proportions of military personnel and their spouses in the DoD survey (39, 55) reported that their last move had caused problems, some serious, for family members finding employment. Unemployment rates are substantially higher for military than civilian wives (28, 39, 40). Family income is lower in military families than civilian families (18), due largely to lack of employment opportunities for wives. For officers' wives, who are more likely to be oriented to a career rather than just to employment, geographic mobility interferes with normal career progression. Even if they can find work in their field, they lose seniority when they move. Thus, employment problems create economic hardships for the family and problems of personal identity and worth for the wives.

While the military provides subsidies for moving expenses when a servicemember is transferred to a new location, these are often inadequate, forcing the family to pay some of the expenses (32, 39, 55, 62). Frequent moves result in military families being less likely than civilian families to own their own home. Home ownership is not only a cultural goal in American society, but also is often a family's major financial asset and a buffer against inflation.

One mechanism used by some families to help avoid the stress of frequent mobility is not to accompany the servicemember on a move, even though allowed by the military. This response appears most common in certain circumstances, such as when a move would interfere with the spouse's career or when there is a teenager in the family. Regardless of the reason for this decision, it produces an additional family separation beyond that required by other organizational demands.

Separations

Military demands often necessitate that servicemembers be away from their families. The extent and nature of these requirements vary among and within the services. In peacetime the most common types of assignments that result in family separations include military schooling, field training, sea duty, and unaccompanied tours. There are also assignments on which the family is allowed to accompany the servicemember but chooses not to for various reasons. The length of peacetime separations generally varies from a few days to a year; wartime separations can be much longer and indefinite. Certain types of military personnel (e.g., submariners and combat troops) experience frequent or prolonged separations due to deployment of forces for training or military missions.

Results of the 1985 DoD survey showed that 72 percent of enlisted personnel and 79 percent of officers with spouses and/or children had been separated from their families for some time during the preceding year; 30 percent of enlisted people and 18 percent of officers had spent at least five months away from their families. Navy and Marine Corps personnel (both enlisted and officer) had spent more time separated from their families than Army and Air Force personnel (55, 62).

Although the effects of separations on families may vary depending on the type of separation, others are common to most, if not all, families. Separations always require adjustments by servicemembers and their spouses and children. Since little attention has been given to servicemembers either in research or in the provision of services, we know less about their reactions to separations than about those of their wives. The most common problems experienced by the latter are loneliness, problems with children, physical illness, and loss of their usual social role in the community (21, 26, 68, 74, 89, 96). The wife is thrust into the role of sole parent. Research on military children with psychological problems has often identified the absence of the father as a contributing factor (45, 67). Even when families cope well with separation, most still view it as a stressful experience.

Wartime separation carries special problems and stresses. Concern for servicemembers' safety can be paramount. Research on the families of prisoners of war and those missing in action shows that families often go through the stages of grief, but they cannot complete the process and return to normal lives because they are "in limbo" (46, 64, 90).

Discontinuities in a married couple's interaction created by geographical separation interfere with the usual processes of shared social construction of the world, of their marriage, and of their self-perceptions. Individual experiences and perceptions of reality during separation are likely to necessitate adjustments following reunion (86).

The reunion process is clearly stressful for families who have been separated for a long time and/or for returning prisoners of war. While less severe for peacetime separations, reunion requires readjustments under the best of circumstances and can precipitate family problems, including family violence. Ironically, some evidence shows that certain successful strategies for family coping during the separation result in greater difficulties reintegrating the servicemember into the family (42, 63).

Separations also have some beneficial effects. They allow for individual growth and for development of the marital relationship. Some relationships benefit from a period of less intense interaction. Military members and their spouses sometimes say a separation makes them appreciate each other more and adds novelty and romance to their relationships. But most families view the difficulties of separations as outweighing the benefits (39).

Long Working Hours and Shift Work

The individual servicemember does not have control over his/her time, as the organization can demand work at any time. In the institutional military, this power is seen as legitimate, both in a legal and normative sense, because of the mission of the organization. The value changes associated with movement toward an occupational military include the lessened legitimacy of this organizational demand under routine conditions. It is generally expected and perceived as legitimate in emergency situations, and comparable to other occupations subject to being on call, such as police officers, fire fighters, and physicians. Even in peacetime, military working hours are often long and uncertain; some jobs require shift work. Military units practice for emergencies by using unexpected call-ups, which may require members to report for duty in the middle of the night. These exercises may suddenly separate families for days at a time.

Requirements to work beyond usual duty hours, especially when they are imposed without notice, can interfere with family members' time together, recreational plans, the spouse's employment, and the fulfillment of family responsibilities. In research on work and family issues, time is often cited as a factor in conflicts by both civilian workers (57, 76, 78) and military personnel (33, 58). Last-minute work demands are particularly disruptive and stressful when the servicemember routinely takes care of his/her children while the spouse works. This is not an uncommon practice among American families, whether civilian or military. Presser (79, 80) has called attention to the large number of families where the father is the children's principal caregiver while the mother works. This is especially prevalent among young couples or when the mother works part time and/or does shift work. In the military it is more common among enlisted personnel than officers (39).

While the military can exact long hours from servicemembers, which can conflict with family functioning, it can also be flexible in adapting to family needs. Accommodation to families is in some ways easier than in other occupations and organizational settings. Since work in the military is not hourly, even for low-ranking employees, supervisors can grant time off for family responsibilities and activities without loss of wages or vacation time (33). Thus, while mission requirements often necessitate long hours and days away from families, on other occasions servicemembers can be allowed time off without interfering with mission effectiveness.

Residence in Foreign Countries

Because of the United States' role in the balance of world power, even in peacetime, substantial proportions of U.S. military personnel are stationed overseas. The numbers of troops in particular places vary as a function of U.S. foreign policy and world events. According to the *Defense Almanac* (30), as of March 31, 1987, 38 percent of all military personnel were assigned outside of the continental United States, including 23 percent who were outside of the U.S. states and territories. At the time of the DoD survey in March 1985 (55), 26 percent of enlisted personnel and 19 percent of officers were stationed overseas; 22 percent of enlisted personnel and 15 percent of officers were stationed outside of the United States and territories. Army personnel were the most likely to be overseas (42 percent of enlisted personnel and 30 percent of officers), followed by Air Force (26 percent of enlisted and 16 percent of officers) and Navy (13 percent of enlisted and 12 percent of officers), with the Marine Corps servicemembers least likely to be overseas (5 percent of enlisted and 4 percent of officers).

To get a sense of the extent of overseas living for service members in the course of their careers, we can examine how much time military personnel have spent in overseas duty according to length of service. Across all services, 54 percent of enlisted personnel and 35 percent of officers with four to six years of service have spent at least one year overseas. For those with seven to ten years of service, the corresponding figures are 74 percent and 64 percent respectively.

Comparisons across military services show that, among those who have served between four and six years, the percentage of enlisted personnel with at least one year overseas is largest for the Army (78 percent) and smallest for the Navy (35 percent). (Most Navy personnel at sea are not counted as "overseas"; 73 percent with four to six years of service have spent at least one year on sea duty.) For officers, the Army again has the largest percentage (55 percent); the Air Force has the smallest (25 percent). For those with seven to ten years of service, fully 93 percent of Army enlisted personnel and 71 percent of officers have been overseas for at least one year; those with at least three years overseas constitute 61 percent of these enlisted personnel and 44 percent of these officers.

Periodic foreign assignments bring to the military family both benefits and hardships. Relocation adjustments are experienced in extreme form (e.g., 56). While they vary according to how different the host culture is from American society, even in those most similar to the United States (industrialized Western democracies) the initial reaction can be one of "culture shock." Behavioral norms differ on matters both serious and mundane; language barriers can lead to feelings of isolation and even fear (56, 67). Perceptions of a hostile environment are aggravated by terrorist attacks (56).

While most families eventually cope with living abroad—and many thoroughly enjoy the experience—some encounter severe difficulties. Economic problems are prevalent when the foreign currency exchange rate is unfavorable to the U.S. dollar. Spouses have difficulty obtaining employment. Families who are not command-sponsored (not provided with such support as transportation to the location for family members or housing on post) must live "on the economy" and tend to be isolated from formal and informal military institutional supports. Even for families who are eligible for it, on-post housing may not be available at the beginning of the servicemember's tour of duty. Thus, the family must either make two moves (the first to offpost housing) or experience a period of family separation; with the latter option, adjustment to the foreign culture is coupled with reunion adjustments.

A different kind of consequence for families of having U.S. military personnel in foreign countries is the formation of transcultural marriages. Differences among categories of military personnel (e.g., by service and by rank) in the prevalence of marriages to foreign-born spouses mirrors fairly closely the pattern of occurrence of overseas assignment. Those most likely to have spouses who were born outside the United States to non-military parents are enlisted men in the Army (17 percent) (39). Transcultural marriages may entail more difficult interpersonal adjustments of the partners to each other and generally require adaptation of the foreign-born spouse to American culture (53). While many bicultural couples show successful adjustments, there are also indications that they have lower levels of marital satisfaction and commitment (15).

Normative Constraints

While the military organization affects family life via demands on service members, it also exercises more direct constraints on families through normative pressures on the behavior of spouses and children. Family members informally carry the rank of the servicemember, and behavioral prescriptions vary accordingly. In the traditional institutional military, wives of service personnel "are expected to initiate and take part in a panoply of social functions and volunteer activities" (73, p. 381). Wives of officers and senior noncommissioned officers are integrated into a military social network with clearly defined role obligations and benefits determined by their husbands' ranks and positions.

Wives are socialized through various mechanisms. Traditional expectations (especially for officers' wives) are clearly spelled out in handbooks, such as *The Army Wife* (88), which cover a broad range of topics, including military customs, rank courtesy, entertaining, etiquette, and calling cards. Wives are informed that their husbands owe their primary loyalty to the military, not the family. Wives are told how to act at military social functions and are given "tips and taboos." There are special prescriptions regarding rank, and various social obligations are specified. While some of these prescriptions do not carry the normative force they have had traditionally, most are still communicated and enforced through informal interpersonal processes.

Family members learn that their behavior is under scrutiny and that the degree to which it conforms to normative prescriptions can affect the servicemember's career advancement. Social pressures to conform are especially exerted on officers' wives and, to a lesser extent, on senior NCO wives. For wives of lower-ranking enlisted men and for military children, there are fewer prescriptive obligations; rather, pressures on them are more proscriptive in nature. Enlisted wives are generally not required to engage in military community activities; they are expected, however, to refrain from "troublesome" behavior. Violations of such norms by enlisted wives or by children that come to the attention of military authorities result in pressure on the service members to control their family members. Such pressures are exerted primarily on families who live on military installations, where they are more subject to military control and attention than are those who live off-post.

While military wives may experience normative constraints as pressures, they may also acquire social psychological benefits when they are incorporated into the military system. With their roles institutionalized, wives have defined social identities and are more readily integrated into supportive social networks. Such integrative social mechanisms are likely to make important contributions to personal well-being, especially during stressful times such as routine family separations, relocation, and combat deployment.

Masculine Culture and Structure

Various elements of military culture, including certain aspects of the predominant masculine ideology, have strong potential for affecting families and family programs. One obvious component of military culture, the acceptance of violence, has ramifications for behavior in the family, including a possible propensity for violence.

Traditional gender role norms prevail in the military. However, movements toward more egalitarian values in the wider society are beginning to permeate the military culture (16). The more such institutional changes take place, the greater will be the adjustments necessary in the way the military operates. At the organizational level, greater priority would be given to family issues. Within the family, we can expect more willingness on the part of military men to accommodate to their wives' needs and wishes and to their children's developmental needs.

The hierarchical structure and task orientation of the military has implications for work and family linkages. One of these impacts can be seen in the development of family programs. In developing programs to respond to family needs, there is a tendency in the military to model these programs after other military organizational units; such structures are often contraindicated for the program objectives. For example, research shows that people prefer to use informal social supports when faced with stressful situations, such as occur during family separations due to deployments (58, 96). To assist spouses, the military can endeavor to facilitate the formation of supportive social networks with other military spouses. However, the actual organizational responses are often formal and dominated by rules, rank hierarchies, and pressures on people to attend meetings; a commander's success in establishing family support is judged by the level of formal activity rather than by the degree to which families actually feel supported. The result is that families feel coerced rather than cared for (58; author's field research observations).

Advantages of Military Life Style to Families

The life style for families in the military institution has some advantages that have not been covered above. These benefits to servicemembers and their families are part of the encompassing nature of the armed forces, but the effects are generally more positive than the life style characteristics discussed above.

Some factors of military work contribute to family financial well-being. Notable here are job security and financial benefits such as retirement (earlier than in comparable civilian jobs) and post exchange and commissary privileges. There are post recreational facilities, as well as the provision of housing on base.

The military institution provides social and psychological benefits. There is at least a strong potential for social solidarity and communality, a sense of social belonging, and interpersonal support. A shared life style and relative separation from the civilian world foster the development of norms for families to help each other. The military community enables many members to have an unambiguous social identity. Successfully adapting to the challenges of such organizational demands as separation and moving produces a sense of personal strength and independence in many family members (86).

SPECIFIC WORK–FAMILY LINKAGE ISSUES: INTERSECTIONS OF CAREER AND FAMILY LIFE CYCLES

The degree of competition between military organizational demands and family demands changes over the course of the career and family life cycles. There are life-cycle stages where certain military demands can be predicted to be especially stressful. The nature of the intersection between family needs and organizational pressures has consequences for both family functioning and organizational performance (e.g., readiness and retention). Identifying the common conflict points can help in developing policies to mitigate stress and conflict at these critical intersections.

Geographic mobility affects families differently, depending on where they are in the life cycle. Moving can be particularly stressful for teenagers (25) and their families (38). Adolescence involves a search for personal identity, which usually requires integration into a peer group. Moving not only disrupts relationships with peers (76), but also hampers participation in extracurricular activities and paid employment, which may be important components of one's self-concept. Relocating while in high school may impede academic performance, leading to difficulties in college admission, especially for those with high aspirations.

Moving is likely to exacerbate the conflict with parents so common in our society during this developmental period. If the adolescent does not want to move or experiences difficulties at the new location, anger toward the military parent may result.

Because of the difficulties associated with relocation, military families with teenage children are likely to resist moving. One possible solution, which may become more common, is for the servicemember to move to a new assignment without his/her spouse and children. Other servicemembers are likely to respond to the conflict between the demands of the military and the needs of their adolescent children by leaving the military. This is a viable option for many families because it is common for servicemembers with teenagers to have already completed twenty years of service (and therefore be eligible for retirement benefits). Among such military personnel are experienced and successful officers and noncommissioned officers crucial to the armed forces. Further, many of these servicemembers are in critical positions; the organization needs them to perform at optimum levels, which is unlikely if they are experiencing family conflicts.

It would be beneficial for the military to anticipate this pressure point, increase its sensitivity to family dynamics and needs, and adopt more flexible reassignment policies. The services should certainly try to accommodate special requests by servicemembers with teenage children to extend the duration of their stay at their current location.

There are points in the life cycle when geographical mobility may not be as stressful and may even be welcomed. Young couples who have no children are likely to view moving as an opportunity to see new places and probably have fewer adjustment problems (39), especially if there is employment available for the spouse, and the servicemember has time to spend with the spouse.

Like geographic mobility, the strains of separation may be especially difficult at certain stages of family life. Newly married couples, who have had less time to solidify their relationships, are especially vulnerable to the disruptions of separation. Young couples depend on time together for the development of intimate bonds, trust, and a shared understanding of reality. New marriages are sometimes too fragile to survive separation. Young families with preschool children who are not near their extended families and long-term friends are more likely to have problems of social isolation and loneliness associated with separation.

Long-term separations during particular family phases are especially disruptive to family functioning and violate social expectations regarding family roles. Men who are away during their wives' pregnancy and/or childbirth miss an important family event. Servicemembers separated from their young children miss periods of rapid growth and change. Similarly, they sometimes are absent for special events in their children's lives (e.g., a child's first step, first word, first bicycle ride, or birthday).

Families often need help during separations and existing programs are viewed as inadequate by many (38). Young families have the fewest resources of their own and therefore need support from the military institution, both in terms of informal social networks and formal programs and services. Preventing and solving family problems during separation improves military performance. It is also beneficial to the military organization to incorporate families into the military institution as early as possible, socializing them to military life in order to develop commitment and cooperation rather than conflict over the servicemember's loyalty. Among the supports that are likely to do this is housing on post. Activities within military units are especially beneficial to new military spouses by providing opportunities to interact with others who can provide social support during separations.

Young families also need affordable and convenient child care, both to enable spouse employment and to provide non-employed spouses with some relief from continuous parental responsibility. Long or unpredictable duty hours and other servicemember absences from home hinder shared parental child care, an economical practice used by many young couples (80).

IMPLICATIONS FOR POLICY AND PRACTICE

Work–family linkages in the military have been in rapid flux over the past few years. Service policies and programs have been somewhat responsive to these dynamics. Attention to family issues is quite recent and has not yet been institutionalized; it is not a fundamental part of the military culture. There are still strong pressures on servicemembers and their families to adapt to the demands of the organization. While programs have been developed to buffer the stress families experience, there are many possible policy changes that can improve family quality of life and satisfaction with the military. The ways in which the military organization and families mutually adapt to each other are dependent on many factors and issues. Two organizational issues are salient.

Of primary importance in policy consideration is the extent to which the military can be responsive to family needs while maintaining or enhancing mission effectiveness. The armed forces have strong traditions that are extremely resistant to change; policy change can come about only with the assurance that national security will not be threatened. Indeed, what often draws organizational attention to family issues is recognition of the important role families play in retention and readiness.

A second issue often raised in discussing military family policy is the extent of the organization's responsibility compared with that of individual servicemembers and their families. The armed forces are wrestling with the question of how far they should go in providing services. Attempts to reach families are often fraught with concerns about the balance between supporting families and invading family privacy. Policy change and intervention strategies are likely to be most effective to the extent that families are made aware of what is available to them, truly encouraged to use policy options and services without detriment to servicemembers' careers, and allowed to choose for themselves the extent of their involvement with the military.

The policies, programs, and practices of the armed forces can accommodate family issues. Research is accumulating that helps in understanding the predictable stressors in the military life style and the dynamics by which these stressors operate under varying conditions (including the family situation) (1, 85). Policy changes can take families into account in ways that serve to reduce family stress without necessarily detracting from mission readiness. Indeed, responsiveness to the family concerns of servicemembers can improve various components of readiness and retention.

The emphasis in recent organizational responses has been on programs and services to assist families in adapting to the military life style and coping with stress. Such developments exist at many levels, including DoD-wide, service-wide, installation-specific, and unit-specific. Programs include legislation granting military spouse hiring preferences and spouse employment services, sponsor programs, exceptional family member services, family housing construction, community representation systems, and family support groups. Child-care facilities, while increasing, are generally still insufficient to meet the growing demand.

Other programs emphasize advice to families on what to expect and how to cope with military stressors, such as geographic mobility and separation. More such programs can be developed using the results of research that identify, for example, the most adaptive strategies for those in different organizational and family situations.

Policy innovations of a different sort are also needed and possible: those that focus on making the military system more adaptive to family concerns. Among the policies that could be targeted are volition in reassignments, tour lengths, relocation notice, housing eligibility policies, timing and control of unaccompanied tours, and quarters clearance procedures. Assignment policies, for example, could be responsive to family needs without career detriment, especially when servicemembers make specific requests. For example, it is predictable that servicemembers with teenage children will sometimes ask to have their current tour extended. Granting such requests, when possible, would often be beneficial to both family and military.

Certain situations can make a family separation particularly detrimental to family and servicemember well-being. Service policies and practices that recognize and respond to such situations with compassion and flexibility can improve long-term morale, retention, and readiness.

There are several specific types of military families where military adaptation can potentially increase the institutional commitment of servicemembers and their families. These include junior enlisted families, military women, and dual-service couples.

The special circumstances of young enlisted families place them at high risk for a host of problems, including poverty, family violence, psychological adjustment difficulties, and marital dissolution. There are potential policies that can ease their burdens while at the same time integrating them into the military institution. For example, provision of on-post housing can relieve some of their financial pressures, facilitate their use of available on-post services, socialize them into the military way of life, and foster their interaction with the single servicemembers who live on post. Further, even without providing on-post housing, the armed forces can offer opportunities for junior enlisted families to develop informal social support networks, which ameliorate the effects of stressful life events. Personnel policies such as the Army's unit rotation can facilitate these opportunities if the units make specific attempts to do so. Incorporating enlisted wives into the military organization in ways similar to the institutionalization of the roles of officers' wives can potentially strengthen their husbands' commitment to the military. Indeed, the direction of social change with regard to women's roles, and the association of social class with these changes, may presage more integration into post life for enlisted wives and less for officers' wives.

Increasing numbers of women in uniform have already required changes in the traditionally male military institution. Further organizational adaptation, especially improvements in the treatment of military women, can foster their morale and career commitments. Specifically regarding family issues, service policies can aim at being partially accommodating to especially greedy family stages. Thus, for example, military members can be allowed to take parental leave, and child-care programs can be expanded and improved.

Dual-service couples offer potentially high commitment to the armed forces. To retain these couples, the major effort required by the military is the provision of coordinated assignments. Although this gets more difficult as the numbers of such couples increase, the gains in institutional dedication may be worth the accommodations necessary.

In general, it is important for the military services to ensure that high-level policy sensitivity to family concerns is carried through the day-to-day operations of the organizations. Leadership training at all levels should include research-based specific guidelines on how best to address the family needs of subordinates. Leaders are evaluated on various dimensions of personnel management; their sensitivity and responsiveness to subordinates' family concerns could be included as well.

The military services must respond to changes in the nature of their forces and to societal changes in family patterns and gender roles. In general, the more the armed forces adapt to family needs, the greater the commitment of both servicemembers and their families to the institution. To the extent that the military views the family as an outside influence with which it competes, the more resistant servicemembers and their families will be to the demands of the organization. To the extent that the military works to incorporate the family and adapt to it, the result will be organizational change that preserves the institutional nature of military organization.

NOTES

1. Barokas, J., and Croan, G. (eds.) (1988) *The Army Family Research Program's Family Factors in Retention, Readiness, and Sense of Community: The Plan for Research*. Fairfax, VA: Caliber Associates. Report to the U.S. Army Research Institute for the Behavioral and Social Sciences.

2. Bartone, P. (1987) Boundary crossers: The role of family assistance officers in the Gander disaster. Paper presented at the meeting of the Inter-University Seminar on Armed Forces and Society, October, Chicago, IL.

3. Bartone, P., Saczynski, K., Ingraham, L., and Ursano, R. (1987a) The impact of a military air disaster on the health of family assistance workers. Paper presented at the meeting of the American Psychological Association, August, New York.

4. Bartone, P., Saczynski, K., Ingraham, L., and Ursano, R. (1987b) Psychological issues in the recovery of an Army unit after traumatic loss. Paper presented at the meeting of the American Psychological Association, August, New York.

5. Berger, P. L., and Kellner, H. (1964) Marriage and the construction of reality. *Diogenes* 46:1–23.

6. Berger, P. L., and Luckmann, T. (1967) *The Social Construction of Reality.* Garden City, NY: Anchor.

7. Bergermaier, R., Borg, I., and Champoux, J. E. (1984) Structural relationships among facets of work, nonwork, and general well-being. *Work and Occupations* 11:163–81.

8. Blucher, J. (1987) The right to work. *Army Times*, August 3, pp. 57, 60–61, 63.

9. Bowen, G. L. (1984) Military family advocacy: A status report. *Armed Forces & Society* 10 (Summer):583–96.

10. Bowen, G. L. (1985) Families in blue: Insights from Air Force families. *Social Casework: The Journal of Contemporary Social Work* 8:459–66.

11. Bowen, G. L. (1986a) A framework for research on career decisions and the military family. In G. M. Croan (ed.), *Career Decision Making and the Military Family: Towards a Comprehensive Model* (Appendix A). Oakton, VA: Caliber Associates.

12. Bowen, G. L. (1986b) Spouse support and the retention intentions of Air Force members: A basis for program development. *Evaluation and Program Planning* 9:209–20.

13. Bowen, G. L. (1987) Changing gender-role preferences and marital adjustment: Implications for clinical practice. *Family Therapy* 14:17–33.

14. Bowen, G. L. (1988) Corporate supports for the family lives of employees: A conceptual model for program planning and evaluation. *Family Relations* 37:183–88.

15. Bowen, G. L., and Henley, H. C. (1987) Asian-wife marriages in the U.S. military: A comparative analysis with white- and black-wife marriages. *Family Perspective* 21:23–37.

16. Bowen, G. L., and Neenan, P. A. (1988) Sex-role orientations among married men in the military: The generational factor. *Psychological Reports* 62:523–26.

17. Bowen, G. L., and Orthner, D. K. (1986) Single parents in the U.S. Air Force. *Family Relations* 35:45–52.

18. Burgess, T. (1984) Three military wives jobless for every civilian one. *U.S. Army Times*, November 5, pp. 3, 66.

19. Campbell, A. (1981) *The Sense of Well-Being in America: Recent Patterns and Trends.* New York: McGraw-Hill.

20. Canadian Forces (1987) Military family study: A promise. *Personnel Newsletter* (Ottawa, Canada: Office of the Assistant Deputy Minister for Personnel, National Defence Headquarters).

21. Carlson, E. C., and Carlson, R. (1984) *Navy Marriages and Deployment.* Lanham, MD: University Press of America.

22. Coates, C. H., and Pellegrin, R. J. (1965) *Military Sociology: A Study of American Military Institutions and Military Life.* University Park, MD: Social Science Press.

23. Coser, L. A. (1974) *Greedy Institutions: Patterns of Undivided Commitment.* New York: Free Press.

24. Coser, L. A., and Coser, R. L. (1974) The housewife and her "greedy fam-

ily." In Coser, L. A. (ed.), *Greedy Institutions: Patterns of Undivided Commitment*, pp. 89–100. New York: Free Press.

25. Darnauer, P. (1976) The adolescent experience in career Army families. In H. I. McCubbin, B. B. Dahl, and E. J. Hunter (eds.), *Families in the Military System*, pp. 42–66. Beverly Hills, CA: Sage.

26. Decker, K. B. (1978) Coping with sea duty: Problems encountered and resources utilized during periods of family separation. In E. J. Hunter and D. S. Nice (eds.), *Military Families: Adaptation to Change*, pp. 113–29. New York: Praeger.

27. Department of the Army. (1984a) *The Army Family Action Plan* (pamphlet 608–41). Washington, D.C.

28. Department of the Army (1984b) *Soldiers Report III: 1984*. Washington, D.C.: Human Resources Development Directorate, Office of the Deputy Chief of Staff for Personnel, U.S. Department of the Army.

29. Department of the Army (1985) *The Army Family Action Plan II* (pamphlet 608–41). Washington, D.C.

30. Department of Defense (1987) *Defense 87 Almanac*, September/October. Alexandria, VA: American Forces Information Service.

31. Dillkofer, H., Meyer, G., and Schneider, S. (1985) *Soziale Probleme von Soldatenfamilien der Bundeswehr* (with English summary). Munich: Sozialwissenschaftliches Institut der Bundeswehr.

32. Doering, Z. D., and Hutzler, W. P. (1982) *Description of Officers and Enlisted Personnel in the U.S. Armed Forces: Reference for Military Manpower Analysis*. Santa Monica, CA: RAND.

33. Emberton, K. D. (1988) *Perceptions by Army Junior Noncommissioned Officers and their Spouses of the Impact of Leader Power and Behavior on their Family Well-Being*. Master's thesis, University of Maryland, College Park.

34. Gerstel, N., and Gross, H. (1984) *Commuter Marriage: A Study of Work and Family*. New York: Guilford Press.

35. Ginovski, J., and Blucher, J. (1987). Air Force wives pressured to quit working, inquiry finds. *Army Times*, October 26, p. 3.

36. Goffman, E. (1961) *Asylums: Essays on the Social Situation of Mental Patients and Other Inmates*. Garden City, NY: Doubleday.

37. Grace, G. L., and Steiner, M. B. (1978) Wives' attitudes and the retention of Navy enlisted personnel. In E. J. Hunter and D. S. Nice (eds.), *Military Families: Adaptation to Change*, pp. 42–54. New York: Praeger.

38. Griffith, J. D., Doering, Z. D., and Mahoney, B. S. (1986) *Description of Spouses of Officers and Enlisted Personnel in the U.S. Armed Forces: 1985. A Report Based on the 1985 DoD Surveys of Officer and Enlisted Personnel and Military Spouses*. Arlington, VA: Defense Manpower Data Center.

39. Griffith, J. D., LaVange, L. M., Gabel, T. J., Doering, Z. D., and Mahoney, B. S. (1986) *Description of Spouses of Officers and Enlisted Personnel in the U.S. Armed Forces: 1985. Supplementary Tabulations from the 1985 DoD Surveys of Officer and Enlisted Personnel and Military Spouses*, Vols. 1–3. Arlington, VA: Defense Manpower Data Center.

40. Grossman, A. S. (1984) *The Employment Situation for Military Wives*. Washington, D.C.: U.S. Department of Labor, Bureau of Labor Statistics.

41. Helmreich, R. J., Spence, J. T., and Gibson, R. H. (1982) Sex role attitudes: 1972–1980. *Personality and Social Psychology* 39:896–908.

42. Hill, R. (1949) *Families under Stress: Adjustment to the Crisis of War Separation and Reunion.* New York: Harper.

43. Holahan, C. J., and Moos, R. W. (1982) Social support and adjustment: Predictive benefits of social climate indices. *American Journal of Community Psychology* 10:403–15.

44. House, J. S. (1981) *Work Stress and Social Support.* Reading, MA: Addison-Wesley.

45. Hunter, E. J. (1982a) *Families under the Flag: A Review of Military Family Literature.* New York: Praeger.

46. Hunter, E. J. (1982b) Marriage in limbo. *U.S. Naval Institute Proceedings* 108/7/953:27–32.

47. Janowitz, M. (1975) *Military Conflict.* Beverly Hills, CA: Sage.

48. Jans, N. A. (1985) Issues in Australian service family life: An empirical study. Unpublished paper.

49. Jans, N. A. (1987) The quality of life in the Australian Defence Force. In J. Kuhlmann (ed.), *Forum International*, Vol. 5, pp. 47–83. Sessions of Research Committee 01: Armed Forces and Conflict Resolution, XI World Congress of Sociology, International Sociological Association, New Delhi, India, August 1986, Munich, Federal Republic of Germany: SOWI (Sozialwissenschaftliches Institut der Bundeswehr).

50. Jans, N. A. (forthcoming) *Careers in Conflict: A Study of Service Officers' Careers and Families in Peacetime.* Canberra: Canberra College of Advanced Education, Monograph Series.

51. Jolly, R. (1987) *Military Man, Family Man.* London: Brassey's Defence Publishers.

52. Kanter, R. M. (1977) *Work and Family in the United States: A Critical Review and Agenda for Research.* New York: Russell Sage.

53. Kim, B. L. C., Okamura, A., Ozawa, N., and Forrest, V. (1981) *Women in Shadows: A Handbook for Service Providers Working with Asian Wives of U.S. Military Personnel.* La Jolla, CA: National Committee Concerned with Asian Wives of U.S. Servicemen.

54. Laharanne, C. (1983) *The French Army NCO's Wife: From Dependence to Interdependence through Negotiation.* Paper prepared for the International Conference of the Inter-University Seminar on Armed Forces and Society, October, Chicago, IL.

55. LaVange, L.M., et al. (1986) *Description of Officers and Enlisted Personnel in the U.S. Armed Forces: 1985. Supplementary Tabulations from the 1985 DoD Surveys of Officer and Enlisted Personnel*, Vols. 1–3. Arlington, VA: Defense Manpower Data Center.

56. Lewis, C. (1987) Dealing with uncertainty: American military families in Europe. In J. Kuhlmann (ed.), *Forum International*, Vol. 5, pp. 3–45. Sessions of Research Committee 01: Armed Forces and Conflict Resolution, XI World Congress of Sociology, International Sociological Association, New Delhi, India, August 1986, Munich, Federal Republic of Germany: SOWI (Sozialwissenschaftliches Institut der Bundeswehr).

57. Love, M., Galinsky, E., and Hughes, D. (1987) Work and family: Research findings and models for change. Unpublished manuscript.

58. Marlowe, D. H., et al. (1987) Unit manning system field evaluation (Tech-

nical Report no. 5). Washington, D.C.: Walter Reed Army Institute of Research, Department of Military Psychiatry.

59. Martin, J. A., and Ickovics, J. R. (1987) The effects of stress on the psychological well-being of Army wives: Initial findings from a longitudinal study. *Journal of Human Stress* (Fall):108–115.

60. Mason, K. O., and Lu, Y. H. (1988) Attitudes toward women's familial roles: Changes in the United States, 1977–1985. *Gender & Society* 2:39–57.

61. McBroom, W. H. (1984) Changes in sex-role orientations: A five-year longitudinal comparison. *Sex Roles* 11:583–92.

62. McCalla, M. E., Rakoff, S. H., Doering, Z. D., and Mahoney, B. S. (1986). *Description of Officers and Enlisted Personnel in the U.S. Armed Forces: 1985. A Report Based on the 1985 DoD Surveys of Officer and Enlisted Personnel*. Arlington, VA: Defense Manpower Data Center.

63. McCubbin, H. I., and Dahl, B. B. (1976) Prolonged family separation in the military: A longitudinal study. In H. I. McCubbin, B. B. Dahl, and E. J. Hunter (eds.), *Families in the Military System*, pp. 112–44. Beverly Hills, CA: Sage.

64. McCubbin, H. I., Dahl, B. B., Metres, P. J., Jr., Hunter, E. J., and Plag, J. A. (1974) *Family Separation and Reunion: Families of Prisoners of War and Servicemen Missing in Action* (Report no. 74–70). San Diego, CA: Naval Health Research Center, Center for Prisoner of War Studies.

65. McKain, J. L. (1976) Alienation: A function of geographical mobility among families. In H. I. McCubbin, B. B. Dahl, and E. J. Hunter (eds.), *Families in the Military System*, pp. 69–91. Beverly Hills, CA: Sage.

66. Meyer, G. M. (1987) Reality experiences in military families of the Bundeswehr. In J. Kuhlmann (ed.), *Forum International*, Vol. 5, pp. 85–120. Sessions of Research Committee 01: Armed Forces and Conflict Resolution, XI World Congress of Sociology, International Sociological Association, New Delhi, India, August 1986, Munich, Federal Republic of Germany: SOWI (Sozialwissenschaftliches Institut der Bundeswehr).

67. Military Family Resource Center (1984) *Review of Military Family Research and Literature*, Vols. 1–2. Springfield, VA: Military Family Resource Center.

68. Montalvo, F. F. (1976) Family separation in the Army: A study of the problems encountered and the caretaking resources used by career Army families undergoing military separation. In H. I. McCubbin, B. B. Dahl, and E. J. Hunter (eds.), *Families in the Military System*, pp. 147–73. Beverly Hills, CA: Sage.

69. Moore, M. (1987) Commanders barred from interfering in military spouses' careers. *Washington Post*, October 27, p. A6.

70. Moskos, C. C. (1977a) From institution to occupation. *Armed Forces & Society* 4 (Fall):41–50.

71. Moskos, C. C. (1977b) The all-volunteer military: Calling, profession, or occupation? *Parameters* 7:2–9.

72. Moskos, C. C. (1978) The emergent military: Calling, profession, or occupation? In F. D. Margiotta (ed.), *The Changing World of the American Military*, pp. 199–206. Boulder, CO: Westview Press.

73. Moskos, C. C. (1986) Institutional/occupational trends in armed forces: An update. *Armed Forces & Society* 12 (Spring):377–82.

74. Nice, D. S. (1979) *The Course of Depressive Affect in Navy Wives during Family Separation*. San Diego, CA: Naval Health Research Center.

75. Orthner, D. K., Giddings, M. M., and Quinn, W. H. (1987) *Youth in Transition: A Study of Adolescents from Air Force and Civilian Families* (AFP 30–48). Washington, D.C.: U.S. Air Force, Office of Family Matters.

76. Piotrkowski, C. S. (1979) *Work and the Family System: A Naturalistic Study of Working-Class and Lower-Middle-Class Families.* New York: Free Press.

77. Pleck, J. H. (1977) The work–family role system. *Social Problems* 24:417–27.

78. Pleck, J. H., and Staines, G. L. (1982) Work schedules and work–family conflict in two-earner couples. In J. Aldous (ed.), *Two Paychecks: Life in Dual-Earner Families*, pp. 63–87. Beverly Hills, CA: Sage.

79. Presser, H. B. (1982) Working women and child care. In P. W. Berman and E. R. Ramey (eds.), *Women: A Developmental Perspective.* Washington, D.C.: U.S. Department of Health and Human Services.

80. Presser, H. B. (1988) Shift work and child care among young dual-earner American parents. *Journal of Marriage and the Family* 50:3–14.

81. Repetti, R. L. (1985) The social environment at work and psychological well-being. Doctoral dissertation, Yale University.

82. Repetti, R. L. (1987) Individual and common components of the social environment at work and psychological well-being. *Journal of Personality and Social Psychology* 52:710–20.

83. Segal, M. W. (1986a) Enlisted family life in the U.S. Army: A portrait of a community. In D. R. Segal and H. W. Sinaiko (eds.), *Life in the Rank and File: Enlisted Men and Women in the Armed Forces of the United States, Australia, Canada, and the United Kingdom*, pp. 184–211. Washington, D.C.: Pergamon-Brassey's.

84. Segal, M. W. (1986b) The Military and the Family as Greedy Institutions. *Armed Forces & Society* 13 (Fall):9–38.

85. Segal, M. W. (1986c) *Plan for Research on Army Families.* Alexandria, VA: U.S. Army Research Institute for the Behavioral and Social Sciences.

86. Segal, M. W., Kammeyer, K. C. W., and Vuozzo, J. S. (1987) The impact of separation on military family roles and self-perceptions during peacekeeping duty. Paper presented at the meeting of the Inter-university Seminar on Armed Forces and Society, October, Chicago, IL.

87. Segal, M. W., and Segal, D. R. (1983) Social change and the participation of women in the American military. In L. Kriesberg (ed.), *Research in Social Movements, Conflicts and Change*, Vol. 5, pp. 235–58. Greenwich, CT: JAI Press.

88. Shea, N. (revised by A. P. Smith) (1941–1966). *The Army Wife.* New York: Harper & Row.

89. Snyder, A. I. (1977) *Sea and Shore Rotation: The Family and Separations. A Bibliography of Relevant Material.* Pearl Harbor, HA: Mental Health Clinic, Naval Regional Medical Clinic.

90. Stratton, A. (1978) The stress of separation. *U.S. Naval Institute Proceedings* 104 (July):53–58.

91. Szoc, R. (1982) *Family Factors Critical to the Retention of Naval Personnel.* Washington, D.C.: Family Support Program, NMPC-66, Naval Military Personnel Command.

92. U.S. Bureau of the Census (1985a) *Current Population Reports* (Series P–20, no. 398). Washington, D.C.: U.S. Government Printing Office.

93. U.S. Bureau of the Census (1985b) *Current Population Reports* (Series P–20, no. 402). Washington, D.C.: U.S. Government Printing Office.

94. U.S. Bureau of the Census (1985c) *Current Population Reports* (Series P–23, no. 145). Washington, D.C.: U.S. Government Printing Office.

95. U.S. Department of Labor, Bureau of Labor Standards (1985) *Employment and Earnings.* Washington, D.C.: U.S. Government Printing Office, January.

96. VanVranken, E. W., Jellen, L. K., Knudson, K. H. M., Marlowe, D. H., and Segal, M. W. (1984) *The Impact of Deployment Separation on Army Families* (Report NP–84–6). Washington, D.C.: Walter Reed Army Institute of Research.

97. Voydanoff, P. (1987) *Work and Family Life.* Beverly Hills, CA: Sage.

98. *Washington Post* (1987) 2 Air Force officers' wives were pressured to quit jobs. October 15, p. A23.

99. Wickham, J. A., Jr. (1983) *Chief of Staff White Paper 1983: The Army Family.* Washington, D.C.: Department of the Army.

100. Willis, G. (1987) DoD letter affirms spouses' right to work. *Army Times,* November 2, pp. 3, 72.

101. Woelfel, J. D., and Savell, J. M. (1978) Marital satisfaction, job satisfaction, and retention in the Army. In E. J. Hunter and D. S. Nice (eds.), *Military Families: Adaptation to Change,* pp. 17–31. New York: Praeger.

2

Family Factors and Member Retention: A Key Relationship in the Work and Family Equation

Gary L. Bowen

The retention of military personnel has become an issue of national concern. It has been the subject of congressional hearings and public debates, and retention concerns are among the top priorities of military leadership (11). Retention concerns have extended beyond first-term members, where re-enlistment rates are traditionally low, to include second-term, mid-career, and even late-career officers and noncommissioned officers. Importantly, goals have expanded from "retention" per se to the "retention" of high-quality performers and individuals in critical manpower shortage areas (13, 34).

Given the extensive amounts of both time and money required to recruit and train personnel, as well as the "lost investment" in senior enlisted and officer members who leave while still eligible to continue active-duty military service, it is vital that military decision makers understand the factors that influence the career commitments of servicemembers. Only then can they endorse and develop policies and programs that help reduce the turnover rate of experienced and qualified members, thereby increasing the "readiness" of the armed forces.

This chapter is a revised version of a more extensive manuscript prepared under contract no. DAAG29-81-D-0100, Delivery Order 1684 for the Army Research Institute's panel on retention and the military family. Support for the revision was provided by an IBM Junior Faculty Development Award, the University of North Carolina at Chapel Hill Foundation. An earlier version was presented at the Ninety-Fourth Annual Convention of the American Psychological Association, Washington, D.C., August 1986. The views and opinions contained in this chapter are those of the author and should not be construed as an official Department of Army position, policy, or decision, unless so designated by other documentation. Grateful appreciation is expressed to Drs. Paul Gade, Glenda Nogami, and Truman Tremble of the Army Research Institute and to Mr. Gerald Croan of the Caliber Associates for their valuable comments on an earlier version of this chapter.

Over the last decade, the military services have demonstrated an increased interest in the influence that family factors have on the retention decision-making process of military members. Stimulated by a substantial increase in the proportion of members with family responsibilities (3, 9) as well as a shifting value among military members to better balance the meaning and priority of work with family goals and interests (28), this interest parallels the growing recognition of the interdependence among personal and family well-being, recruitment and retention decisions, and job satisfaction and productivity (6, 14, 20). This recognition has provided the impetus for the increasing incorporation of support programs and services for military personnel and their families (10, 20, 23).

Despite a proliferation of research on work–family linkages in the military community over the last decade (2, 10), little attention has been directed toward modeling the influence of family factors on the retention decision-making process of military members. Given the importance of empirical integration for providing a conceptual underpinning for future research activities, the purpose of this chapter was to develop a comprehensive, conceptual model of linkages between family factors and the retention decision-making process of military members.

In addition to its heuristic implications, such a model should have important implications for policy and program planners in the military community. However elementary, the model should be helpful to planners in identifying potentially promising policy, program, and organizational interventions to enhance the retention of desired personnel, and in developing models to predict quantitative impacts of family-related interventions on retention.

Such a model should also be of interest to civilian employers who are faced with a changing U.S. workforce, which includes an increasing number of married women with children and a new dynamic between the work and family lives of employees. This is especially the case for those with employees who share demands similar to those faced by military personnel (e.g., police and fire department personnel, senior corporate executives). Paralleling the interest of their military counterparts, these employers too have become increasingly interested in better understanding the connection between organizational policies and practices, employee morale and commitment, and the family demands and satisfactions of employees (7). Despite the extensive research on the turnover process among civilian employees across a broad range of employment settings, researchers have only begun to understand how, for whom, and under what conditions family factors influence voluntary turnover decisions (7, 25).

The model developed in this chapter is based upon a literature review of studies concerning the nature of work and family linkages within the military community. The review was guided by three objectives: (a) to identify how and under what conditions family factors have been found to impact upon the career decision-making process of military members, (b) to critique the nature and limitations of the knowledge base to date, and (c) to identify implications for further research activity exploring the interplay of work and family variables in the military community. The overall aim of the review was to generate hypotheses for modeling purposes, to develop "grounded theory" (17). Although the bidirectional pathway between work and family variables is increasingly recognized (12, 41), this chapter focuses primarily upon one direction of influence: the family's influence on work, in particular, the family's influence on the retention intentions and behaviors of military members.

A LITERATURE CRITIQUE

Although the issue of employee retention has sustained the interest of personnel researchers since the turn of the century (25), the study of retention in the military services has only recently become a focus of study. The transition to an all-volunteer force in 1973, the need for a large standing peacetime force that supports allies worldwide, a declining service-age youth cohort, coupled with the increased technological sophistication required to operate modern weapons, have generated increased concern about the retention of trained personnel among both congressional and military leaders (10, 35). The relationship between family factors and retention in the military is even more recent. Given recent research that suggests the inextricable link between family responsibilities and satisfactions of employees and employee morale and commitment, it is no longer possible to deny the critical influence that families have on work (7, 35).

Until recently there was only limited research, largely anecdotal, to suggest the influential role that family factors play in the retention decision-making process. However, since the early 1970s there has been an increasing number of studies that have reported a link between family factors and retention (6, 14). Unfortunately, as will be discussed in more detail below, many of these studies have suffered from methodological limitations, including small, often nonrepresentative or narrowly defined samples (e.g., officer members only), and inadequate statistical controls.

Nonetheless, there is a growing body of literature that attests to the linkages between family factors and retention (29). In fact, one family variable, spouse support for the member's career, has been identified consistently in the research literature to date as a positive and direct predictor of the retention decision-making process of military members (6, 18, 28, 29, 38). However, with the exception of spouse support, there has been a lack of consistency in the findings of studies examining the links between family factors and the retention intentions and decisions of military members.

Despite the growing body of literature investigating the influence of family factors on the retention decision-making process of military members, a number of conceptual and methodological issues continue to plague the research. Since the purpose of this chapter is to generate hypotheses for modeling purposes using a grounded theoretical approach, it is important to briefly discuss a select number of these issues to highlight some of the challenges to model development and research in this area of study.

Variation in the Specification of the Dependent Variable

The lack of consistency between studies in the conceptualization of the dependent variable poses special challenges to comparing results from research in this area of inquiry. Although most studies have focused on the retention intentions of members (6), other studies have focused on the actual behavior decisions of members to continue or terminate military service (19). In addition, some studies have used an expanded definition of retention intention, combining this variable with other job indicators, such as job performance and satisfaction with military life and current assignment (29). More attention needs to be directed to studying the advantages and disadvantages of using various operational definitions of retention at the individual level.

A Negative View Toward Intentions to Leave and Turnover Behavior

Studies to date have implicitly viewed loss/turnover behavior as negatively valued. However, recent work in the civilian community suggests that not all turnover is "dysfunctional" to the organization (15). For example, although turnover can result in the loss of high performers, productivity loss, and replacement costs, it can have positive implications if it results in the displacement of poor performers, increased chances of promotion for those remaining in service, and the infusion of new knowledge and technology via replacements (24). To fully understand the implications of turnover, future studies need to examine the consequences of loss as well as its causes.

Reliance on Member's Perceptions of Family Factors

In recent years it has become evident that in every marriage there is really two marriages—his and hers (39, 42). In only a few cases, however, have military researchers investigating work and family linkages in the military community employed samples of both husbands and wives (28). For example, most studies that have explored the relationship between spouse support and the retention decision-making process of military members have operationalized the independent variable, spouse support, based on the member's perceptions of the spouse's support rather than the actual stated support of the spouse. In a recent analysis Bowen found that the actual stated support of the spouse for the member's career to be a better predictor of the member's retention intention than the perception of the member toward the level of spouse support (6). To determine the full impact of family factors on the retention intentions and decisions of military members, it will be important in future studies to include the perceptions and attitudes of other family members besides the military member in the sample.

Neglect of the Anticipated Impact of Family Life on the Retention Decision-Making Process of Single Members

To date there has been a lack of research investigating the perceptions of single members toward the military community as a place to be married and have a family. It is likely that the perceptions of single members toward the compatibility between the military way of life and family life will have an influence on their decisions about a career in the military. In addition, it will be important to investigate the impact that the nonmarital relationships of single members have on their decisions to continue or terminate their military careers.

Lack of Stage-Specific Analysis

To date, research examining the links between family factors and retention intentions/decisions in the military have failed to consider how such relationships vary across stages of the career and the family life cycle, especially the latter. For example, it is likely that the influence of family factors on the retention decision-making process of military members will vary by tenure group (e.g., first term, second term, and so forth).

Selected studies have attempted to control for the tenure group of the sample by limiting the sample to certain groups, often specified by years of service or rank. For example, Bowen, in his analysis of family and retention linkages in the Air Force, restricted his sample to those members with less than ten years of service (6). In general, however, there is a lack of consistency across studies in specifying the tenure groups included in the analysis.

Other Issues

In addition to the issues outlined above, there has also been an overdependence in past studies on cross-sectional as compared with longitudinal designs, a focus on bivariate as compared with multivariate analysis, an overreliance on quantitative as compared with qualitative methods for model building, an underanalysis of data sets, and a failure to separate marital and family interactional variables from variables dealing with levels of marital and family life satisfaction. There has also been a service imbalance in the research on the influence of family factors on the decision-making process of military members. By far the greatest number of studies have been conducted in the Navy context, where interest in the retention of naval petty officers started in the mid-1970s. Paralleling the services' differential retention problems within population subgroups and differences in their need for technically trained personnel, there has also been a tendency for the various services to focus differentially on various aspects of personnel loss, with the Army focusing most on first-term attrition, the Air Force concentrating more heavily on officer retention, and the Navy placing greater attention on retention after a second tour of duty.

Although the combined influence of these issues limits the use of a grounded theoretical approach to generate models of work–family linkages, substantial progress has been made over the last decade in studying the influence of family factors on the retention decision-making process of military members. However, it is clear that continued conceptual clarification as well as additional methodological and statistical rigor are needed in this important area of policy and program research. This is especially the case if the purpose is to create explanatory and predictive models for guiding policy and program development.

A CONCEPTUAL MODEL

The aim of this section of the chapter is to outline a model hypothesizing the direct as well as the indirect paths of influence of family factors on the retention decision-making process of military members. An attempt is also made to depict factors that indirectly influence the retention intentions and decisions of military members through their impact on family-related factors. Following the turnover research of Mobley et al. in the civilian sector (25) and Orthner and Pittman in the military sector (29), satisfaction with marital and family life is depicted as a major mediator between antecedent and outcome variables in the model.

Using an inductive theoretical approach, the process of constructing the model involved first identifying the nature of relevant data and then summarizing the source of the data, the nature of hypotheses tested, and the major findings. The development of the model relied primarily on 18 empirical studies, selected primarily for their methodological soundness and their use of multivariate analysis (4, 5, 6, 8, 18, 19, 21, 22, 27, 28, 29, 30, 31, 32, 36, 38, 40, 43).

Since the nature of relationships between variables is an essential focus of inquiry when using an inductive theoretical approach, relationships between variables in each study were examined closely for direction, shape, amount of influence, and length of time involved in the relationship. In the process, careful attention was given to evaluating the unique limitations of the data and the data analysis that impact upon the confidence that can be

TABLE 2.1
Variable Domains: A Synopsis of the Literature

Family Life Cycle (X1)
(Y1)
  Marital status
  Years married
  Presence of children
  Number of children
  Age of youngest child

Career Life Cycle (X1)
(Y1)
  Years of service
  Rank (M)
  Employment status (S)

Job Demands (X2)(Y2)
  Work hours
  Family separations (M)
  Temporary duty assign-
    ments (M)
  Remote tours (M)
  Extra-duty assign-
    ments (M)
  Swing shifts (M)
  Frequency of PCS (M)
  MOS (M)
  Nature of job (S)

Community Embedded-
ness and Satisfaction
(X3)(Y3)
  Satisfaction with
    location
  Good environment
    for family
  Size of personal network
  Relationships: Personal
    network
  Base responsiveness to
    families

Marital/Family Interaction
(X4)(Y4)
  Gender role attitudes
  H/W problem solving
  Marital communication
  H/W time together
  H/W sexual relationship
  H/W role sharing
  H/W ease of communication
  Parent/child companionship
  Parent/child time together
  Religious participation

Marital/Family Life Satisfaction
(X5)(Y5)
  Satisfaction: Marital relationship
  Satisfaction: Parent/child
    relationship

Satisfaction with Military Life
(X6)(Y6)
  General satisfaction: Military life
  Military/family conflict
  Like the military way of life (S)
  Feel proud to be part of
    military (S)
  Satisfaction: Military social
    life/protocol (S)

Retention Intention
(X7)
  Reenlistment intent
  Extension behavior

Desirability of Con-
tinuing Military Life
(Y7)
  Desire to remain in
    military

Spouse Support (Y8)
  Desire: member to
    continue military

Turnover (X8)
  Decision to con-
    tinue/terminate
    military service

Note: M = Member only; S = Spouse only; H/W = Husband and wife/ PCS = Permanent change of
    station; MOS = Military occupational status.

TABLE 2.2
Toward a Specification of Propositions Concerning the Relationship Between Family Factors and the Retention Decision-Making Process of Military Members: A Foundation for Model Development

FIRST-ORDER PROPOSITIONS	SECOND-ORDER PROPOSITIONS

Turnover (X8)

The greater the retention intention, the lower the chance for turnover behavior (19).

Retention Intention (X7)

The greater the spouse's support for the member's career, the higher the retention intention of the member (6, 18, 19, 22, 29, 30).

The greater the member's satisfaction with military life, the higher the retention intention (6, 27).

The more the member is satisfied with military life, the higher the retention intention.

The fewer the conflicting demands between military service and family life, the higher the retention intention (38).

The higher the member's marital satisfaction, the higher the retention intention (29).

Spouse Support (Y8)

The greater the spouse's desire to remain in the military, the higher the spouse's support of the member's career (6).

The higher the retention intention of the member, the higher the spouse's support of the member's career (22, 38).

Table 2.2 (continued)

FIRST-ORDER PROPOSITIONS	SECOND-ORDER PROPOSITIONS

Desirability of Continuing Military Life (Y7)

The more the spouse agrees with military rules, the greater the desire to continue military life (19).

The more the spouse likes the military, the greater the desire to continue military life (19).

The more the spouse feels proud of the military, the greater the desire to continue military life (19).

The greater the spouse's satisfaction with military life, the greater the desire to continue military life.

The more the spouse feels that his/her participation in the military provides a contribution to society, the greater the desire to continue military life (19).

The greater the spouse's satisfaction with military social life and protocol, the greater the desire to continue military life (22).

The greater the spouse's satisfaction with military life, the greater the desire to continue military life (6, 18).

The more satisfied the spouse is with parent/child relationships, the greater the desire to continue military life (6).

The higher the spouse's marital and family life satisfaction, the greater the desire to continue military life.

The more satisfied the spouse is with marriage, the greater the desire to continue military life (6).

Table 2.2 (continued)

FIRST-ORDER PROPOSITIONS	SECOND-ORDER PROPOSITIONS
The more time that the member spends away from home because of job demands, the greater the interference with home life (32, 43).	
The more frequent the member's separation from the family, the higher the spouse's parent-child relationship stress (40).	
	The greater the respective job demands of members and spouses, the less frequent and positive the marital and family interaction.
The more frequent the member's separation from the family, the greater the spouse's feelings of loneliness (40).	
Members and spouses in marriages where the spouse works part-time are more likely to experience lower marital companionship than members and spouses in marriages where the spouse is not employed or works full-time (30).	
Parents of adolescents are more likely to experience lower marital companionship than childless couples and parents of younger children (28).	
	Parents of adolescents are more likely than other parents to experience less positive marital and family interaction.
Parents of adolescents are more likely to experience higher parent-child relational stress than parents of younger children (28).	

Community Embeddedness and Satisfaction (X3; Y3)

Members and spouses in the senior enlisted and officer ranks are more likely to have weaker community relationships with friends and neighbors than more junior enlisted and officer members and spouses (4).

Table 2.2 (continued)

FIRST-ORDER PROPOSITIONS	SECOND-ORDER PROPOSITIONS
	The greater the marital and family interaction, the greater the marital and family satisfaction.
The greater the role sharing in marriage, the greater the marital and family life satisfaction (8, 28, 31).	
The greater the ease of communication between spouses, the greater the marital and family life satisfaction (21, 28).	
The greater the sexual satisfaction, the greater the marital and family life satisfaction (28).	
The greater the joint church attendance, the greater the marital and family life satisfaction (5).	
The greater the joint church attendance, the greater the parent-child relationship satisfaction (5).	
The more positive the perceptions toward base responsiveness to families, the greater the marital and family life satisfaction (29, 30).	
	The more embedded and satisfied with the military community, the greater the marital and family life satisfaction.
The greater the social support network, the greater the marital and family life satisfaction (29, 30, 36, 38).	

Marital and Family Interaction (X4; Y4)

The more positive the member's marital and family interaction, the more positive the spouse's marital and family interaction, and vice versa (8).

The more embedded and satisfied with the military community, the more positive the marital and family interaction (28, 36).

Table 2.2 (continued)

FIRST-ORDER PROPOSITIONS	SECOND-ORDER PROPOSITIONS
The more positive the military atmosphere is viewed by the spouse as a place to rear children, the greater the desire to continue military life (6, 30).	
	The more embedded and satisfied the spouse is with the military community, the greater the desire to continue military life.
The more embedded the spouse is in the military community, the greater the spouse's desire to continue military life (6, 30).	

Satisfaction with Military Life (X6; Y6)

The greater the spouse's support for the member's career, the higher the member's satisfaction with military life (6).

The greater the marital satisfaction, the greater the satisfaction with military life (21, 38).

The greater the member's satisfaction with military life, the greater the spouse's satisfaction with military life, and vice versa (28).

Marital and Family Life Satisfaction (X5; Y5)

The greater the member's satisfaction with marital and family life, the greater the spouse's satisfaction, and vice versa (8).

The more effective the problem-solving in marriage, the greater the marital and family life satisfaction (28).

The greater the companionship in marriage, the greater the marital and family life satisfaction (28).

Table 2.2 (continued)

FIRST-ORDER PROPOSITIONS	SECOND-ORDER PROPOSITIONS

Job Demands (X2; Y2)

The higher the rank of the member, the more hours worked per week (28).

The job demands of members and spouses vary over the family and work life cycles.

Childless spouses and those with children older than six years of age are more likely to be employed than spouses with children under age six (28).

Source Documents

4   Bowen (1985)

5   Bowen (1986a)

6   Bowen (1986b)

8   Bowen and Orthner (1983)

18 Grace and Steiner (1978)

19 Holoter et al. (1974)

21 Lavee, McCubbin, and Patterson (1985)

22 Lund (1978)

27 Mowbray and Scheirer (1984)

28 Orthner and Bowen (1982)

29 Orthner and Pittman (1986)

30 Orthner, Pittman, and Monroe (1984)

31 Patterson and McCubbin (1984)

32 Raney (1980)

36 Stawarski and Bowen (1988)

38 Szoc (1982)

40 Van Vranken (1984)

43 Woelfel and Savell (1978)

the presence or expected future presence of a spouse, child, or other family member.

The Proposed Model

Figure 2.1 identifies the major components of the family/turnover model and the hypothesized relationships between components. Table 2.2 should be consulted both for the nature of the relationship between components as well as for the respective sources of empirical support. Briefly summarizing with the aid of Figure 2.1, it is predicted that the turnover behavior of members (x8) will be directly and positively affected by their retention intentions (x7). The level of support from the spouse for the member's career (y8) is hypothesized to have a positive and reciprocal relationship with the retention intentions of the member (x7). The level of spouse support (y8) is also predicted to indirectly impact upon the retention intentions of the member through its indirect and positive impact on the member's level of satisfaction with military life (x6). In addition, the retention intentions of members are also hypothesized to be directly affected by the member's satisfaction with military life (x6) and by the member's marital and family life satisfaction (x5)—hypothesized to both directly affect retention intentions and to indirectly affect retention intentions through a positive and direct influence on the member's satisfaction with military life. The level of satisfaction of the member and spouse with military life (x6 and y6, respectively) is hypothesized as reciprocal.

Like the member, the spouse is also hypothesized to have an attitude toward the desirability of staying in or leaving the military (y7), which will directly affect the level of support given to the member for continuing the military career (y8). This attitude for spouses (y7) is predicted to be directly affected by their satisfaction with military life (y6), by their satisfaction with marital and family life (y5), and by their level of community embeddedness and satisfaction (y3). In addition, the impact of spouses' satisfaction with marital and family life (y5) on their feelings about the desirability of continuing or leaving military life (y7) is also hypothesized as indirect as well as direct through their satisfaction with military life (y6).

It is predicted that the satisfaction of the member and spouse with marital and family life (x5 and y5, respectively) are strongly interrelated. The evaluation of marital and family life by both the member (x5) and spouse (y5) is hypothesized to be directly affected by their respective perceptions toward marital and family interactions (x4 and y4, respectively), which are predicted to be interrelated, and by their respective levels of community embeddedness and satisfaction (x3 and y3, respectively). In addition, the member's and spouse's levels of community embeddedness and satisfaction (x3 and y3, respectively) are predicted to indirectly affect their levels of marital and family life satisfaction (x5 and y5, respectively) through a positive and direct impact on their respective perceptions toward marital and family interaction (x4 and y4, respectively). The level of marital and family interaction of the member and spouse is also predicted to vary depending on the respective job demands of both the member and the spouse (x2 and y2, respectively).

Last, the job demands, the level of community embeddedness among members (x3) and spouses (y3), and the level of marital and family interaction among members (x4) and spouses (y4) are predicted to vary over the family/work life cycle for members (x1) and spouses (y1). The family/ work life cycle serves as the exogenous variable in the model and will be discussed in the following section.

THE NEED FOR A LIFE-COURSE PERSPECTIVE

Families are dynamic institutions whose membership, function, and needs vary over time. Work careers are similarly dynamic, changing in both form and function over the years (26). As a consequence, to understand variations in work–family linkages, it is necessary to employ a process model. The life-course perspective and role-strain theory provide useful concepts for this type of analysis (41).

The concept of work and family "career" is essential to understanding the influence of family factors on the retention decision-making process of military members. In its most general sense, the concept of "career" refers to a patterned sequence of activities throughout the life cycle, and includes stages and critical transition points (1, 16, 41). Stages are divisions within the career (or life cycle) that are different enough from one another to constitute separate periods (e.g., the transition from single life to marriage). From the process or life-course perspective, the intersections and interdependences of work and family career lines may involve competing demands that require scheduling, coordinating, and time and resource management (41). The expanding and contracting demands of work and family roles across the life cycle may create role strain and/or conflict at certain intersections, which may have consequences for both work and family performance and stability.

To date, little theoretical or empirical attention has been directed toward examining the interactions of work–family linkages across the life cycle. This is true whether we examine military or civilian literature. Research is required in the military community that traces family–work dynamics over time, exploring the consequences of this process for family dynamics as well as for the retention decision-making process of military members. It is likely that there are pressure points at certain intersections of work and family careers. For example, many couples attempt to begin their careers and their families simultaneously. The responsibilities for the early development needs of children combined with the heightened pace and expectations of a new job often present considerable pressures on young adults and their families.

The Rapoports have labeled the intermeshing of work and family careers as "role cycling" (33). These intersections become natural intervention points for studying the consequences of transitions in either the work career, the family career, or both for family dynamics and the retention decision-making process of the military members.

CONCLUSION

Despite the proliferation of research on work–family linkages in the military community over the last decade, there has been a limited theoretical effort at modeling the influence of family factors on the retention decision-making process of military members. Although a number of conceptual and methodological issues limit the comparability of research in this important area of inquiry, a theoretical model is outlined using an inductive theoretical approach. A key aspect of the model is the inclusion of both member- and spouse-related variables—a serious limitation in most prior research.

Given the limitations in synthesizing existing literature exploring the influence of family factors on the retention decision-making process of military members, the model is offered as a conceptual and theoretical straw man. By attempting to integrate the research literature to date, the model should have heuristic implications as well as implications for policy and program planners in developing interventions to enhance the retention of desired personnel.

As a straw man it is hoped that the model will help focus future inquiries into the influence of family factors on the retention decision-making process of military members. It is suggested that a combination of quantitative and qualitative methodologies be used to test relationships hypothesized in the model, especially those that incorporate longitudinal designs that follow panels of military members and their spouses over time who are at different stages in the family/career life cycle. The use of qualitative decision-making frameworks are also particularly recommended for tracing the process by which members and their spouses make a decision about continuing or discontinuing military service.

The testing and refining of the model will depend on careful development of operational definitions and empirical measures of its conceptual domains. To date there has been a general lack of comparability in the definition and measurement of key constructs in the model. It is hoped that the model presented will stimulate greater attention to measurement issues.

As a beginning framework it is recommended that military leaders sponsor research to explore the validity of the model not only within the military services, but also within the civilian employment sector. At present there is a dearth of comparative research on work–family linkages between the military services and civilian employers. A better understanding by military policy and program planners of how the work–family dynamic varies between the military and civilian employment sectors can promote the development of policy and program initiatives that focus on institutional strengths. Such initiatives will enhance the ability of the military services to compete with civilian employers to retain high-quality performers and individuals with advanced skills.

NOTES

1. Aldous, J. (1978) *Family Careers: Developmental Change in Families.* New York: John Wiley and Sons.

2. American Family (1985) Military family services and research on the rise. *American Family* (April):2–7.

3. Armed Services YMCA (1984) *American Military Families: Basic Demographics.* Springfield, VA: Military Family Resource Center.

4. Bowen, G. L. (1985) Families in blue: Insights from Air Force families. *Social Casework* 8:459–66.

5. Bowen, G. L. (1986a) Opportunities for ministry: The Air Force chaplain as a resource. *Military Chaplain Review* 15(2):61–75.

6. Bowen, G. L. (1986b) Spouse support and the retention intentions of Air Force members: A basis for program development. *Evaluation and Program Planning* 9:209–20.

7. Bowen, G. L. (1988) Corporate supports for the family lives of employees: A conceptual model for program planning and evaluation. *Family Relations* 37:183–88.

8. Bowen, G. L. and Orthner, D. K. (1983) Sex-role congruency and marital quality. *Journal of Marriage and the Family* 45:223–30.

9. Bowen, G. L., and Orthner, D. K. (1986) Single parents in the U.S. Air Force. *Family Relations* 35:45–52.

10. Bowen, G. L., and Scheirer, M. A. (1986) The development and evaluation of human service programs in the military: An introduction and overview. *Evaluation and Program Planning* 9:193–98.

11. Callander, B. (1982) Manpower: Rosy now, but thorny ahead. *Air Force Times* (April):21, 26.

12. Crouter, A. C. (1984) Spillover from family to work: the neglected side of the work–family interface. *Human Relations* 37:425–42.

13. Croan, G. M. (1986) *Career Decision Making and the Military Family: Toward a Comprehensive Model.* Alexandria, VA: U.S. Army Research Institute.

14. Croan, G. M., Katz, R., Fischer, N., and Smith-Osborne, A. (1980) *Roadmap for Navy Family Research.* Arlington, VA: Office of Naval Research.

15. Dalton, D. R., Krackhardt, D. M., and Porter, L. W. (1981) *Functional Turnover: An Empirical Assessment* (NTIS no. ADA 103 355). Eugene, OR: University of Oregon.

16. Feldman, H., and Feldman, M. (1975) The family life cycle: Some suggestions for recycling. *Journal of Marriage and the Family* 37:277–84.

17. Glaser, B. G., and Straus, A. S. (1967) *The Discovery of Grounded Theory: Strategies for Qualititive Research.* New York: Aldine.

18. Grace, G. L., and Steiner, M. B. (1978) Wives' attitudes and the retention of Navy enlisted personnel. In E. Hunter and D. Nice (eds.), *Military Families: Adaptation to Change*, pp. 42–54. New York: Praeger.

19. Holoter, H. A., Stehle, G. W., Conner, L. V., and Grace, G. L. (1974) *Impact of Navy Career Counseling on Personnel Satisfaction and Reenlistment: Phase 2 (TR3)*. Santa Monica, CA: System Development Corporation.

20. Hunter, E. J. (1982) *Families under the Flag*. New York: Praeger.

21. Lavee, Y., McCubbin, H. I., and Patterson, J. M. (1985) The double ABCX model of family stress and adaptation: An empirical test by analysis of structural equations with latent variables. *Journal of Marriage and the Family* 47:811–25.

22. Lund, D. A. (1978) Junior officer retention in the modern volunteer Army: Who leaves and who stays? In E. J. Hunter and D. S. Nice (eds.), *Military Families: Adaptation to Change*, pp. 32–41. New York: Praeger.

23. Military Family Resource Center (1984) *Review of Military Family Research and Literature*. Springfield, VA.

24. Mobley, W. H. (1982) Some unanswered questions in turnover and withdrawal research. *Academy of Management Review* 7(1):111–16.

25. Mobley, W. H., Griffeth, R. W., Hand, H. H., and Meglino, B. M. (1979) Review and conceptual analysis of the employee turnover process. *Psychological Bulletin* 86(3):493–522.

26. Moen, P. (1983) The two provider family: Problems and potentials. In D. H. Olson and B. C. Miller (eds.), *Family Studies Review Yearbook* Vol. 1 pp. 397–427. Beverly Hills, CA: Sage.

27. Mowbray, E., and Scheirer, M. A. (1984) *Variables Influencing the Reenlistment of Army Enlisted Personnel: A Critical Review*. Rockville, MD: Westat.

28. Orthner, D. K., and Bowen, G. L. (1982) *Families in Blue: Insights from Air Force Families in the Pacific*. Greensboro, NC: Family Development Press.

29. Orthner, D. K., and Pittman, J. F. (1986) Family contributions to work commitment. *Journal of Marriage and the Family* 48:573–81.

30. Orthner, D. K., Pittman, J. F., and Monroe, P. (1984) *Preliminary Impact Assessment of U.S. Air Force Family Support Centers: Development of an Impact Model*. Washington, D.C.: Department of the Air Force.

31. Patterson, J. M., and McCubbin, H. I. (1984) Gender roles and coping. *Journal of Marriage and the Family* 46:95–104.

32. Raney, J. L. (1980) *Relationship between Marital Status and Reenlistment Intent of U.S. Army Reservists*. Alexandria, VA: U.S. Army Research Institute.

33. Rapoport, R., and Rapoport, R. (1978) *Dual-Career Families Re-examined*. New York: Harper & Row.

34. Rimland, B., and Larson, G. E. (1981) The manpower quality decline. *Armed Forces and Society* 8:21–78.

35. Segal, M. W. (1986) The military and the family as greedy institutions. *Armed Forces and Society* 13:9–38.

36. Stawarski, C. A., and Bowen, G. L. (1988) *Family Adaptation: An Empirical Analysis of Family Stressors and Family Resources*. Alexandria, VA: U.S. Army Research Institute.

37. Stoloff, P. (1972) *An Analysis of First Term Reenlistment Intentions*. Arlington, VA: Center for Naval Analysis.

38. Szoc, R. (1982) *Family Factors Critical to Retention.* San Diego, CA: Naval Personnel Research and Development Center.

39. Thompson, L., and Walker, A. J. (1982) The dyad as the unit of analysis: Conceptual and methodological issues. *Journal of Marriage and the Family* 44:889–900.

40. Van Vranken, E. W. (1984) *The Impact of Deployment Separation on Army Families.* Washington, D.C.: Walter Reed Army Institute of Research.

41. Voyandoff, P. (1980) *Work–family life cycles.* Paper presented at the workshop on theory construction, National Council on Family Relations, October, Boston, MA.

42. Walters, L. H., Pittman, J. F., and Norrell, J. E. (1985) Development of a quantitative measure of a family from self-reports of family members. *Journal of Family Issues* 5:497–514.

43. Woelfel, J. C. and Savell, J. M. (1978) Marital satisfaction, job satisfaction, and retention in the Army. In E. J. Hunter and D. S. Nice (eds.), *Military Families: Adaptation to Change*, pp. 17–31. New York: Praeger.

3

Marital Quality and Job Satisfaction of Male Air Force Personnel: A Test of the Spillover Hypothesis

Peter A. Neenan

Few topics have generated as much attention in the literature of organizational behavior and occupational sociology as job satisfaction. Locke noted over a decade ago that more than 3,000 published research studies focusing on this area had appeared in the 40 years preceding his review (19). Even a cursory glance at the number of publications related to this construct that have appeared since Locke's analysis indicates that the level of interest in exploring the patterns and sources of job satisfaction has not waned. Given the influence that job satisfaction is often presumed to exert at individual, organizational, and societal levels, as well as its status as a primary social indicator of the quality of work life (25), such a high level of scholarly interest is not surprising.

However, despite this considerable interest in job satisfaction, there has been a paucity of research assessing the possible interrelationships between perceptions of quality of life in both work and nonwork domains. Until recently researchers investigating job satisfaction generally conceptualized the relationship between work and nonwork areas of life as "segmented," assuming that events that occur in one domain lack consequences for events that occur in the other. Kanter has referred to this stance as the "myth of separate worlds," an orientation that she contended served the perceived interests of employers by permitting them to deny the possibility of any spillover of negative or dysfunctional effects of organizational policies and procedures upon the family life of employees (14).

The data for this study were collected under USAF Contracts F33600–70–C–0423 and F33600–70–81–R–0290. Any opinions, findings, or conclusions expressed in this publication are those of the author, and do not necessarily reflect the views of the Department of the Air Force.

There has been an increasing acceptance by employers that organizations ignore the family life dimension of employees at their own peril (1). Even so, examination of the degree to which family factors and characteristics affect employees' perceived level of job satisfaction has remained relatively unexplored. Instead, most investigations probing familial effects and impacts upon the workplace have tended to concentrate upon the extent to which temporal constraints imposed by the family system have affected such factors as employee labor market experience and absenteeism (5).

This chapter explores the extent to which the quality of marital life of employees contributes to their overall level of job satisfaction. It focuses specifically on an occupational category markedly different from those in which most marital and job linkage studies have been undertaken: married male members of the U.S. Air Force.

MODELS OF WORK–FAMILY LINKAGES

Increasing attention has been directed to the question of the extent to which work and family are interconnected and, if so, to what degree and in what direction. Mortimer and London have summarized the broad areas in which this interconnection has been identified (23). In addressing ways in which work influences the family, they note that the primary spheres of influence consist of the social status and economic resources that work provides for the family. In addition, work sets external constraints on family organization and activities and shapes the attitudes, values, and personalities of its members both through socialization processes as well as their experiences at work.

In considering the influences that flow from the family to work, Mortimer and London point to the socialization function of the family, which instills fundamental values and attitudes toward work and affects its members' occupational choices, career paths, and eventual occupational attainment. Additionally, the evolution of family organizational structures and roles assumed by family members has begun to exert its influence on the nature of work roles and requirements, as employing institutions attempt to retain their employees and foster high levels of organizational commitment on their part. While they observe that work-related experiences exercise their influence upon family members, no mention is made of the possibility of a reciprocal influence in which individual attitudes and experiences of family members are carried over to the workplace. The question thus remains: What effect does marital quality have on the level of job satisfaction?

Voydanoff has identified four possible ways in which the linkage between work and family systems might occur (33). The first of these is a "spillover" relationship, in which attitudes and outlooks in one system carry over directly and positively into the other. From this orientation, if one experiences a high degree of satisfaction with his or her family life, that satisfaction would be expected to carry over into the work domain and manifest itself in terms of increased satisfaction on the job. Conversely, strains and dissatisfactions arising from work would be anticipated to be reflected by similar experiences in the family.

A second possible relationship between work and family systems identified by Voydanoff has been referred to as the "compensatory" model. As with the spillover model, attitudes from one area carry over into the other. However, in contrast to the former model, the relationship is inverse—people who fail to find satisfaction in one life area (e.g., work or family) make up for this deficiency by finding satisfaction in the other.

A third possible relationship between family and work is that of "opposition." This is predicted to occur when demands in one sphere prevent performance in the other. Thus, excessive demands arising from work, such as long hours or extended travel, might preclude individual performance of particular family roles.

A fourth possibility is that there is no direct relationship between work and family, either positive or negative. This latter model has received some empirical support in the literature, yet has failed to attain the degree of consensus that is generally accorded the spillover model of work–family linkage, which has become the predominant research perspective in recent years (5).

The assumption that a positive "spillover" relationship exists between marital and job satisfaction has been an important element undergirding the development of corporate and organizational responses (1). These responses are designed to enhance employee productivity, commitment, and job satisfaction by addressing concerns that have the potential to decrease marital satisfaction and thus adversely affect employee performance at the workplace. While existing empirical research generally tends to support the spillover model, most often through assessment of the degree of correlation between satisfaction with marital quality and satisfaction with job or work, little substantive research exists that probes the degree to which marital quality contributes to job satisfaction over and above factors related to the job itself, as well as demographic characteristics of the individual worker. This chapter undertakes such an assessment, providing an opportunity to critically examine the ability of the spillover model to uniquely account for increased levels of job satisfaction for male members of the U.S. Air Force.

Before turning to a consideration of the extent to which satisfaction with marital quality contributes to overall job satisfaction for these Air Force members, this chapter will first consider other factors possibly related to job satisfaction, elements that will serve as important control variables in this investigation.

JOB SATISFACTION AND ITS PRECURSORS

Demographic Characteristics

Throughout the extensive body of literature probing the nature and patterns of job satisfaction, several common themes have emerged. The first of these is that demographic characteristics of the individual worker appear to bear significant relationship to his or her reported level of job satisfaction. Among these "person characteristics," age, race, educational level, and occupational prestige have often been reported as significantly associated with differing levels of job satisfaction.

Age appears to be positively associated with an individual's level of job satisfaction; older workers tend to report higher levels of job satisfaction than their colleagues who are younger (13, 17, 34, 37). Hall holds open the possibility that this relationship exists because of variations in expectation between younger and older workers—the former expect more but get less, while the latter expect less and get it (9).

Most studies of job satisfaction that examine differences between black and white workers indicate that the former report lower levels of satisfaction (21, 29, 36). While differences continue to exist, perhaps due in large degree to persisting patterns of discrimination, the disparity between reported job satisfaction levels between blacks and whites has decreased over the years. In general, a condition of parity seems to exist with respect to job satisfaction level for black and white workers when other occupational and demographic conditions are controlled (34, 35).

The association between educational attainment level and reported level of job satisfaction shows a mixed pattern. While some investigations report a direct and positive relationship—the greater the educational attainment, the higher the reported level of job satisfaction (8)—others have found an inverse relationship between educational level and reported job satisfaction (25, 32). One possible explanation that has been offered for these seemingly discrepant findings relates to the concept of "overeducation." For example, Quinn and his associates noted that job dissatisfaction appeared to be particularly high for blue-collar workers with one or more years of college education (25). In a similar vein, Burris noted that workers who are very highly overeducated and who feel underemployed report lower levels of job satisfaction (3). However, even in his study, there essentially appeared to be little or no substantive relationship between moderate levels of overeducation and job satisfaction level.

Occupational prestige also appears to bear some relationship to reported level of job satisfaction. Mortimer has noted that investigations of this relationship consistently find that incumbents in professional, technical, and administrative positions show the highest levels of job satisfaction, while workers in middle- and lower-level occupations report correspondingly lower levels of overall job satisfaction (22).

While demographic characteristics such as those described above appear to manifest some relationship with level of job satisfaction, research suggests their importance as meaningful predictors effectively disappears when characteristics more closely related to the job itself are introduced as controls (34, 35).

Job-related Characteristics

While various specifications of the types of characteristics related to work and its outcomes exist, most current research has tended to adopt the view that there are two broad domains of work-related variables. The first of these embraces characteristics that are inherent in the job itself, such as the degree of stimulation and challenge the job provides, the opportunity it allows an individual to develop and use his or her talents, and the degree of autonomy and self-direction present in the job. In contrast, a second category of job-related variables comprises features that relate more to environmental conditions surrounding the job, such as pay and benefits, working conditions, relations with co-workers, and issues related to management and administrative policy, such as equitable treatment by supervisors, recognition for job performance, and perceptions of organizational rules and regulations.

This dual specification reflects the research perspective of Frederick Herzberg and his colleagues, who identified the former category of job-related variables as "intrinsic" and the latter as "extrinsic" sources of satisfaction and motivation (11). In their investigations of the sources of job satisfaction conducted with engineers and accountants in the Pittsburgh metropolitan area, these investigators observed that it was the intrinsic job factor that tended to contribute to worker satisfaction. The greater the individual's satisfaction with the intrinsic components of the job, the higher the level of overall reported job satisfaction.

On the other hand, worker satisfaction with the extrinsic components of work did not appear to contribute meaningfully to his or her overall level of reported job satisfaction. Instead, lower levels of satisfaction with these extrinsic job characteristics contributed to worker dissatisfaction. This finding led Herzberg to formulate his "two factor" theory of job satisfaction. Conceptualizing job satisfaction and dissatisfaction as two distinct dimensions, he contended that extrinsic components were incapable of contributing to job satisfaction; their only role came into play with respect to job dissatisfaction. Only intrinsic job characteristics could contribute to job satisfaction.

Herzberg's approach to the measurement of the sources of job satisfaction and dissatisfaction has come under considerable scrutiny since its emergence. Fein contends that Herzberg and others have developed a model that applies only to an elite group of workers, and that for most employees pay and job security remain the primary sources of motivation (7). King has noted that Herzberg set forth a variety of different interpretations of his model, none of which appears completely consistent with empirical findings (15). Still others have faulted perceived methodological deficiencies and limitations, as well as the inconsistent results from attempted replications (6, 12, 18).

Notwithstanding these criticisms of Herzberg's methodology and specification of the theory and its components, broad conceptualization of intrinsic and extrinsic job-related factors remains a predominant paradigm for describing and categorizing sources of job satisfaction (16, 30). The degree to which intrinsic and extrinsic job-related factors do, in fact, contribute to reported job satisfaction for the respondents who are the focus of this chapter will be considered in the subsequent discussion of analysis.

In addition to assessing intrinsic and extrinsic satisfaction, this investigation also examined the level of respondent satisfaction with management policy, a construct that has likewise been identified in the literature as a significant component of job satisfaction (18, 24).

METHOD

Sample Profile

This investigation is a secondary analysis of data collected in 1979–1981 from a subsample of 865 male members of the United States Air Force, married to civilian spouses. This group of respondents was drawn from a worldwide sample of 992 Air Force service personnel, including both males and females. The subsample randomly selected for this investigation consisted of 91 black and 774 white males, of whom 359 were officers and 506 enlisted personnel. The mean age for this sample was 34.5 years, while the average length of service for these respondents was 11.4 years. Approximately four-fifths (81.3 percent) of these participants were in their first marriage at the time of the survey, and 77.5 percent indicated that they had children living at home. The mean number of years of formal education attained by these members was 14.7.

It should be noted that the occupational environment for these survey participants differs considerably from the milieus within which most assessments of job satisfaction and its components have typically occurred. In contrast to the civilian sector, the military has been described as a form of a "greedy" institution, one that places considerably higher demands on both the member and his or her family (27). In this sense, the institution is perceived as legitimately able to absorb a greater part of an individual's (and, by extension, his or her family's) total life than is the case for institutions and organizations that do not manifest this characteristic. As a result, it would appear much less likely that these respondents would be able to draw as clear a line of distinction between work and nonwork domains as might be the case for individuals in most civilian occupations; one remains at least potentially "on duty" as an Air Force member twenty-four hours a day, seven days a week.

Job Satisfaction: The Dependent Variable

The dependent variable in this investigation consisted of a single-item global measure of a respondent's self-reported level of job satisfaction. Participants were asked to describe their level of job satisfaction on a five-point Likert-type scale, with possible score values ranging from zero to four. The following response categories were possible: "very dissatisfied," "somewhat dissatisfied," "mixed feelings," "fairly satisfied," and "very satisfied."

Respondents as a group tended to report fairly high levels of job satisfaction on this global measure, a finding that seems to parallel investigations conducted on civilian populations over the past two decades (17). The group as a whole reported a mean value of 2.82, with a standard deviation of 1.29. Of the 865 Air Force members responding to this item, only 7.7 percent indicated they were very dissatisfied with their job, while 10.9 percent stated they were somewhat dissatisfied. A somewhat greater proportion of respondents said they had mixed feelings toward their job (14.7 percent). Approximately one-fourth of survey participants (24.6 percent) indicated they were fairly satisfied with their job, while 42.1 percent of all respondents said they were very satisfied with their jobs. Analysis of differential response rates in level of job satisfaction by age, race, occupational status (military rank), parental status, and years of service in the military failed to reveal any statistically significant differences in level of job satisfaction on these characteristics.

Intrinsic Job Satisfaction: A Control Variable

In addition to the global measure of job satisfaction, respondents assessed their level of satisfaction with two broad sets of facet-specific indicators that have been identified in the literature as potential contributors to overall job satisfaction level. The first set of indicators consisted of eight measures of intrinsic satisfaction with work. This set included five items measuring the extent to which respondents (a) enjoyed performing day-to-day job activities; (b) felt that factors at work encouraged them to work hard; (c) gained a sense of accomplishment from the job; (d) felt that their co-workers functioned as a team; and (e) felt that their interests matched their Air Force job specialty. Each of these five items was measured on a five-point Likert-type scale, with possible responses ranging from "very little extent" to "very great extent." In addition to these five items, three other questions were asked of survey participants. These included perceived importance of the mission assigned to the present command, the importance that the respondent himself ascribed to his present job, and the respondent's level of interest in his present job. Both the perceived importance of the mission assigned to the present command and the respondent's assessment of the importance of his job were measured on a four-point Likert scale ranging from 0 ("not important at all") to 3 ("very important"). Level of respondent interest in his job was also assessed using a four-point Likert scale, ranging from 0 ("uninterested") to 3 ("very interested").

Principal components factor analysis and subsequent assessment of the psychometric properties of these eight items suggest the suitability of treating these measures as an additive scale measuring respondent affect toward the intrinsic aspect of his job. Scale reliability was favorable, with a standardized Cronbach coefficient alpha of .81 (4). For the composite scale formed by these eight items pertaining to intrinsic job satisfaction, possible score values could range from a low score of 0 to a high of 29. As a group, respondents reported a mean of 19.84, with a standard deviation of 5.31.

Extrinsic Job Satisfaction: A Control Variable

In addition to the measure of intrinsic satisfaction described above, a series of questions were asked of respondents to ascertain their level of satisfaction with aspects of life in the service other than those that are intimately connected with their jobs. These items were selected, on the basis of factor analysis and assessment of their psychometric properties, from a larger pool of items reflecting satisfaction with Air Force employment conditions, services, and benefits. Items selected for inclusion measured respondent satisfaction with the following seven areas: (a) pay and allowances; (b) job security; (c) medical care; (d) dental care; (e) base exchange; (f) commissary; and (g) recreational facilities. Each of these items was assessed using a five-point Likert scale, with values ranging from 1 ("very dissatisfied") to 5 ("very satisfied").

For purposes of this investigation, these seven items were summed to form an additive scale, with an overall standardized Cronbach reliability coefficient of .73. For this composite measure of extrinsic satisfaction, possible values ranged from 7, for respondents indicating they were very dissatisfied with each of these items, to a score of 35 for individuals who reported they were very satisfied with each of these areas. The group of respondents as a whole reported a mean score of 24.07, with a standard deviation of 4.32.

Satisfaction With Management Policy: A Control Variable

This investigation also assessed the level of respondent satisfaction with management or administrative policy through three Likert-type items measuring satisfaction with military rules and regulations, management of personnel, and treatment by Air Force superiors. As was the case with the measures of extrinsic satisfaction employed in this inquiry, these three items were selected for inclusion on the basis of factor analysis and evaluation of their psychometric properties. Respondents were asked to rate their level of satisfaction with these items on a five-point scale ranging from 1 ("very dissatisfied") to 5 ("very satisfied"). When summed to form an additive scale, the composite measure of satisfaction with management policy yielded a Cronbach coefficient alpha reliability of .80. Possible score values on this aggregate measure ranged from a low of 3 to a possible high score of 15. Respondents as a group reported a mean score of 9.63 with a standard deviation of 2.29.

Measures of Marital Quality: The Independent Variable

In order to assess the extent to which marital quality affected the level of job satisfaction for these Air Force members, a shortened and slightly modified set of indicators based largely on the Dyadic Adjustment Scale developed by Spanier was asked of respondents (28). Factor analysis of these items indicated that they encompassed five separate dimensions, relating to: (a) marital satisfaction; (b) marital consensus; (c) affectional expression; (d) marital tension; and (e) marital companionship.

Marital Satisfaction

Respondents in this study were asked to assess their perceived level of marital satisfaction by responding to four Likert-type items measuring the extent to which they felt (a) things were going well between the respondent and his spouse; (b) the participant confided in his mate; (c) the respondent regretted his marriage; and (d) the extent to which the participant desired his marriage to succeed. The first three of these items employed a six-point Likert scale. Possible response categories included: 1 ("all of the time"), 2 ("most of the time"), 3 ("more often than not"), 4 ("occasionally"), 5 ("rarely"), and 6 ("never"). Assessment of the extent to which respondents desired their marriages to succeed, expressed in behavioral terms, was also undertaken using a six-point Likert scale: 0 ("I would go to almost any length"), 1 ("I would do all I can"), 2 ("I would do my fair share"), 3 ("It would be nice, but I can't do more than I am now doing") 4 ("It would be nice, but I refuse to do any more than I am now doing"), and 5 ("I can't do anything, there is no more I can do").

For purposes of analysis, these four items were combined into an additive scale after recoding to ensure unidirectionality of responses among all items, resulting in a range of possible values extending from 3 to 23. This scale of marital satisfaction has a standardized coefficient alpha of .72. The group as a whole reported a mean score of 19.58, with a standard deviation of 2.18.

For this recoded scale, the higher a respondent's score, the higher his level of reported marital satisfaction.

Marital Consensus

Seven items were used to measure participants' perceived level of marital consensus. Each of these items employed Likert-type scales with four possible response categories: 0 ("always agree"), 1 ("almost always agree"), 2 ("occasionally disagree"), and 3 ("disagree"). These seven items assessed the reported extent of agreement between the respondent and his spouse in the following areas: (a) handling family finances, (b) friendships, (c) parents and in-laws, (d) aims and goals in life, (e) major decisions, (f) career decisions, and (g) child rearing and discipline.

These items were combined to form an additive scale, with a standardized alpha coefficient of reliablity of .74. The group as a whole reported relatively high levels of marital consensus, as assessed by this composite indicator. From a possible range of values extending from 0 to 21, the mean across all respondents was 8.35, with a standard deviation of 3.06. In contrast to the composite indicator of marital satisfaction discussed above, the lower a respondent's score on this marital consensus scale, the higher his reported level of spousal agreement.

Affectional Expression

This domain of marital quality was assessed using three items designed to ascertain each respondent's perception of the quality of physical love and sexual relationships with his spouse, the extent of agreement between the respondent and his spouse concerning demonstrations of affection, and the extent of agreement between the participant and his spouse concerning sexual relations. The first of these items was measured on a three-point scale, including 0 ("very good"), 1 ("ok"), and 2 ("not so good'). The latter two items were measured on the same four-point scale as that employed for the assessment of marital consensus: from 0 ("always agree") to 3 ("disagree").

Combining these three items into an additive scale yielded a composite measure with a standardized reliability coefficient of .78. Possible values ranged from 0 (positive evaluation of affectional expression) to 8 (the most negative possible assessment of this dimension). The group as a whole reported a mean value of 2.48 for this composite measure, with a standard deviation of 1.70.

Marital Tension

Yet another indicator used to assess marital quality was composed of measures designed to elicit respondents' perceived level of marital tension. Four Likert-type items measured the frequency with which (a) respondent and spouse "got on each other's nerves"; (b) the participant left the house after a disagreement; (c) the respondent and his wife quarreled; and (d) the couple discussed divorce or separation. Each of these items was measured on a six-point Likert scale. Possible response categories included 1 ("all of the time"), 2 ("most of the time"), 3 ("more often than not"), 4 ("occasionally"), 5 ("rarely"), and 6 ("never"). For each of these items, the lower score, the higher the degree of perceived tension with respect to the item.

When combined into a composite indicator of marital tension, the resulting scale had a standardized reliability coefficient alpha of .68. Possible values on this measure of marital tension ranged from 4 to 24, with the lower the score, the higher the reported level of marital tension. The group mean for this measure was 19.63, with a standard deviation of 1.90.

Marital Companionship

The final indicator of marital quality employed in this investigation measured respondents' perception of the level of marital companionship between themselves and their spouses. Four items were used to assess this domain. The first of these entailed a measure of the perception of companionship between respondent and spouse. The remaining three items consisted of assessments of the extent of agreement between respondent and spouse concerning matters of recreation, time spent together, and leisure time activities. Perception of respondent–spouse companionship was assessed using a three-point Likert scale (0, "very good"; 1, "ok"; and 2, "not so good"), while the three remaining items were measured on the same four-point scale employed in the assessment of marital consensus (0, "always agree"; 1, "almost always agree"; 2, "occasionally disagree"; and 3, "disagree").

When combined as an additive scale, this composite indicator yielded a standardized reliability coefficient of .72. Across all respondents, the mean score on this measure was 4.30, with a standard deviation of 1.95. Possible scale values ranged from 0 (indicating a high degree of marital companionship) to 11.

In all, five indicators employing a total of 22 variables were used to assess respondent perception of marital quality. Given that item response categories were not uniform across all individual items used in the construction of scales, each component item was standardized by z-score transformation to ensure comparability among items and scales. For purposes of subsequent analysis, all individual variables and multiple-item scales used in this investigation were similarly standardized.

ANALYSIS

In examining the contribution, if any, that marital quality makes to overall level of job satisfaction, it becomes possible to test the applicability of the "spillover" model of the relationship between marital and work domains. In particular, this investigation enables assessment of the relationship between marital quality and job satisfaction over and above selected control variables, both demographic and work related, that prior research has suggested are associated with overall job satisfaction.

As a means of assessing the relative importance of these factors to job satisfaction, three hierarchical multiple regression models were employed. These models sequentially incorporate increasingly elaborate specifications of variables that have often been identified as contributing to job satisfaction. The first of these assessed only the influence of selected demographic characteristics as they related to variation in global job satisfaction. These variables included respondents' race, occupational status, educational attainment level, presence or absence of children living at home, and length of service as an Air Force member. For purposes of analysis these variables were force-entered as a block.

The second model was built upon the first by adding to the block of respondent demographic characteristics the following three job-related controls: intrinsic satisfaction, extrinsic satisfaction, and satisfaction with management policy. These three indicators were also force-entered as a block of variables, thus affording a test of the extent to which each contributes to respondent job satisfaction over and above variation associated with demographic characteristics alone, as well as the two other job-related controls.

Finally, a third, fully saturated model was specified. This model built upon both the first and second models by entering the five indicators of marital quality (marital satisfaction, marital consensus, affectional expression, marital tension, and marital companionship) discussed previously. As was the case for the two restricted models outlined above, these five indicators were also force-entered as a block. This model thus allows assessment of the extent to which these components of marital quality contribute to respondent job satisfaction over and above the demographic and work-related variables used in this study, as well as with one another.

RESULTS

Model I: Demographic Characteristics

The first of these models consisted of the dependent variable, job satisfaction, regressed on selected demographic characteristics of respondents. These characteristics included respondent race, educational level, date of entry into the service, presence of children living at home, and occupational status.

Race of respondent was treated as a dummy variable for purposes of analysis, in which white respondents were classified as 0 and black members were coded as 1. In addition to race, both occupational status and presence of children at home were also treated as dummy variables, with officers coded 0 and enlisted personnel coded 1, while respondents with children at home were classified as 0 and those without children at home were assigned a value of 1.

Educational attainment level and date of entry for respondents each consisted of interval-level measures. Educational level was assessed by asking the number of years of school completed by respondents, while length of service was determined by asking the participant's date of entry.

When only these five demographic characteristics were considered in relation to respondent job satisfaction, two variables, date of entry and presence of children at home, appeared to be significantly related to respondent job satisfaction as shown in Table 3.1. Individuals with earlier date of entry into the service were more likely to report higher levels of job satisfaction than respondents with fewer years in the Air Force (Beta = $-.173$; $t_{(856)} = -4.82$; $p < .001$), while members with children at home were similarly likely to report greater job satisfaction than did those without (Beta = $-.086$; $t_{(856)} = -2.43$; $p < .02$). No statistically significant association appeared to exist between race, occupational status, and educational level and overall reported level of job satisfaction for these Air Force members. Taken as a group, these five demographic variables, when considered by themselves, accounted for approximately 4 percent of the variance in respondent job satisfaction (Table 3.1).

Model II: Demographic and Work-Related Characteristics

This second hierarchical model was built upon the preceding specification by adding to it, as a force-entered block, the three work-related indicators of extrinsic satisfaction, intrinsic satisfaction, and satisfaction with management policy. Once again the dependent variable in this analysis consisted of overall respondent job satisfaction.

As Table 3.1 indicates, this second-level model attenuated the statistically significant relationships found to exist between job satisfaction and both length of service and presence of children at home in the demographic-only model.

Intrinsic satisfaction emerged as strongly associated with respondent job satisfaction: the higher the level of intrinsic satisfaction for these respondents, the higher their level of overall job satisfaction (Beta = $.628$; $t_{(785)} = 22.17$; $p < .001$). Respondent satisfaction with management policy was also significantly associated with job satisfaction for these participants: the higher their level of satisfaction with management policy, the higher their level of overall job satisfaction (Beta = $.148$; $t_{(785)} = 4.95$; $p < .001$). Extrinsic satisfaction, on the other hand, was not significantly associated with respondent job satisfaction.

As Table 3.1 shows, this second-order model, incorporating both the work-related and demographic variables employed in this study, explains approximately 50 percent of respondent variance in job satisfaction, in contrast to the 4 percent explained by the demographic model alone.

Model III: Demographic, Work-Related, and Marital Quality Dimensions

This fully specified model examines the influence of the indicators of marital quality probed in this study as they contribute to respondent job satisfaction over and above both demographic and work-related characteristics. As indicated in Table 3.1, these five indicators, taken individually or together, added no statistically significant contribution to the explanation of variation in respondent job satisfaction. Indeed, incorporating these variables into the regression equation actually slightly reduced the proportion of adjusted variance in the dependent variable accounted for by all independent variables (see Table 3.1). This statistical artifact arises from the inability of these indicators to contribute more explanatory power than is removed by the adjustment in degrees of freedom resulting from their incorporation into the model, thus demonstrating their irrelevance as contributors to job satisfaction level for these respondents (31). Within the context of this fully saturated model, these marital quality indicators, along with extrinsic satisfaction, were the least predictive of member job satisfaction.

DISCUSSION

Clearly, this analysis of the contributory effects of marital quality to job satisfaction does not lend support to the existence of a spillover relationship for the married male Air Force members who are the focus of this inquiry. At the same time, the question must be asked as to whether the results presented here allow for categorical rejection of such an interconnection. Prior to assuming such a stance, it is important to note several cautionary observations.

First, the possibility should be kept in mind that for different persons, different patterns of marital–work interface may well be operative. Rather than assuming that the preponderance of respondents would behave in the same manner in relating these two spheres of their lives, this perspective leaves open the possibility that each pattern of relationship—spillover, compensatory, opposition, and no relationship—will be the case for certain segments of respondents. Hence, these differing patterns of work and family linkages may, when viewed in the aggregate, negate one another, yielding a finding of no relationship between marital quality and job satisfaction.

It is also possible that satisfaction and dissatisfaction with marital quality pose different implications for job satisfaction. Much like the Herzberg two-factor theory of job satisfaction discussed previously (11), the possibility must at least be left open that there is a similar relationship between marital quality and work satisfaction. When viewed from this perspective, while high levels of marital quality may not contribute to overall job satisfaction, low

TABLE 3.1
Contribution of Demographics, Work-Related Variables, and Marital Quality Indicators to Job Satisfaction

Variable	Model I		Model II		Model III	
	Beta	*t*-value	Beta	*t*-value	Beta	*t*-value
Education	−.004	−.07	−.026	−.54	−.026	−.54
Children at home	−.086	−2.43*	−.045	−1.76	−.043	−1.68
Race	−.024	−.70	−.037	−1.45	−.035	−1.36
Date of entry	−.173	−4.82**	−.031	−1.16	−.028	−1.05
Rank	−.056	−.86	−.018	−.39	−.022	−.46
Extrinsic satisfaction			−.004	−.16	−.004	−.16
Intrinsic satisfaction			.628	22.17**	.627	22.00**
Satisfaction with management policy			.148	4.95**	.146	4.87**
Affectional expression					.017	.54
Marital tension					.026	.81
Marital consensus					.011	.34
Marital companionship					.013	.39
Marital satisfaction					.022	.65
R^2	.049		.508		.509	
R^2 (adjusted)	.043		.503		.501	
R^2 change	—		.459		.001	

*$p < .02$.   **$p < .001$.

levels may possibly contribute to job dissatisfaction. Such a nonlinear explanation of these findings merits further exploration.

A third caveat concerns the nature of the participants examined in this study. It was noted previously that the military, unlike many if not most civilian occupations, exhibits many of the features of a "greedy" institution, one that allows for less marked differentiation between work and other life spheres of its members. To the extent that these institutional and organizational characteristics actually serve to blur the distinction between occupational and nonoccupational sectors, the ability of either a spillover or compensatory interaction to operate might well be limited. Should subsequent investigation suggest such a pattern, it would appear to lend support to a variant of the "opposition" model articulated by Voydanoff and discussed previously in this chapter (33). Hence, caution should be exercised in generalizing the findings of this investigation to populations within civilian occupations without further research.

Another concern related to the nature of the organizational context of these military members is the possibility that the construct of job satisfaction may not possess the same meaning as is the case with civilian groups. Rather than satisfaction with a specific job in the military, it may be satisfaction with life in the military itself that is the analogous variable to job satisfaction in the civilian sector. Subsequent research should assess the extent to which the indicators described in this inquiry, including overall job satisfaction for individuals, contribute to satisfaction with life in the military. As a part of such investigation, the contributory power of marital quality, if any, to satisfaction with military life should be examined again.

A final consideration that should be borne in mind is that interconnections between family and work life may operate differently for men and women. The paucity of research that has been conducted probing the contribution of marital satisfaction and quality of marital life to job satisfaction has tended to focus, by and large, on female samples. While there is evidence of changing gender roles and relationships between men and women in both civilian (10, 20) and military settings (2), further research is needed that explores the possibility that males, whether in civilian or military contexts, are more likely to operate from a separate-spheres model than are women, for whom either a spillover or compensatory model may be more likely to operate.

CONCLUSIONS AND IMPLICATIONS

Three major findings have emerged from this investigation of the interrelationship between marital quality and job satisfaction. First, already discussed at some length, it is not possible to accept the spillover hypothesis that perception of marital quality will contribute, in a positive and direct way, to overall job satisfaction for the Air Force members who are the subject of focus in this study. Virtually no additional variance in respondent job satisfaction was accounted for by the five indicators of marital quality employed in this inquiry, either singly or in combination.

Equally striking is the extent to which respondent satisfaction with non-monetary, work-related variables accounted for the preponderance of variation in overall job satisfaction for these participants. The only other construct that was significantly related to member job satisfaction was satisfaction with management policy. In contrast to the thrust of much prior research, none of the demographic variables examined in this inquiry explained a significant amount of variation in job satisfaction when work-related variables were incorporated into the model. These findings point to the utility of further examination concerning ways in which the military organization can enhance and strengthen these major contributors to the job satisfaction of its members.

Finally, the failure of satisfaction with extrinsic, monetary-related factors to contribute to respondent job satisfaction highlights once again the relative lack of importance of such incentives in relation to job satisfaction, at least in the military context that informs the background for this study. This finding thus appears to challenge, at least in part, criticisms that have been leveled against the theoretical importance of intrinsic, as opposed to extrinsic, factors in terms of their relative contribution to job satisfaction.

NOTES

1. Bowen, G. L. (1988) Corporate supports for the family lives of employees: A conceptual model for program planning and evaluation. *Family Relations* 37:183–88.

2. Bowen, G. L., and Neenan, P. A. (1988) Sex role orientations among married men in the military: The generational factor. *Psychological Reports* 62:523–26.

3. Burris, V. (1983) The social and political consequences of overeducation. *American Sociological Review* 48:454–67.

4. Cronbach, L. J. (1951) Coefficient alpha and the internal structure of tests. *Psychometrika* 16:297–334.

5. Crouter, A. C. (1984) Spillover from family to work: The neglected side of the work–family interface. *Human Relations* 37:425–42.

6. Dunnette, M. D., Campbell, J. P., and Hakel, M. D. (1967) Factors contributing to job satisfaction and job dissatisfaction in six occupational groups. *Organization Behavior and Human Performance* 2:143–74.

7. Fein, M. (1976) Motivation for work. In R. Dubin (ed.), *Handbook of Work, Organization, and Society*, pp. 465–530. Chicago, IL: Rand McNally.

8. Glenn, N., and Weaver, C. N. (1982) Further evidence on education and job satisfaction. *Social Forces* 61:46–65.

9. Hall, R. H. (1986) *Dimensions of Work*. Beverly Hills, CA: Sage Publications.

10. Helmreich, R. J., Spence, J. T., and Gibson, R. H. (1982) Sex role attitudes: 1972–1980. *Personality and Social Psychology* 39:896–908.

11. Herzberg, F., Mausner, B., and Snyderman, B. B. (1959) *The Motivation to Work*. New York: John Wiley.

12. Hulin, C. L., and Smith, P. C. (1965) A linear model of job satisfaction. *Journal of Applied Psychology* 49:209–16.

13. Janson, P., and Martin, J. K. (1982) Job satisfaction and age: A test of two views. *Social Forces* 60:1089–1102.

14. Kanter, R. M. (1977) *Work and Family in the United States: A Critical Review and Agenda for Research and Policy*. (*Social Science Frontiers*, no. 9). New York: Russell Sage Foundation.

15. King, N. (1970) Clarification and evaluation of the two-factor theory of satisfaction. *Psychological Bulletin* 74:18–31.

16. Landy, F. J. (1985) *Psychology of Work Behavior*. Homewood, IL: Dorsey Press.

17. Levitan, S. A., and Johnson, C. M. (1982) *Second Thoughts on Work*. Kalamazoo, MI: W. E. Upjohn Institute for Employment Research.

18. Locke, E. A. (1965) The relationship of task success to task liking and satisfaction. *Journal of Applied Psychology* 49:379–85.

19. Locke, E. A. (1976) The nature and causes of job satisfaction. In M. D. Dunnette (ed.), *Handbook of Industrial and Organizational Psychology*, pp. 1297–1350. Chicago, IL: Rand McNally.

20. McBroom, W. H. (1984) Changes in sex-role orientations: A five-year longitudinal comparison. *Sex Roles* 11:583–92.

21. Moch, M. K. (1980) Job involvement, internal motivation, and employees' integration into networks of work relationships. *Organizational Behavior and Human Performance* 25:15–31.

22. Mortimer, J. T. (1979) *Changing Attitudes Toward Work. (Work in America Institute Studies in Productivity,* no. 11). Scarsdale, NY: Work in America Institute.

23. Mortimer, J. T., and London, J. (1984) The varying linkages of work and family. In P. Voydanoff (ed.), *Work and Family: The Changing Roles of Men and Women,* pp. 20–35. Palo Alto, CA: Mayfield Publishing.

24. Pritchard, R. D., and Karasick, B. (1973) The effects of organizational climate on managerial job performance and job satisfaction. *Organizational Behavior and Human Performance* 9:126–46.

25. Quinn, R. P., Staines, G. L., and McCullough, M. R. (1974) *Job Satisfaction: Is There a Trend? (Manpower Research Monograph* no. 30). Washington, D.C.: U.S. Department of Labor Manpower Administration.

26. Seashore, S. E., and Taber, T. D. (1975) Job satisfaction indicators and their correlates. *American Behavioral Scientist* 18:333–68.

27. Segal, M. (1986) The military and the family as greedy institutions. *Armed Forces and Society* 13:9–38.

28. Spanier, G. B. (1976) Measuring dyadic adjustment: New scales for assessing the quality of marriage and similar dyads. *Journal of Marriage and the Family* 38:15–28.

29. Staines, G. L., and Quinn, R. P. (1979) American workers evaluate the quality of their jobs. *Monthly Labor Review* 102:3–12.

30. Steers, R. M., and Porter, L. W. (1987) *Motivation and Work Behavior,* 4th edn. New York: McGraw-Hill.

31. Studenmund, A. H., and Cassidy, H. J. (1987) *Using Econometrics.* Boston, MA: Little, Brown and Company.

32. Tannenbaum, A. S., Kavcic, B., Rosner, M., Vianello, M., and Weisser, G. (1974) *Hierarchy in Organizations.* San Francisco, CA: Jossey-Bass.

33. Voydanoff, P. (1980) *The Implications of Work–Family Relationships for Productivity. (Work in America Institute Studies in Productivity,* no. 13). Scarsdale, NY: Work in America Institute.

34. Weaver, C. N. (1977) Relationships among pay, race, sex, occupational prestige, supervision, work autonomy, and job satisfaction in a national sample. *Personnel Psychology* 30:437–45.

35. Weaver, C. N. (1978) Black–white correlates of job satisfaction. *Journal of Applied Psychology* 63:255–58.

36. Weaver, C. N. (1980) Job satisfaction in the United States in the 1970s. *Journal of Applied Psychology* 65:364–67.

37. Wright, J. D., and Hamilton, R. F. (1978) Work satisfaction and age: Some evidence for the "job change" hypothesis. *Social Forces* 56:1140–58.

II

SPECIAL POPULATION GROUPS

4

Single Parents in the Workplace: Conserving and Increasing Human Capital

David W. Wright

Mary and Robert are single parents. She is an office manager for a large Fortune 500 firm who is rearing two young boys aged 8 and 9. He is a staff sergeant in the Army with custody of two teenagers, a 13-year-old daughter and a 15-year-old son. Both of these single parents enjoy their work and are committed to pursuing careers within their respective work organizations, despite demands of single parenting. In fact, both see their careers as a major factor in their effectiveness as single parents even though the demands of parenting combined with the responsibilities of careers constitute a tightrope for them. Although Mary and Robert often feel inadequate and frustrated that they must make so many compromises in the two most satisfying domains of their lives, their overall well-being remains quite intact. Both feel the variety of role strain and parenting issues they face could be eased by some reasonable changes in the policies and practices of their employers.

Mary and Robert are part of a large group of parents comprising slightly more than one-quarter of all family units in 1984 (65). Their impact in the work world is reflected in the estimate that as many as one-third of all employees may be single parents at some time during their work life and many will remain so (8). These employees either will become single parents during their employment or, like many women, enter the work world as single parents. As workers, single parents can no longer be viewed as expendable by employers because they struggle with a complicated nexus between their family lives and their work lives that does not fit some traditional norm.

In fact, much of the complexity in the relationship between single parents and their work organizations is not unique to them. They, like other working parents, take a variety of family factors into account when considering the jobs they take, their schedules, their career commitment, and their perceptions of success (7, 31, 45, 51, 52, 64). Unfortunately, many work organizations still underrate how important these family factors are to their employees (31), although some are discovering a diversity reflected in employee desires on which they can capitalize. Moreover, a growing shortage of workers in many occupations combined with high training costs is increasing the value of all employees. Work organizations simply cannot afford to let good single-parent employees slip away due to difficulty in making adjustments to their unique needs and concerns. Making those adjustments is now a matter of maintaining productivity and a long-term conservation and accumulation of human capital.

Despite recognition of the unique needs and concerns of single parents, their exact nature and, therefore, the required adjustments, are not yet clear to many managers and administrators. Indeed, the issues single parents face have received attention only recently in the research literature. It is the purpose of this chapter to examine those issues and to propose ways work organizations can make adjustments to maintain and increase the productivity of single parents and to capitalize upon this viable source of human capital. Issues concerning role strain and parenting will be highlighted first, followed by an assessment of single parents' well-being. The chapter concludes by discussing the policies and practices that can foster the well-being of single parents by addressing role strain and parenting issues. In addition, a brief overview of future research needs is presented. Special attention is given to single parents in the military. Since military management policies, work responsibilities, and personnel are increasingly similar to their counterparts in the private sector, the intimate link between the work organization and family found in the military helps in forming a model that can be used by work organizations in the civilian sector.

ROLE STRAIN

Traditionally, an adult's most salient roles have been associated with work and family, but until 1970 little effort was made to fully understand how workers divided their time and commitment between these worlds. Most studies viewed the organization and the family as institutions in competition for the time and energy of the employee (12). They described the effects of the work world on the family via the worker (3, 10, 44, 46, 55, 58). However, recent empirical support has emerged for alternate models viewing the relationship between workers and their employer organizations as more interdependent. While workers must still accommodate to the demands of the two major institutions of work and family, their commitment to either is dependent on collaboration between the two. But, at best, this collaboration is an uneasy one and strain between roles exists.

Several authors have described work-family-related strain as especially high for individuals who are working parents (5, 56, 67), but it is probably greatest for working single parents. They must often learn family roles that have typically been the domain of the opposite sex and blend them effectively with ones they already know. While living this nontraditional life style, these parents must attempt to fulfill unclear expectations as well as balance work and family roles. Their ability to balance the dual demands from work and family is critical since job-family role strain is the most important predictor of decreased levels of well-being, especially for single mothers (9).

Income

Compounding the role strain problem for single parents is the fact that, regardless of their income group before becoming single parents, they commonly experience a reduction in income persisting for at least five years, especially if remarriage does not occur (72). Divorced mothers are especially at risk in this regard because their financial problems are usually related to lower overall income; whereas for divorced fathers, it is generally concluded financial strain is largely due to the loss of nonmonetary contributions, formerly made by their spouses, for which they must now pay (1, 9, 11, 14, 24, 25, 29, 42, 72, 73). Furthermore, the lack of comparable worth, valued job skills, and the cost of childcare all combine to make the feminization of poverty an increasingly common and disturbing phenomenon, although parents of either sex are especially vulnerable to unemployment if they have young children or teenagers (38). It should not be surprising that many single parents attempt to hold second jobs even though to do so compounds their role strain problems.

Time

Having more discretionary time or more flexible work schedules could help reduce single parents' role strain in several ways, but seldom are they available. Single mothers, in particular, suffer a major lack of discretionary time (9). Based on Burden's (9) study, their responsibilities as both parents and workers required 10 to 20 hours more work per week than single fathers and 20 to 30 more hours per week more than non-parents. However, the situation should not be construed as easy for men. Of the single fathers they questioned, Keshet and Rosenthal (28) reported that 63 percent said their lives were hampered by working hours.

Having discretionary time does not merely allow a single parent to fulfill various role demands. Time is also important because its lack disrupts a family's interaction with others and the outside world. When this occurs, they will have a more difficult time developing a consensually agreed-upon definition of reality (18) and clear role structures. This need is especially great for newly formed single-parent families. During this important period, especially if it follows divorce, death of a spouse, or adoption of a child by a single person, each individual in the family needs the support of other members while they grieve losses or make adjustments to all the things a new life style brings. Young children, in particular, need a safe and reliable structure while they reestablish a sense of security.

Military Single Parents

Compared with their counterparts in the civilian sector, the strain between work and family for military single parents appears to be quite similar. They struggle to balance most of the same demands implicit in parenting and work roles. Because of the pay and benefit structure along with job security inherent in enlistment and commissions, financial strain is generally less of a problem for military service members. However, especially for those in the lower-level enlisted ranks, financial strain is a major problem for some. In terms of time demands, there are indications that work weeks for military single parents are similar to those of married military parents and that work weeks, in general, are fairly similar to those of civilians (6, 45). Furthermore, single parents in Orthner's (45) study were just as likely to work extra duty on evenings and weekends and did not request or receive any more special work considerations than did married parents.

However, the military poses special challenges related to travel, readiness, relocations, and risk. For instance, about one-half of Navy fathers are in deployable units that regularly go to sea for several months at a time (50). In the Air Force about one-third of single fathers and one-quarter of single mothers had to serve temporary duty assignments averaging 10 nights away from home a year. However, more than two-thirds of single parents experiencing these temporary duty assignments reported no associated difficulties (6). In fact, in Orthner's study (45) fewer single parents reported problems with temporary duty assignments than did married men, although problems are greater for those with young children. Despite these findings military single parents must be in a constant state of readiness to travel and periodic relocations are common. Such demands when combined with the usually high family role demands that single parents confront can lead easily to a situation of role overload and strain, especially when coping resources and supports are not readily available.

Summary and Conclusion

Single parents have to struggle with role strain on several dimensions. Some of those struggles are similar to those experienced by married working parents, but the nature of the single parent's role strain has some unique aspects. As for married working parents, the role strain derives from conflicts between external demands and internalized beliefs and role conflict. It is especially high when major differences exist between values prevailing at work and at home (40, 75), since placing an emphasis on one area of one's life often means the other suffers. For instance, if a single parent's work environment is very competitive and nonsupportive, while his or her home life involves considerable companionship and support, shifting between the two could be difficult.

Another factor contributing to role strain is the fact women traditionally were expected to fit careers around child rearing and family needs while complementary expectations existed for men to find success in work outside their homes. Although changes have occurred in the role responsibilities for both men and women in our society, without a second parent in the household single parents must juggle both instrumental and expressive roles. The more traditional the roles a single parent played prior to their new status, the more confusing his or her new roles will be and the more likely roles inconsistent with long-held values and attitudes will be encountered, thus intensifying role strain. To help prevent role strain, single parents must have an income adequate to meet family obligations. They must also be supported by institutional attitudes that are contemporary and flexible. Only then will they be able to successfully resolve issues concerning conflicts of roles, financial strain, and the lack of discretionary time.

PARENTING ISSUES AND CHALLENGES

It should come as little surprise that the family concerns of working single parents center on rearing children. In many respects, their major areas of concern are not different from those of other working parents: parent–child relationships, childcare, and co-parenting. It is important single parents feel satisfied with their parenting since they generally draw a good deal of their self-esteem from that role. When they experience problems in that area of their lives, their work performance as well as their interpersonal relations at work are likely to be affected. As a consequence the wisdom of employers who understand and address these issues is not trivial.

Parent–Child Relations

Just as Mary and Robert feel inadequate at times about their success in performing their parenting roles, many single parents wonder if they put enough energy into their children, possibly because they have higher expectations of themselves or a greater sensitivity to parent-child relationships. However, several studies show that while single parents undervalue their parenting role performance, they actually are quite involved with their children (13, 27, 28, 48, 61, 63). Even if single parents do spend less time with their children as compared with other parents, conclusions about the quality of parent–child relationships on that basis alone are risky; many variables must be considered. For instance, many divorced parents report decreased stress between themselves and their children's other parent, thereby improving the parent–child relationship and offsetting lack of time together (6, 28). Furthermore, even though they might want improvements, few single parents believe their one-parent homes are inherently worse than a traditional two-parent home (47). Still, some feel they have failed their children by obtaining a divorce or fear the children would prefer to be with the other parent (28).

Similar to other parents in the military, single parents serving in the armed forces find separation from their children and long duty hours to be stressful. However, it is less stressful for parents of adolescents compared with those of younger children. In addition, acceptance of the military's values and life style make it less stressful (45). Despite the possibility of greater stress on parent–child relationships among single parents in the military, 56 percent of Air Force single parents report the Air Force to be a good place to raise children (6, 45). Although very few viewed it negatively, about one-third had mixed feelings.

Childcare

Childcare during work hours is quite possibly the greatest parenting concern among working single parents. Like other working parents, they want and need high-quality childcare that is reasonable in cost, with flexible hours of availability. For single parents the need for childcare varies considerably with the type of work they do. For parents like Mary, whose children are young, childcare during work hours is crucial. However, since her job demands little outside the typical 40-hour week, the hours of care can be fairly standard. The situation is different for parents like Robert. His job may require him to travel periodically and to put in extra duty hours. Undoubtedly, there are going to be times when these situations will be preceded by little notice, so the type of childcare for parents in jobs like his must be much more flexible in hours of availability. Furthermore, since Robert's children are teenagers they may not require supervised childcare as much as organized activities and resources to draw on when separated from their father. For single parents in the Air Force, Bowen and Orthner (6) report the most common form of childcare used was in-home care by a friend, neighbor, or adult relative. Slightly more than one-half of this childcare occurred in the home of the provider. However, there are data that single fathers prefer nurseries or childcare facilities to in-home caretakers, even though they are sometimes uncertain about how to make good choices in this regard (28, 37).

Co-parenting

Most single parents must deal with co-parenting relationships. For divorced individuals, good ones are not common enough, especially during the first year after divorce (22, 23, 69, 71). However, there is some indication single fathers have better relationships with their former spouses than do single mothers with theirs, probably because men have less financial dependence on their former spouses (20, 48).

Noncustodial mothers and noncustodial fathers appear to have similar visitation arrangements with their children (13). Summers are the most common time for visitation, followed by weekends and holidays. However, frequent contact may have a negative effect on single parents' personal adjustment (54) and, for most single fathers, frequent visitation may intensify their fears about losing custody. Similarly, Bowen and Orthner (6) report that even though nearly one-third of single fathers and over one-half of single mothers in the Air Force reported their children never saw the other parent, 84 percent of them were very satisfied with these custody arrangements.

It is likely co-parenting issues will continue to be prominent for single parents as various forms of joint custody become more common. As of 1984, 30 states had statutes authorizing joint custody, and the U.S. Supreme Court has steadily increased the rights of absent parents, especially of fathers (36). As co-parental relationships become increasingly salient, it is more likely the special needs of these parents will be addressed. However, an increase in joint custody also means there will be many more parents who will fill the role of single parent at least some of the time, further swelling those ranks.

Summary and Conclusion

Flexibility within the work environment goes a long way in helping single parents to be effective. Employers must be sensitive not only to the needs of their single-parent employees to spend time with their children, but also to the fact that parenting often requires time during work hours for such things as school meetings and doctor appointments. Of particular importance to single parents is the availability of flexible and affordable childcare. Large work organizations can make the lives of their employees much easier, as well as increase employee production and reduce absenteeism, by providing childcare or making it easy to obtain. Finally, there is considerable evidence that relationships between divorced parents continue after divorce. The quality of these relationships varies considerably, but they can have a great effect on parents' general well-being as well as the nature of the parent–child relationship.

PERSONAL WELL-BEING

It would be easy to assume single parents pay a high price in their general well-being given the combination of role strain and parental demands. In fact, most parents are well adjusted and satisfied with their lives (54). For instance, Bowen and Orthner (6) found four of five Air Force single parents to be satisfied with their lives overall. Similarly, the single parents Hanson (21) studied reported fairly high levels of physical and mental health. Loveland-Cherry (32) found no differences in personal health practices by family type and concluded single parents have the ability to meet their health needs as well as parents in other family types.

Several authors have examined the differences between single fathers and single mothers on adjustment and personal well-being. Pett (54) found few significant differences between the two groups on general well-being and, furthermore, scores of these single parents did not differ substantially from those obtained from a national sample of divorced individuals. Similarly, Lowenstein and Koopman (33) found few differences between fathers and mothers on measures of self-esteem, although Fine, Schwebel, and Myers (15) found middle-class single mothers to have lower self-esteem, more depression and anxiety, and less satisfaction with motherhood than their counterparts with spouses. However, these women were functioning in normal ranges.

After reviewing research on job satisfaction, another indicator of well-being, Forgionne and Peeters (16) found little association between gender and job satisfaction. However, although inconsistent in their specific findings, some researchers have found job satisfaction to vary by gender (26, 30) and others that it did not (74). Benin and Nienstadt (4) surmise the relationship between gender and job satisfaction may differ according to the control varibles used. For instance, there is some indication job satisfaction varies across the life cycle for men, but not for women (26) and that women's work and family role expectations may change more than men's during the course of professional training (19).

Social Well-Being

Hanson's (21) work established a correlation between social support and single parents' mental health. Reducing distress, especially depression, can be achieved by receiving help and assistance with domestic tasks and childcare (29). Unfortunately, many single parents experience social isolation even when they remain involved in their communities (6, 60), although it remains unclear how and why this occurs. Some contributing factors include inability of single parents to coordinate their schedules with those of other parents, a lack of free time, and a preference for spending their free time with their children. Single mothers have been found to maintain smaller social networks than fathers (9, 15, 35) and many single parents, especially fathers, experience a variety of social prejudices about their role (17, 59, 66) even if they do stay connected socially. Pett (54) concluded the best predictor of social adjustment is a parent's subjective feelings of well-being and inner emotional state, along with an absence of distressing situations.

One reason many single parents may give their relationships with their children a higher priority than other parents is because their social networks are often unfulfilling (28, 49). In fact, many single parents do not use a social network even when it is valued and available. There are indications that, although they do participate to some extent in social organizations, single fathers do not become heavily involved (17, 49) and many do not experience them as helpful. Many single fathers report shifts in their social networks from married couples to other single parents (2), but they still find it difficult to develop meaningful relationships (53). For instance, men in Weiss' 1973 study (70) did not find Parents Without Partners valuable for friendship opportunities with the same sex, and they had to deal with rivalry between cliques and contradicting messages about Parents Without Partners as a source of dating relationships. But not all single parents suffer socially. Gasser and Taylor (17) discovered many men made new friends after becoming single parents; some even reported having more friends, but not seeing them as often.

Single parents in Bowen and Orthner's (6) Air Force study reported parents and relatives as their most valued sources of support, although only slightly more than one-half said they would consult them in times of personal crisis. Furthermore, while slightly less than half felt close to their friends, a relatively small percentage would consult them in times of personal crisis. Santrock and Warshak (57) reported that single fathers were more likely to seek support, whereas others have found the opposite (21, 37, 41). However, studies with military populations suggest social isolation is not unique to single parents. For example, several studies show social isolation from the surrounding community is a major problem for all military families and that they are not likely to seek support from sources outside of the military (34, 39). Furthermore, about one-half of all personnel enter the Navy health care system because of problems caused or aggravated by social and emotional needs (43).

Summary and Conclusion

Together, these studies suggest single parents, as a group, are healthy individuals who maintain a sense of well-being despite the issues and challenges they face. This speaks quite highly of their resilience and character in the face of difficulties, and underscores their excellent potential as employees. Since so many single parents experience some degree of social isolation, it also can be seen that well-being in a social context involves more than maintaining contact and involvement. Social and support networks, whether they are formal or informal, need to be sensitive to the special needs of single parents. In particular, for single parents in the military, there is a need for the civilian sector to be better informed about problems unique to military families and for the development of community resources sensitive to their needs. Since children and work are the two major priorities of most working single parents, work organizations might provide opportunities where single parents can associate with one another in activities, at least some of which include children.

IMPLICATIONS FOR POLICY AND PRACTICE

There currently exists considerable diversity in the structures of American families, and one increasingly common form is the single-parent family. As these families have increased, so too has their representation in the work world. Furthermore, there are indications their numbers will continue to be large. In many ways, single parents are like other working parents; they value their jobs and careers as well as their families. But there are some important differences between single parents and other working parents. Foremost, single parents may not have another adult with whom to share the day-to-day burdens associated with rearing children. Their solitary efforts to balance these burdens with responsibilities and opportunities at work often result in role strain. Many, especially women, suffer financial strain and most do not have adequate discretionary time available to them. Despite these strains, they continue to invest considerable energy in being good parents and most believe they are doing a good job. Probably because of that belief, most single parents are quite well-adjusted and healthy individuals who are assets to their employers. Furthermore, their desire to provide good lives for their families makes them dedicated to their jobs or careers. Those who are in the military are like their civilian counterparts in these respects, although they must deal with special constraints in the areas of readiness, travel, childcare needs, risk, and relocations. Although studies suggest most single parents are doing fairly well, the special characteristics of single parents and their families have implications at the level of both policy and practices.

Policies

Thompson and Gongla (62), commenting that bureaucracies, especially governmental ones, are likely to become increasingly involved in the lives of single-parent families, caution that this involvement must be based on a realistic perspective of contemporary family structures. In particular, policies affecting families must clearly recognize there is nothing inherently wrong with single parents and single-parent families. They should address specific issues single parents struggle with, but they must also recognize the diversity across single-parent families.

Burden (9) has recommended a number of policies for the government and employers in both the private and public sectors. At the government level, policies are needed to address affirmative action plans: on-the-job training (in particular, for women with low levels of job skills who have ended marriages), comparable worth legislation, incentives for employers to develop support programs for single parents, more accessible childcare programs, employment and training opportunities, and enforcement of child support programs. In addition, policies increasing opportunities to obtain mediation counseling or conciliation counseling would help prevent extended resource-consuming battles between parents about co-parenting issues. Policies for employers must reflect a greater willingness to implement flexible hours and work schedules; provision of childcare programs either on-site, by contract, or through the use of vouchers; staff training on work–family issues affecting single parents; expanded employee assistance programs; and vigorous affirmative action policies (9).

Each branch of the military currently has policies restricting enlistment of single parents. It is believed by senior leadership personnel that single parents may be unable to cope with the demands of active duty or will not maintain a commitment to the service. Policies dictate specific conditions to be met by those who become single parents while on active duty, but who wish to remain servicemembers. These conditions generally involve providing proof that childcare plans have been made so that single parents will not be restricted in carrying out their duties. In fact, however, there is little data to support the fears of the military and more data to allay them. A foremost consideration is that the services represent considerable security for single parents and many are quite willing to comply with regulations allowing them to maintain and keep this security. Given the anticipated shortages of manpower, the military might benefit by reconsidering its recruitment policies and allowing single parents to enlist if they can meet the necessary childcare requirements. Furthermore, most adjustments required of the military to respond to single parents' needs are very similar to those increasingly being made to increase the desire to remain in the military for servicemembers in two-parent families or those where both parents are military members. For instance, issues related to frequency of change of duty station, separation from family, child care, and medical benefits are all shown to decrease a soldier's intention to remain in the Army (64). These issues are increasingly capturing the attention of military policy makers who appreciate high training costs and projected manpower shortages.

Practice

Childcare

Probably foremost among program areas where organizations and employers might provide support to single parents is childcare. Indeed many professionals and parents regard adequate and affordable childcare as the single most important social issue of the next decade. It should be clear that when adequate and affordable childcare is not available, single parents are more likely to suffer distress over the welfare of their children and increased role strain. To the extent that an organization can make available high-quality childcare that inspires the single parent's confidence, these effects will be reduced. One major factor increasing this confidence is the degree to which programs facilitate children's development rather than merely providing custodial care. Of course, childcare programs must also be reasonable in cost and offer flexible hours of availablity.

Family Support Programs

A variety of family support programs also hold promise for improving the interaction between single parents and organizations. The military has been at the forefront in implementing this kind of programming with its family support or service centers, which provide direct and indirect services to servicemembers and their families. Similarly, many companies now have employee assistance programs that meet various needs of their employees and their families. However, there are some important issues for these programs to address.

First, concerning direct services, Bowen and Orthner (6) found only about one-half of the Air Force single parents they surveyed were aware of support groups available to them, and only 20 percent had participated in such a group. Participation was especially unlikely among parents of adolescent children and among junior-grade enlisted personnel. Ironically, almost two-thirds of their sample reported interest in participating in a support group, and those most interested were junior enlisted men and women, parents of preschoolers, and those who felt low levels of satisfaction with their parent–child relationships. Assistance programs must work especially hard to let an organization's members know about their existence through active outreach efforts.

Second, many single parents pride themselves on being self-reliant. Although this is generally a positive quality that helps them cope with the circumstances they encounter, it can also contribute to social isolation, especially in stressful situations. When encountering difficulties, they may not expect to find help, so programs should include a broad outreach strategy. Furthermore, many single parents are of the opinion that social service professionals are biased against single-parent families. For example, dissatisfaction with family counseling has been expressed by Air Force single parents (6). Parents of teens appear especially unlikely to attend counseling compared with those with young children. Other studies suggest many single parents, especially fathers, do not feel counselors are tuning into their feelings and fully appreciating their struggles. Directors of programs must ensure their staffs are well trained to understand single-parent family life and that they broaden their conceptions of parenting.

RECOMMENDATIONS FOR FURTHER STUDY

Although the literature on single-parent families has grown considerably over the last ten years, there is still a great deal more to be learned. In particular, four prevailing themes about single parents need continued study. The first is that single-parent families are broken families. Less emphasis should be placed on examining the deleterious effects of growing up in single-parent families and more on the positive effects. More comparisons need to be made between growing up in single-parent families and conflicted two-parent families. Second, single-parent families are commonly viewed as a homogeneous group. Although recent studies have made distinctions between these families more clear, additional efforts are needed to better define and clarify the differences. Third, research efforts to understand single-parent families have typically been both conceptually and methodologically simplistic. More sophisticated models of single-parent life need to be formulated and tested. Fourth, the single-parent family is too often seen as a temporary step to remarriage. Even though this is often the case, researchers need to provide a better understanding of *process* of adjustment to the single-parent role using longitudinal studies.

Finally, more research is needed to help clarify the relationships single parents have with their work. There are a number of indications that single parents may be especially dedicated workers, possibly even more so than their single non-parent and married counterparts. Unfortunately, almost no comparison information exists to test this notion. Many inferences about this relationship currently rely on military samples. More comparisons are needed between military personnel and workers in the civilian sector.

CONCLUSION

The single-parent family is an increasingly common nontraditional family form. Based on the present review, single parents are shown to adjust well to the circumstances leading to their roles. However, like other families, they vary considerably along a number of dimensions. It is important that single-parent families be considered on a case-by-case basis. However, single parents do have to cope with some circumstances and situations that generally are not problems for parents in two-parent families, including: (a) managing a household with one income at a time when many two-parent families find it difficult to manage with two incomes; (b) fulfilling, by themselves, all of the adult-parent roles required in a household, including ones they may be uncomfortable and unfamiliar with; (c) dividing a finite amount of time between work, children, and self without the back-up of another parent or adult; (d) maintaining a satisfactory relationship with their children; and (e) finding easily accessible, high-quality childcare with hours flexible enough to accommodate their hectic schedules.

The fact that so many single parents are well adjusted suggests they cope with these problems quite well, albeit often in an atmosphere of social isolation. Moreover, their circumstances and problems combine to make most single parents motivated employees. Since many face or experience financial strain, they are likely to strive to seek and keep jobs. Because many struggle to contain the level of chaos in their lives, they are often moved to find stability in their relationships with their work organizations. Finally, the fact so many are well adjusted, despite the difficult circumstances they must cope with, suggest they are quite capable individuals and they can be exceptional employees in organizations sensitive to their special needs. In conclusion, although appeals to work organizations to make changes in how they influence the family lives of their employees largely have been based on ethical or moral positions (68), there is evidence such changes can also improve the effectiveness of company operation and profits because they constitute long-term investments in human capital.

NOTES

1. Bane, M. J., and Weiss, R. S. (1980) Alone in the world of single parent families. *American Demographics* 2(5):11–14, 48.

2. Bartz, K. W., and Witcher, W. C. (1978) When father gets custody. *Children Today* 7:2–6.

3. Beck, R. A., and Beck, S. F. (1979) *Labor and Leisure and Home*. Beverly Hills, CA: Sage.

4. Benin, M. H., and Nienstedt, B. C. (1985) Happiness in single and dual-earner families: The effects of marital happiness, job satisfaction, and life cycle. *Journal of Marriage and the Family* 47(4):975–84.

5. Bohen, H. H., and Viveros-Long, A. (1981) *Balancing Jobs and Family Life*. Philadelphia, PA: Temple University Press.

6. Bowen, G. L. and Orthner, D. K. (1986) Single parents in the U.S. Air Force. *Family Relations* 35:45–52.

7. Bowen, G. L. (1986) Spouse support and the retention of Air Force members: A basis for program development. *Evaluation and Program Planning* 9:209–20.

8. Brandwein, R. A. (1977) After divorce: A focus on single parent families. *Urban and Social Change Review* 10:21–25.

9. Burden, D. S. (1986) Single parents and the work setting: The impact of multiple job and homelife responsibilities. *Family Relations* 35:37–43.

10. Clark, R. A., Nye, F. I., and Gecas, V. (1978) Husbands' work involvement and marital role performance. *Journal of Marriage and the Family* 40:9–22.

11. Corcoran, M. E. (1979) The economic consequences of marital disolution for women in the middle years. *Sex Roles* 5 (March):343–53.

12. Coser, L. A. (1974) *Greedy Institutions: Patterns of Undivided Commitment*. New York: Free Press.

13. DeFrain, J., and Eirick, R. (1981) Coping as divorced single parents: A comparative study of fathers and mothers. *Family Relations* 30:265–74.

14. Epenshade, T. J. (1979) The economic consequences of divorce. *Journal of Marriage and the Family* 41:615–25.

15. Fine, M., Schwebel, A. I., and Myers, L. J. (1985) The effects of world view on adaptation to single parenthood among middle-class adult women. *Journal of Family Issues* 6(1):107–27.

16. Forgionne, A. F., and Peeters, V. E. (1982) Differences in job motivation and satisfaction among female and male managers. *Human Relations* 35:101–18.

17. Gasser, R. D., and Taylor, C. M. (1976) Role adjustment of single parent fathers with dependent children. *The Family Coordinator* 25:397–403.

18. Gramling, R., and Forsyth, C. (1987) Work scheduling and family interaction. *Journal of Family Issues* 8(2):163–75.

19. Grant, L., Ward, K. B., Brown, D. R., and Moore, W. E. (1987) Development of work and family commitments: A study with women and men medical students. *Journal of Family Issues* 8(2):176–98.

20. Greif, G. L. (1984) *The Impact of the Visiting Mother's Involvement.* Paper presented at the Annual Meeting of the National Council on Family Relations, October, San Francisco, CA.

21. Hanson, S. M. H. (1986) Healthy single parent families. *Family Relations* 35:125–32.

22. Hetherington, M. B., Cox, M., and Cox, R. (1978) The aftermath of divorce. In J. H. Stevens, Jr., and M. Mathews (eds.), *Mother–Child, Father–Child Relations,* pp. 149–76. Washington, D.C.: National Association for the Education of Young Children.

23. Hetherington, M. B., Cox, M. and Cox, R. (1975) *Beyond Father Absence: Conceptualization of Effects of Divorce.* Presented to the Society for Research in Child Development, April, Denver.

24. Hoffman, S. (1977) Marital instability and the economic status of women. *Demography* 14(February):67–76.

25. Hoffman, S., and Holmes, J. (1976) Husbands, wives and divorce. In G. J. Duncan and J. N. Morgan (eds.), *Five Thousand American Families: Patterns of Economic Progress,* Vol. 4, pp. 23–75. Ann Arbor, MI: University of Michigan, Institute for Social Research.

26. Kalleberg, A. L., and Loscocco, K. A. (1983) Age differences in job satisfaction. *American Sociological Review* 48:78–90.

27. Katz, A. J. (1979) Lone fathers: Perspective and implications for family policy. *The Family Coordinator* 28:521–28.

28. Keshet, F. H., and Rosenthal, K. M. (1978) Single parent fathers: A new study. *Children Today* 7:13–17.

29. Keith, P. M., & Schafer, R. B. (1982) Correlates of depression among single parent, employed women. *Journal of Divorce* 5(3):49–59.

30. London, M., Crandall, R., and Seals, G. W. (1977) The contribution of job and leisure satisfaction to quality of life. *Journal of Applied Psychology* 62:328–34.

31. Louis Harris and Associates (1981) *Families at Work: Strengths and Strains.* Minneapolis, MN: General Mills.

32. Loveland-Cherry, Carol J. (1986) Personal health practices in single parent and two parent families. *Family Relations* 35:133–39.

33. Lowenstein, J. S., and Koopman, E. J. (1978) A comparison of self-esteem between boys living with single-parent mothers and single-parent fathers. *Journal of Divorce* 2(2):195–208.

34. McEvoy, P. (1982) *Navy wives' knowledge of, interest in and willingness to utilize naval and civilian support services during deployments.* Dissertation, United States International University, San Diego.

35. McLanahan, S. S. (1983) Family structure and stress: A longitudinal comparison of two-parent and female-headed families. *Journal of Marriage and the Family* 45:347–57.

36. Melli, M. S. (1986) The changing legal status of the single parent. *Family Relations* 35:31–35.

37. Mendes, H. A. (1976) Single fatherhood. *Social Work* 21:308–12.

38. Moen, P., Kain, E. L., and Elder, G. H., Jr. (1983) Economic conditions and family life: Contemporary and historical perspectives. In R. R. Nelson and F. Skidmore (eds.), *American Families and the Economy: The High Cost of Living,* pp. 213–59. Washington, D.C.: National Academy Press.

39. Montalvo, F. (1976) Family separation in the Army: A study of the problems encountered and the caretaking resources used by career Army families undergoing military separation. In H. McCubbin, B. Dahl, and E. Hunter (eds.), *Families in the Military System,* pp. 147–73. Beverly Hills, CA: Sage.

40. Mortimer, J. T., Hall, R., and Hill, R. (1978) Husbands' occupational attributes as constraints on wives' employment. *Sociology of Work and Occupations* 5:285–313.

41. Neito, D. S. (1982) Aiding the single father. *Social Work* 27:473–78.

42. Nestel, G., Mercier, J., and Shaw, L. (1982) Economic consequences of midlife change in marital status. In L. B. Shaw (ed.), *Unplanned Careers: The Working Lives of Middle-Aged Women,* pp. 109–25. Lexington, MA: Lexington.

43. Nice, D. (1979) The military family as a social support: Implications for biosocial health. Paper presented at the Joint Inter-University Seminar–Air University Symposium on "Changing Military Manpower Realities: Strategic and Organizational Implications in the 1980s," June, Maxwell Air Force Base, Montgomery, AL.

44. Olson, D., McCubbin, H., Barnes, H., Larsen, A., Muxan, M., and Wilson, M. (1983) *Families: What Makes Them Work.* Beverly Hills, CA: Sage.

45. Orthner, D. K. (1980) *Families in Blue: A Study of Married and Single Parent Families in the U.S. Air Force.* Washington, D.C.: Department of the Air Force.

46. Orthner, D. K., and Axelson, L. (1980) The effects of wife employment on marital sociability. *Journal of Comparative Family Studies* 11:531–45.

47. Orthner, D. K., and Bowen, G. L. (1985) Fathers in the military. In S. M. H. Hanson and F. W. Bozett (eds.), *Dimensions of Fatherhood,* pp. 307–26. Beverly Hills, CA: Sage.

48. Orthner, D. K., and Brown, R. J. (1978) Single-parent fathers: A study with implication for military families. In E. J. Hunter and D. S. Nice (eds.), *Military Families: Adaptations to Change,* pp. 88–102. New York: Praeger.

49. Orthner, D. K., Brown, T., and Ferguson, D. (1976) Single parent fatherhood: An emerging family life style. *Family Coordinator* 25:429–37.

50. Orthner, D. K., and Nelson, R. (1980) *A Demographic Profile of U.S. Navy Personnel and Families.* Washington, D.C.: U.S. Department of the Navy.

51. Orthner, D. K., and Pittman, J. F. (1986) Family contributions to work commitment. *Journal of Marriage and the Family* 48(August):573–81.

52. Osherson, S., and Dill, D. (1983) Varying work and family choices: Their impact on men's work satisfaction. *Journal of Marriage and the Family* 45:339–46.

53. Petronio, S., and Endres, T. (1985) Dating and the single parent: Communication in the social network. *Journal of Divorce* 9(2):83–105.

54. Pett, M. A. (1982) Predictors of satisfactory social adjustment of divorced single parents. *Journal of Divorce* 5(5):1–17.

55. Piotrkowski, C. S. (1979) *Work and the Family System*. New York: Free Press.

56. Pleck, J. H. (1979) Work–family conflict: A national assessment. Paper presented at the annual meeting of the Society for the Study of Social Problems, Boston, MA.

57. Santrock, J. W., and Warshak R. A. (1979) Father custody and social development in boys and girls. *Journal of Social Issues* 35:112–25.

58. Scanzoni, J. (1970) *Opportunity and the Family*. New York: Free Press.

59. Schlesinger, B. (1978) Single-parent fathers: A research review. *Children Today* 7(3):12, 18–19, 37–39.

60. Smith, M. (1980) The social consequences of single-parenthood: A longitudinal perspective. *Family Relations* 29:75–81.

61. Tedder, S. L., Libbee, K. M., and Scherman, A. (1981) A community support group for single custodial fathers. *Personnel and Guidance Journal* 60:115–19.

62. Thompson, E. H., and Gongla, P. A. (1983) Single-parent families: In the mainstream of society. In E. Macklin and R. Rubin (eds.), *Contemporary Families and Alternative Lifestyles: A Handbook on Research and Theory*, pp. 97–124. Beverly Hills, CA: Sage.

63. Todres, R., and Schlesinger, B. (1976) Motherless families: An increasing social pattern. *Child Welfare* 55:533–58.

64. U.S. Department of the Army (1971) *Survey Estimate of Dependent and Off-Duty Employment of Army Personnel*. Report 53-71-E. Washington, D.C.: Personnel Management Development Office.

65. U.S. Bureau of the Census (1985) Household and family characteristics: March 1984. *Current Population Reports, series P-20, no. 398*. Washington, D.C.: U.S. Government Printing Office.

66. Victor, F. K., and Winkler, W. A. (1977) *Fathers and Custody*. New York: Hawthorne.

67. Voydanoff, P. (1980) Work–family life cycles. Paper presented at the Workshop on Theory Construction and Research Methodology, National Council on Family Relations, Portland, Oregon.

68. Voydanoff, P. (1984) *Work and Family: Changing Roles of Men and Women*. Palo Alto, CA: Mayfield.

69. Wallerstein, J. S., and Kelly, J. B. (1980) *Surviving the Breakup: How Children and Parents Cope with Divorce*. New York: Basic Books.

70. Weiss, R. S. (1973) The contributions of an organization of single parents to the well-being of its members. *The Family Coordinator* 22:321–26.

71. Weiss, R. S. (1979) *Going It Alone: The Family Life and Social Situation of the Single Parent*. New York: Basic Books.

72. Weiss, R. S. (1984) The impact of marital dissolution on income and con-

sumption in single-parent households. *Journal of Marriage and the Family* 46(1):115–27.

73. Weitzman, L. J. (1985) *The Divorce Revolution*. New York: Free Press.

74. White, T. H. (1981) The relative importance of work as a factor in life satisfaction. *Relations Industrielles* 36:179–91.

75. Yogev, S. (1983) Women in medicine and law: A conceptual viewpoint of competing approaches. In A. C. Kerchoff (ed.), *Research in Sociology of Education and Socialization,* Vol. 4. Greenwich, CT: JAI Press.

5

The Dual-Career Couple: Challenges and Satisfactions

Barbara J. Janofsky

The dual-career couple is no longer considered a new phenomenon. Researchers have studied the dual-career couple since the 1950s, its emergence, formation, convergence, and sometimes collision with normative patterns in our society. Today, over 65 percent of women with children under the age of 18 are gainfully employed, and 52 percent of women with children under six are in the work force (42). Yet our understanding of the dual-career couple still contains many inconsistencies and contradictions. Do women work for psychological well-being, economic well-being, or both? Are men really more likely to participate in household tasks when their wives are employed or is it that women participate less? Finally, what does adaptation mean for the dual-career couple—some quotient of satisfaction across life domains or merely survival on a day-to-day basis?

The purpose of this chapter is to increase our understanding of the challenges and satisfactions faced by dual-career couples in the U.S. military, couples where both the husband and the wife are active duty members of the military. More importantly, it considers how these challenges and satisfactions impact upon their level of satisfaction with military life.

The dual-career family, whether military or civilian, is an integral part of the organization family. When both members of a couple are involved in the same corporate culture, the reciprocal impact of the organization and the family is of considerable importance. Thus, this chapter is an attempt to illuminate one pattern of interface between the organization and the family.

The data for the study were collected under U.S. Air Force contracts F336600–70–C–0423 and F336600–70–81–R–0290. Any opinions, findings, or conclusions expressed in this paper are those of the author only and do not necessarily represent the views and opinions of the Department of the Air Force.

The data for this chapter are based on a sample of 151 Air Force (AF) dual-career couples; the study specifically seeks to identify factors that impact upon the level of satisfaction dual-military members report with regard to the military environment. For purposes of comparison, a selected review of dual-career literature within the civilian context is provided, followed by a review of literature about dual-career couples in the military.

The analyses include both descriptive and inferential statistics. Descriptive analyses will be used to describe the sample, and the similarities or differences between husbands and wives on key variables in the analysis. Inferential analyses will be used to identify the subset of factors in the analysis that influence the level of satisfaction with military life among dual military couples.

DEFINITIONS

In past literature, the terms 'dual earner' and 'dual career' have sometimes been used interchangeably. At other times they have been used to designate different groups, based on such indices as level of education, type of employment, and potential for advancement. For example, in a recent study by Hertz (22), very strict employment and income standards for dual-career couples were set. On the other hand, Repetti (37), in her study of female bank employees, made no distinction between dual-career and dual-earner couples. Despite these differences in definitional criteria for their samples, the results of these two studies are very similar in nature, describing two-provider households as having similar problems and frustrations. Perhaps, as Hiller and Dyehouse (23) have suggested, the criteria for inclusion of couples in the dual-career category may be arbitrary and in the long run not particularly meaningful. For the purposes of this study, no distinctions are made between dual-career and dual-earner couples. Dual-career couples are defined as any married couple in which both partners are employed outside the home.

CIVILIAN DUAL-CAREER COUPLES

The problems and challenges faced by individual dual-career couples emerge as key societal issues. As over two-fifths of the work force are now spouses in dual-earner households, issues such as childcare, role overload, and relocation become paramount concerns and surface as important issues that an increasing proportion of the adult population face (1). The present dual-career work force represents 47 million people, and stands in stark comparison to 1960, when fewer than 20 million people were in dual-earner households.

Role overload is one of the most serious challenges affecting women in dual-career marriages (10, 22). The conflict between one's duties in the home and one's duties in the workplace often place women in an untenable position. The reapportionment of household tasks to include husbands, children, and hired service providers appears to be the best way to lower the frustration and guilt often associated with role overload (36, 39). Attitudinal support on the part of the husband has also been found to be beneficial in relieving the role overload of employed women (6).

Childcare issues, including adequate numbers of slots and satisfactory providers, continue to be major problems for dual-career couples who have children (1, 8). Catalyst (10) reports that finding and keeping satisfactory childcare and providing "adequate" parenting for their children are high-priority concerns of dual-career couples. In her qualitative study of managerial-level couples, Hertz (22) found that finding adequate childcare is a constant task. Although most of these couples could afford live-in childcare providers, they rarely reported that a childcare arrangement lasted longer than six months, at which point couples often had to start from scratch at finding a suitable provider. In addition, it was usually the wife who assumed the duty of finding new childcare, regardless of her occupation or financial status.

The issue of relocation for occupational advancement, and the impact it has on families, becomes increasingly important for dual-career couples. Many companies require relocation to move up the corporate ladder, and historically families have generally packed up and moved when this was required (usually because of the husband's career). However, the decision to move is becoming increasingly difficult for families (40). Relocation packages provided by companies that include aid for the displaced spouse in finding a new position are becoming more common (1). On the other hand, couples are becoming more resistant to moving when it means one spouse will be required to give up lucrative and personally fulfilling employment (29).

Although dual-career couples must deal with many challenges and overcome both internal (e.g., role overload) and external (e.g., finding childcare) strains, there are satisfactions. Women are most likely to report personal growth, independence, and increased self-worth. On the other hand, men enjoy the increase in total family income and find that they and their spouse have more in common and more to talk about (10, 39). Other satisfactions or rewards include greater family security and the ability of parents to provide their children with both male and female work role models.

MILITARY DUAL-CAREER COUPLES

Dual-career couples are increasingly common to the military services and their numbers continue to grow. According to a recent breakdown of survey statistics, 100,000 members of the Armed Forces are married to other servicemembers (35). Data from the 1985 Department of Defense (DoD) survey reveal that 7 percent of married enlisted personnel and 6 percent of married officers have spouses who are in the armed forces. By service branch, one-third of Army women are married to fellow soldiers (35), while in the

Air Force approximately 40 percent of married Air Force women are married to military men (12).

Childcare may be an even larger problem for the dual-military couple than it is for their civilian counterparts. In the military it is nearly impossible for a woman to take time from her career to tend to the needs of a family in its early stages (41). The pregnant woman is generally given just four weeks' maternity leave before returning to her duties.

In addition, military personnel may be asked to work extended and irregular hours that often do not match to hours when daycare is provided. Even on-post facilities are usually not adequate for most dual-military couples, as the servicemember is required to be prepared for emergency deployment and is often absent from home for extended periods of time with very little advance notice.

The re-enlistment intentions and actions of female servicemembers in dual-career marriages have become of great interest to military leadership. A disproportionate number of dual military members do not re-enlist because of family separations and the stress it places on the family (41). Usually it is the woman who chooses to leave the service and take more responsibility for the family, especially after the birth of children. Unfortunately, in many cases, the military services lose the best servicemember in the wife's decision not to re-enlist.

Even in the military, women tend to take on the "corporate wife" standard in shouldering responsibility for entertainment and other duties expected to further their husband's career (43). Women are also more likely to put their husband's careers ahead of their own and to receive less support from their husbands for their career (15, 26). This may be one explanation of why women report that they would be the one to leave the military if a long family separation was necessary—women tend to have a lower level of commitment to a military career (28). This finding is similar to that for the civilian world, where women are more likely to give up employment for their husbands' career.

Segal (38) reports that the dual military couple may in fact be advantageous for the armed services by having both members of a couple formally linked to the military life style. However, their commitment may be dependent on the ability of the military to accommodate their needs for co-location and, if children are present, upon the quality and availability of childcare.

Despite its challenges, military couples report satisfaction with the military life style. The job and the opportunity to serve one's country are major satisfactions. The ability to travel is also seen as a reward for enduring the hardships often faced in military life (28). However, Raiha (35) has found dual military couples are less satisfied than military members married to civilian spouses, but more satisfied than single soldiers. This finding may be due to the hardships presented earlier for dual military couples, such as separations and difficulty finding and keeping childcare. In marriages where one spouse is a civilian, that person often becomes responsible for keeping the day-to-day routines intact; for the dual military couple, there is no one left at home to handle those responsibilities.

FACTORS INFLUENCING SATISFACTION WITH MILITARY LIFE

Many factors have the potential for influencing the level of satisfaction achieved by dual military couples with military life, including: rank, age, military benefits, and number of children in the family. The variables chosen for inclusion in the present analysis are supported by previous literature from both military and civilian sectors.

Family Influences

Sex-Role Attitudes

Sex-role attitudes, especially those of the husband, play an important part in understanding adaptation. Husbands' expressing liberal sex-role attitudes, by believing for example that women should have opportunities to pursue careers, have been shown to be important for women in their pursuit of careers (2, 6).

Perception of Spouse Support

Spouse support may be at least partially determined by a reciprocal exchange of support—husband to wife to husband (27). The perception among active-duty military members of their spouses' support for their work in the military is strongly related to their job and career commitment (7, 33).

Presence of Children

The number and ages of children have been shown to have an impact on the employment of women, and in turn, on the adaptation of the family (11). Having several young children has been found to be negatively related to the wife's employment (18). However, economic need and the importance placed by the husband and wife on women being home with young children has been found to mediate the participation of women in the labor force (14).

Division of Household Labor

Historically, women have continued to perform the majority of household tasks even when employed (4, 16). However, the division of household labor between husbands and wives in marriage seems to be influenced by husbands' income and sex-role attitudes. The more equal the economic status of the partners, the more likely husbands are to participate in household tasks. Ericksen, Yancey, and Ericksen (13) found that the husband's success as an income provider was the best predictor of his assistance with housework, with those in the higher-income brackets contributing the least. In the same vein, having sex-role attitudes supportive of women's employment has been found to be predictive of husbands increasing their participation in household tasks (21).

Marital Quality

Marital quality in relation to dual-career couples has often been examined for the effect of the wife's career on the marriage. As early as 1957 it was found that husbands who disapproved of their wives working produced more disharmony in the marriage and lower marital quality (17). Bailyn (3) has found that happy dual-earner marriages are those where wives are not solely responsible for the care of the house and the children, and when income is high.

Work Influences

Job Morale and Career Commitment

Job morale and career commitment for dual-earner couples often means accommodation; spouses often give less time and/or emotional energy to their jobs because greater demands are placed on them to accommodate to the work of the other spouse (19). When the husband is less involved with his job, the result is often positive for the working wife (20, 24, 25). Additionally, the more absorbed the husband and wife are in their work, the more stress is placed on the family structure (9). In other words, individuals in jobs that require extended hours or travel may place more stress on the family than those people who work only eight hours a day.

Mobility

Mobility in the military is somewhat different from that of the civilian sector. In the military one must relocate when permanent Change of Station (PCS) orders arrive. For the dual military couple this may mean relocating without your spouse, at least initially. PCS moves have been found to be a major drawback for dual military couples remaining in the military (41).

METHOD

Source of Data

The data for the study were collected from 151 dual military couples who were active-duty members of the U.S. Air Force in 1979–1981 (32). Each

TABLE 5.1
Sample Profile

Characteristic	Husbands ($n = 151$)	Wives ($n = 151$)
Age (Mean age)	29.0	27.0
Race		
White	77.5%	80.0%
Black	15.0%	13.3%
Other	5.5%	6.7%
Education		
High school diploma	28.0%	36.0%
Some college/Completed college	47.6%	37.3%
Post-graduate schooling	21.0%	20.0%
Other	4.6%	6.0%
Rank		
Enlisted	70.4%	70.0%
Officers	29.6%	30.0%
Re-enlistment intentions		
Definitely/Probably pursue career	66.6%	50.0%
Undecided	15.6%	20.5%
Definitely/Probably not pursue career	17.7%	29.5%

married couple was randomly selected across nine U.S., seven European, and eight Pacific bases from lists of AF personnel supplied by the AF Manpower and Personnel Center. Personal interviews were conducted with all participants in the study using a structured questionnaire format, with each husband and wife pair interviewed separately and by different interviewers. Table 5.1 presents the demographic profile of the sample husbands and wives.

Profile of Husbands

The husbands ranged in age from 18 to 46, and the majority of men (56.8 percent) were between the ages of 25 and 33. There was a wide range of educational attainment among the husbands. Approximately two-thirds (68.6 percent) had at least some college. The distribution of rank among the sample husbands closely parallels the averages for the Air Force (12).

Approximately two-thirds of the sample husbands (66.6 percent) were definitely or probably planning to pursue a military career, 15.6 percent were still undecided, and 17.7 percent were definitely or probably not planning to pursue a career in the military.

TABLE 5.2
Descriptive Statistics for Dependent and Independent Measures

Measure	Mean		SD		Number of items	Alpha	
	H	W	H	W		H	W
General sat. w/AF life	3.7	3.9	.9	.9	1	—	—
Extramarital supports	1.3	1.3	.41	.36	6	.659	.413
AF environment for children	1.1	1.2	.85	.81	1	—	—
Job morale	2.9	2.6	.83	.84	6	.843	.823
Career commitment	2.5	1.9	1.1	1.2	3	.737	.768
Extramarital closeness	1.2	1.1	.83	.73	5	.670	.500
Marital quality	2.9	3.1	.39	.43	29	.813	.857
Sex-role attitudes	.68	.66	.51	.56	5	.733	.766
Division of household tasks	2.5	2.7	.56	.65	3	.524	.546
Satisfaction w/PCS moves	3.3	3.5	1.0	.88	1	—	—
Spouse's sat. w/R's military service	1.7	1.4	1.1	1.4	1	—	—
Number of base assignments	5.0	2.4	3.9	1.5	1	—	—

Notes: H = Husband; W = Wife; AF = Air Force; PCS = Permanent Change of Station; R = Respondent

Profile of Wives

The women in this sample ranged in age from 18 to 40 years, and more than one-half (57.3 percent) had attended at least some college. Seventy percent of the women were enlisted; 30 percent were officers. The children in these families ranged in age from one to seventeen. Sixty percent of the families were currently rearing one child.

Compared with their member husbands, a lower proportion of wives were probably or definitely planning a career in the Air Force (50.0 percent). Alternately, women were more likely to be undecided (20.5 percent), or to state that they were probably or definitely not planning to pursue a career in the Air Force (29.5 percent).

Measures

The means and standard deviations for each item or scale in the regression analyses are presented in Table 5.2. In addition, the reliability coefficient for each scale is also presented. Each item or scale is briefly described below, beginning with the dependent variable: general satisfaction with AF life.

General Satisfaction with AF Life

This item was measured on a five-point scale from 1 ("Very dissatisfied") to 5 ("Very satisfied").

Extramarital Supports

This scale consisted of six items, involving the likelihood of turning to the following people with a personal or family problem: (a) friends, (b) neighbors, (c) parents or other relatives, (d) chaplain, (e) job supervisor, and (f) work associates. Respondents rated each item on a three-point scale, ranging from 0 ("Very likely") to 2 ("Very unlikely"). For purposes of analysis this scale was reverse coded from "Very unlikely" to "Very likely."

AF Environment for Raising Children

This item was measured on a three-point scale: 0 ("Yes," the AF is a good environment), 1 ("Mixed feelings" about the AF environment for children), and 2 ("No," the AF is not a good environment for raising children).

Job Morale

This scale consisted of six items measuring various aspects of the work environment: (a) enjoyment of daily job activities, (b) sense of accomplishment from job, (c) degree to which interests match AF specialty, (d) interest in AF job, (e) importance that is assigned to AF job, and (f) satisfaction with job. The first four items were measured on five-point scales ranging from 0 ("Very little extent") to 4 ("Very great extent"). The fifth item was measured on a four-point scale from 0 ("Not important at all") to 3 ("Very important"), and the last item was measured on a five-point scale from 0 ("Very dissatisfied") to 4 ("Very satisfied").

Career Commitment

This scale measured the respondents' overall commitment to the military and consisted of three items: (a) feelings about an AF career, (b) plans to pursue or continue an AF career, and (c) total number of years expected to spend in the AF. The first item was measured on a three-point scale from 0 ("One of least satisfying careers") to 2 ("Only career that could satisfy"). The second item was measured on a five-point scale from 0 ("No, definitely not") to 4 ("Yes, definitely"). The last item was recoded to give equal weight to all items in the scale. This scale was constructed to range from zero to four such that the higher the score, the higher the level of career commitment.

Extramarital Closeness

The scale consisted of five variables on which respondents were asked to indicate their closeness to each person: (a) parents, (b) parents-in-law, (c) friends, (d) siblings, and (e) other relatives. All items were measured on a three-point scale from 1 ("Very close") to 3 ('Not close"). This scale was recoded for purposes of analysis to range from "Not close" to "Very close."

Marital Quality

This scale comprised 29 items. Twelve items measured level of agreement between spouses on marital/family issues and were measured on a four-point scale from 0 ("Always agree") to 3 ("Disagree"). Nine items assessed marital communication on a five-point scale from 0 ("Strongly agree") to 4 ("Strongly disagree"). The final eight items assessed general marital satisfaction, companionship, and sexual relations; these were measured on a six-point scale from 1 ("All of the time") to 6 ("Never"). For purposes of analysis, this scale was recoded so that the higher the score, the higher the marital quality.

Sex-role Attitudes

The five items on this scale were all short items expressing either "traditional" or "modern" sex-role attitudes. Each was measured on a five-point scale from 0 ("Strongly agree") to 4 ("Strongly disagree"). This scale was constructed such that the higher the score, the more "traditional" the sex-role attitude.

Division of Household Tasks

This scale measured the division of three general household tasks: (a) housecleaning, (b) doing the dinner dishes, and (c) caring for children's daily needs. These items were measured on a five-point scale: 0 ("Husband always"), 1 ("Husband more than wife"), 2 ("Husband and wife equally"), 3 ("Wife more than husband"), and 4 ("Wife always"). For purposes of analysis this variable was recoded such that the greater the sharing of household tasks, the higher the score.

Satisfaction with PCS Moves

This item assessed overall satisfaction with PCS moves on a five-point scale from 1 ("Very dissatisfied") to 5 ("Very satisfied").

Spouse's Satisfaction with Respondent's Military Service

This item asked respondents to identify how much they wanted their spouse to pursue an AF career, and involved a four-point scale ranging from 0 ("Great extent") to 3 ("Very little extent").

Number of Permanent Base Assignments

Respondents were asked to indicate the total number of base assignments they had had since entering the AF.

DATA ANALYSIS

The primary analysis consisted of multiple regression analyses, with general satisfaction with AF life as the dependent variable. Regression analyses were conducted separately for husbands and wives. Both forced-entry and stepwise regression methods were employed. The forced-entry method was used to control for the potential influence of three demographic variables: age, rank, and number of children in the home. The stepwise method was then used to identify the subsets of variables in the analysis that explained significant levels of variation in the dependent variable.

T tests were also conducted on a subset of variables in the analysis to identify those variables on which husbands and wives differed significantly. These results are presented in the first part of the results section.

RESULTS

Paired *T* Test Analyses

The results of the *t* tests are presented in Table 5.3. Of the ten variables included in the analyses, husbands and wives were significantly different on four. The first variable on which husbands and wives differed significantly was "Job morale." Husbands were more likely to express higher levels of job morale than were their wives about their AF jobs.

Second was "Career commitment," and again, husbands were likely to be more committed to their AF careers than were their wives. "Marital quality" was the third variable on which husbands and wives differed significantly. In this case wives expressed higher levels of marital quality than husbands. Finally, husbands and wives differed significantly on "division of household tasks." Compared with husbands, wives reported more equal sharing of household tasks between their husbands and themselves.

Overall, compared with wives it appears that husbands are more connected to their AF jobs and careers, are less pleased with their marriages, and report less equitable division of household tasks. As compared with husbands, wives report more equitable division of household tasks, are less committed to their AF jobs and careers, and are more pleased with their marriages.

Regression Analyses

Regression analyses were conducted separately for husbands and wives. Although the same independent variables were entered into each equation, only two of the indicators that entered through stepwise regression were significant for both men and women, beyond the influence of the three

TABLE 5.3
Paired t tests for Husbands and Wives

Variable	2-Tailed *t* test	Degrees of freedom	Probability
General satisfaction with AF life	1.78	143	.077
Extramarital closeness	−.73	99	.47
Job morale	−3.34	144	.000
Career commitment	−4.85	144	.000
Extramarital supports	−1.38	145	.168
Marital quality	−2.74	120	.007
Sex-role attitudes	−.52	145	.602
Division of household tasks	4.23	141	.000
AF environment for raising children	1.03	119	.305
Satisfaction with PCS moves	1.97	127	.052

Notes: AF = Air Force; PCS = Permanent Change of Station.

control variables in the analysis: "Job morale" and "Marital quality." The results of these analyses are presented in Tables 5.4 and 5.5.

Husbands

A total of 29.8 percent of the total variance in overall satisfaction with AF life was accounted for by eight indicators. The three control variables entered the equation through forced-entry method first. Together these three variables accounted for 2.7 percent of the overall variance. The results indicate that rank, number of children in the home, and age do make a difference. Older enlisted members with fewer children were more satisfied with the AF life than were officers, younger active-duty members, and those with more children.

The strongest predictor of satisfaction with AF life for husbands was "Career commitment," accounting for 18.1 percent of the total variance. The more men identified with and were committed to their AF careers, the more satisfied they were with AF life. The second predictor that entered the equation for husbands was "Job morale." Men who felt positively toward their jobs were more likely to be satisfied with AF life. This variable accounted for 2.0 percent of the variance. "Husband's extramarital closeness," or the people men reported feeling close to, was the third significant predictor in the model. This variable accounted for 2.3 percent of the variance. The closer that husbands felt to their extramarital social network, the more likely they were to be satisfied with AF life. The next to the last variable to significantly enter the equation was "Marital quality," accounting for 3.0 percent of the variance. Men who reported higher marital quality were more satisfied

TABLE 5.4
Regression Model: General Satisfaction with AF Life for Husbands

Variable	Multiple R	Adjusted R^2	Beta	t
Current Rank			−.023	
Number of children living in home			−.047	
Age	.217	.027	−.211	.017
Career commitment	.479	.208	.507	.000
Job morale	.504	.228	.164	.029
Extramarital closeness	.530	.251	.166	.024
Marital quality	.561	.281	.193	.009
Satisfaction w/PCS moves	.579	.298	.149	.040

Notes: AF = Air Force; PCS = Permanent Change of Station.

with AF life. Finally, "Satisfaction with PCS moves" entered the equation last, and accounted for 1.7 percent of the variance. The more satisfied individuals were with the moves they had made to date, the more satisfied they were with AF life.

Wives

Seven variables entered significantly into the equation for wives, and accounted for 24.0 percent of the variance in their level of satisfaction with AF life. As for husbands, all three of the control variables significantly entered the equation, and accounted for 2.5 percent of the variance. Women who were older and of officer rank and who reported more children living in the home were more satisfied than were younger, enlisted members with fewer children living in the home.

Interestingly, the first variable to enter the model through the stepwise

TABLE 5.5
Regression Model: General Satisfaction with AF Life for Wives

Variable	Multiple R	Adjusted R^2	Beta	t
Current Rank			.038	
Number of children living in home			.042	
Age	.211	.025	−.183	.039
AF good for raising children	.408	.142	−.358	.000
Job morale	.481	.203	.259	.000
Marital quality	.503	.221	.151	.043
Division of household tasks	.525	.240	.163	.034

Notes: AF = Air Force.

method was "AF is a good environment for raising children." This variable accounted for 11.7 percent of the variance. Not surprisingly, women who believed the AF was a good environment for children were more likely to be satisfied with AF life. Following the pattern for husbands, "Job morale" entered the equation second, and accounted for 6.1 percent of the variance. As for husbands, higher job morale was associated with higher satisfaction with AF life. "Marital quality" was the third significant indicator. Higher marital quality was related to higher satisfaction with AF life. Marital quality accounted for 1.8 percent of the variance. Finally, "Division of household tasks" entered the equation fourth, and accounted for 1.9 percent of the variance. The more equally household tasks were shared between couples, the more satisfied women were with AF life.

DISCUSSION

The purpose of this chapter was to identify the individual factors for men and women in dual military marriages that influence their level of satisfaction with Air Force life. Multiple-regression analyses were conducted separately for husbands and wives, controlling for rank, the number of children living in the home, and the age of the respondent. The analyses resulted in quite different predictive models for husbands and wives, with husbands placing relatively more emphasis on external AF-related factors and wives placing relatively more emphasis on marital and family life indicators.

In addition, paired *t* tests resulted in identifying four indicators on which husbands and wives differed significantly. All four of these variables entered into the regression analysis significantly. Two, "Job morale" and "Marital quality," entered the models for both husbands and wives. On the other hand, "Career commitment" entered into the husbands-only model, while "Division of household tasks" entered into the model for wives only.

For husbands, "Career commitment" was the strongest predictor of satisfaction with AF life. It was also a variable where husbands reported significantly higher levels of career commitment than wives. For wives, the strongest predictor of satisfaction with AF life was the "AF environment for raising children."

As predicted in previous work, husbands appeared from the analysis to put more emphasis on their career than did wives (5, 41). On the other hand, wives were more concerned with the welfare of their children, possibly because they have greater responsibility for their children (22). These findings seem to be consistent for both military and civilian couples. Even when women are gainfully employed outside of the home, they tend to have greater responsibility for the children. This responsibility may lead them to place greater emphasis than husbands on factors related to children.

"Job morale" was the second factor that entered the model for both husbands and wives. Satisfaction with the job that they are currently performing is apparently important to their level of satisfaction with the overall AF environment in which they live and work.

An interesting finding for husbands was the importance of the support network. Past literature has reported that men generally have a small support network and few close friends (30). However, in this analysis the support network was found to be significantly related to their level of overall satisfaction with AF life, at least as measured by the husband's level of extramarital closeness. Those men who had closer ties with outside supports were more satisfied with AF life.

For both husbands and wives, "Marital quality" was a significant predictor of satisfaction with AF life. In both civilian and military literature, marital quality has been found to be important to dual-career couples and to positively impact upon their level of satisfaction with their environment (22, 35, 41). This important relationship continues to be replicated here. High marital quality was found to be a positive predictor of the level of satisfaction that both husbands and wives reported with AF life. This finding underscores the importance of the work–family link.

Finally, for husbands, "Satisfaction with PCS moves" was the last variable to significantly enter the model. This variable was not significant for wives. However, husbands had already made an average of five PCS moves, while wives had made an average of only two. As a consequence, wives had not yet experienced the number of relocations that husbands had experienced, thus restricting the variance of this variable in the analysis for wives.

For wives, the final variable to enter the model was "Division of household tasks." The more equitable the division of tasks, the more satisfied wives were with AF life. The results from this analysis indicated that wives were more likely than husbands to report an equitable division of household labor. However, whether in the civilian or military environment, it has been shown that wives continue to perform the majority of household tasks when they are employed (31, 34). Having a husband who shares responsibility for household chores, thus easing the woman's role demands, appears to be very important to women and their satisfaction with AF life.

IMPLICATIONS FOR CLINICAL AND
COMMUNITY PRACTICE

Although these were exploratory analyses, several of the variables that significantly entered the model point toward the importance of the Air Force providing services that encourage the development of supportive family-oriented communities.

A good environment in which to raise children was very important for women in this sample. Although the military services continue to emphasize the environment for children, by providing new and additional childcare facilities and expanded youth and teen programs, the importance of the environment for children cannot be overstated. If women are in fact measuring their satisfaction with AF life at least partly by their satisfaction with the environment for their children, then services that promote a more positive child-rearing environment should be encouraged. This may include such things as extended childcare hours that meet the needs of dual military couples, additional before- and after-school programs for older children, and a re-examination of pregnancy policies that currently allow just four weeks after the birth of a child before the mother must return to her duties.

Another area in which the military services have an impact is marital quality. First, it is important for leadership to understand how the quality of a marriage can impact on the soldier and his or her ability to perform the mission. If a military member is in an unhappy marriage, this may have an adverse effect on the performance of the mission. In the case of the dual military couple, there are two people who may not be performing up to their capacity.

Second, nearly every military installation offers some sort of marriage enrichment training. These programs should be given more emphasis and couples should be encouraged to attend. Participation in these programs should not only favorably impact upon the quality of the couple's marriage, but also positively influence their satisfaction with the military environment. Third, if couples require more in-depth marital counseling, it should be free from possible negative career repercussions. During the interviews many spouses were reluctant to turn to support programs for marital concerns because of their perceived negative implications for the members' career. Again, in the case of dual military couples, two careers are potentially at stake, if privacy and confidentiality are not preserved.

A final area in which the military organization can have an impact concerns the frequency of PCS moves. Since military members are required to move every few years, dual military couples may find themselves in the position of being required to relocate to different installations, at least for a period of time. Husbands who were more satisfied with their relocations were more satisfied with the military environment. It is likely that joint relocations of dual military couples will promote their level of satisfaction with the AF environment.

The dual military couple is a small but growing segment of the military organization. In many respects it closely resembles the civilian dual-earner couple, and, as in the civilian sector, it is unlikely that the dual military couple will go away. Consequently, it is in the military's best interests to learn more about these men and women, and to work with them to provide an environment in which they can serve their country to the best of their abilities, while at the same time continuing to have a satisfying marital and family life.

NOTES

1. Axel, H. (1985) *Corporations and Families: Changing Practices and Perspectives.* New York: The Conference Board.

2. Axelson, L. J. (1963) The marital adjustment and marital role definitions of working and nonworking wives. *Marriage and Family Living* 25:189–95.

3. Bailyn, L. (1970) Career and family orientations of husbands and wives in relation to marital happiness. *Human Relations* 23:489–95.

4. Beckman, L. J., and Houser, B. B. (1979) The more you have the more you do: The relationship between wives' employment, sex-role attitudes, and household behavior. *Psychology of Women Quarterly* 4(2):160–74.

5. Bernard, J. (1981) The good provider role. *American Psychologist* 36:1–12.

6. Beutell, N. J., and Greenhaus, J. H. (1983) Integration of home and non-home roles: Women's conflict and coping behavior. *Journal of Applied Psychology* 68:43–48.

7. Bowen, G. (1986) Spouse support and the retention intentions of Air Force members: A basis for program development. *Evaluation and Program Planning* 9:209–20.

8. Bureau of National Affairs (1986) *Work and Family: A Changing Dynamic.* Washington, D.C.: The Bureau of National Affairs.

9. Burke, R. J., and Bradshaw, P. (1981) Occupational and life stress and the family. *Small Group Behavior* 12:329–75.

10. Catalyst (1981) *Corporations and Two-Career Families: Directions for the Future.* New York: Catalyst.

11. Clark, R. A., Nye, F. I., and Gecas, V. (1978) Husbands' work involvement and marital role performance. *Journal of Marriage and the Family* 40:9–21.

12. DoD (1985) *Description of Officers and Enlisted Personnel in the U.S. Armed Forces: 1985.* Washington, D.C.: U.S. Department of Defense.

13. Ericksen, J. A., Yancey, W. L., and Ericksen, E. P. (1979) The division of family roles. *Journal of Marriage and the Family* 40:301–13.

14. Ewer, P. A., Crimmins, E., and Oliver, R. (1979) An analysis of the relationship between husband's income, family size and wife's employment in the early stages of marriage. *Journal of Marriage and the Family* 41:727–38.

15. Farkas, A., and Durning, K. (1982) *Characteristics and Needs of Navy Families: Policy Implementations.* San Diego, CA: U.S. Navy Personnel Research and Development Center.

16. Farkas, G. (1976) Education, wage rates, and the division of labor between husband and wife. *Journal of Marriage and the Family* 38:473–83.

17. Gianopulos, A., and Mitchell, H. E. (1957) Marital disagreement in working wife marriages as a function of husband's attitude toward wife's employment. *Marriage and Family Living* 19:373–78.

18. Gordon, H. A., and Kammeyer, K. (1980) The gainful employment of women with small children. *Journal of Marriage and the Family* 42:327–36.

19. Gould, S., and Werbal, J. D. (1983) Work involvement: A comparison of dual wage earner and single wage earner families. *Journal of Applied Psychology* 68:313–19.

20. Greenhaus, J. H., and Beutell, N. J. (1985) Sources of conflict between work and family roles. *Academy of Management Review* 10:76–88.

21. Gross, R. H., and Arvey, R. D. (1977) Marital satisfaction, job satisfaction, and task distribution in the homemaker job. *Journal of Vocational Behavior* 11:1–13.

22. Hertz, R. (1986) *More Equal than Others: Women and Men in Dual-Career Marriages.* Berkeley, CA: University of California Press.

23. Hiller, D., and Dyehouse, J. (1986) Dual-career marriage in the research literature. *Journal of Marriage and the Family* 49:787–96.

24. Holahan, C. K.,and Gilbert, L. A. (1979a) Conflict between major life roles: Women and men in dual-career couples. *Human Relations* 32(6):451–67.

25. Holahan, C. K., and Gilbert, L. A. (1979b) Inter-role conflict for working women: Careers versus jobs. *Journal of Applied Psychology* 64(1):86–90.

26. Janofsky, B. (1986) Spouse support: A structural model of husbands' support for wives' employment. Dissertation, University of Georgia.

27. Janofsky, B. J., and Orthner, D. K. (1985) Factors influencing husbands' support for wives' careers. Paper presented at the National Council on Family Relations, November, Dallas, Texas.

28. Janofsky, B., De Jong, J., and Croan, G. (1987) *Work and Family Themes: Dual-Career Couples in the Military.* Alexandria, VA: U.S. Army Research Institute for the Behavioral and Social Sciences.

29. Levenson, M. K., and Hollmann, R. W. (1980) Personal support services in corporate relocation programs. *Personnel Administrator* (September):45–51.

30. Little, R. (1981) Friendships in the military community. *Research in the Interweave of Social Roles* 2:221–35.

31. Model, S. (1981) Housework by husbands. *Journal of Family Issues* 2:225–37.

32. Orthner, D., and Bowen, G. (1982) *Families in Blue, Phase II: Insights from Air Force Families in the Pacific.* Washington, D.C.: SRA Corporation.

33. Orthner, D., and Pittman, J. (1986) Family contributions to work commitments. *Journal of Marriage and the Family* 48:573–81.

34. Pleck, J. (1979) Men's family work: Three perspectives and some new data. *The Family Coordinator* 28:481–88.

35. Raiha, N. K. (1986) Dual career couples in the U.S. Army: A descriptive study. Dissertation, University of Washington.

36. Rapoport, R., and Rapoport, R. (1978) *Working Couples.* London: Routledge & Kegan Paul.

37. Repetti, R. (1987) Linkages between work and family roles. In S. Okamp (ed.), *Applied Social Psychology Annual. Vol. 7: Family Process and Problems,* pp. 98–127. Beverly Hills, CA: Sage.

38. Segal, M. (1986) *Military Families: Institutional and Occupational Trends.* Washington, D.C.: Walter Reed Army Institute of Research.

39. Sekaran, U. (1986) *Dual-Career Families.* San Francisco, CA: Jossey-Bass.

40. Sharda, B. D., and Nangle, B. E. (1981) Marital effects on occupational attainment. *Journal of Family Issues* 2:148–63.

41. Teplitzky, M., Thomas, S., and Nogami, G. (1987) *Dual Army Career Officers.* Alexandria, VA: U.S. Army Research Institute for the Behavioral and Social Sciences.

42. U.S. Bureau of the Census (1984) *Statistical Abstract of the United States: 1985,* 105th ed., p. 399. Washington, D.C.

43. Williams, J. W., Jr. (1978) Dual-career military families. In E. J. Hunter and D. S. Nice (eds.), *Military Families' Adaptation to Change,* pp. 103–110. New York: Praeger.

6

Growing Up in an Organization Family

Dennis K. Orthner, Martha M. Giddings, and William H. Quinn

CASE 1: KRISTEN TURNER

Kristen Turner is an eleven-year-old girl growing up in a suburb of Los Angeles, California. Her father works for a major high-tech company and her mother teaches at the local middle school. Because her father's company is a major employer in the area where they live, many of her neighbors work for the same company as her dad and many of her friends come from those families. Even though her father has been transferred several times, her best friend is one that she knew as a preschooler when their fathers had both worked together at the same regional headquarters.

Kristen likes many of the things that her dad's company provides for her and her family. They all use the company fitness center and swimming pool. They go on company-sponsored trips when there are major meetings for her dad. She and her friends all use the same health center for their medical check-ups. When they have moved, which has not always been easy, at least her father's company helps them with the move and even provides someone to assist her mother in finding a new teaching job. All in all, Kristen feels pretty good about her life, her family, and the company her dad works for.

The authors acknowledge the support of the Department of the Air Force and the Office of Family Matters for their support of this research. Special thanks is given to Lt. Col. Frankie Jones and Lt. Col. Jerry Murray for their assistance in this effort. It should be noted that the authors of this chapter do not purport to reflect the position of the Department of the Air Force and the Department of Defense.

CASE 2: ROBERT BROWN

Robert Brown is fifteen and he is growing up in a housing area of Fort Bragg near the town of Fayetteville, North Carolina. His dad is a first sergeant in the Army, with responsibility for a transportation unit. His dad is gone quite a bit, but Bobby and his mother feel very much a part of the community and neighborhood in which they live.

Bobby's life revolves around the Army. Most of the schools that he has attended have been on Army posts, but now he goes to a school off-post where most of the other kids are also from Army families. He attends church with his family at the post chapel, plays on the soccer team on-post, and gets all of his medical check-ups from Army doctors who work in the post hospital, not too far from his home. Almost all of his friends come from Army families and he thinks he too will join the Army when he grows up, just like his dad. All in all, he likes the Army way of life.

Both of these youths are growing up in organization families. They did not choose their way of life, but because their parents decided to work for large employers their lives have been shaped by the organizations to which their fathers (and their mothers) have committed themselves. The support systems of either the corporation or the military can become such a dominant feature of everyday life that children become nearly as tied to the work organization as their parents and the organization becomes part of their own identities.

We can see evidence of this close tie in a recent study of adolescents growing up in military families (21). In that study, a national sample of adolescents growing up in military and civilian families was compared. It was found that the youth growing up in military families were twice as likely to believe that they would join one of the armed services as compared with youth growing up in civilian families. In addition, those youth who believed in the values of the military organization (e.g., appropriateness of regulations, patriotism, good place for families, etc.) were much more likely to have military career plans for themselves than those who disagreed somewhat with military values. Overall, the more satisfactorily the youth perceived the military organization and their fathers' roles in the organization and felt that their family situation was close and supportive, the more likely they were to plan on joining the organization themselves when they reached adulthood.

In this chapter we will explore some of the ways in which children and youth are influenced by the organizational work environments of their parents. The potential importance of parental work organizations on children will be examined, as will the role that children can play in parental work performance and commitments. Children growing up in military work environments will be the primary focus of the research and data analysis reviewed in this chapter, although comparisons are made with other work environments, including corporate organization families. The chapter will conclude with recommendations for further research and implications will be discussed for practice and policies that deal with organization families and their children.

YOUTH FROM MILITARY FAMILIES: A RESEARCH STUDY

The data to be reviewed in this chapter were gathered from probability samples of adolescents between 11 and 19 years of age from five communities across the United States. In order to better understand the needs of youth growing up in military families, the U.S. Air Force Office of Family Matters commissioned a "Youth in Transition" study in which adolescents from military families could be compared with those growing up in nonmilitary, civilian families (21). This study was a follow-up to an earlier investigation that focused solely on the needs and concerns of Air Force youth (20). The new study was to determine whether youth from these different homes have unique needs or problems that should be better understood by those who provide support services to them.

The sample for this study was designed to be representative of both military and nonmilitary teens living in several areas of the United States. The adolescents were selected from their schools by random selection of classes, coordinated by the research team and school personnel.

Five communities were selected as sites for data collection. For each community the researchers determined the specific middle and high school that served the highest percentage of military youth. Permission to conduct the study was sought from all the school systems involved as well as the parents of the subjects. Research teams were sent into each school on a prearranged date at which time classes were assigned for the survey. Questionnaires were distributed to the students in group sessions. These took about 40 minutes to complete and included questions on a variety of adolescent experiences and personal and relational well-being issues.

A total of 2,435 students participated in the survey. This represented an 82 percent response rate. Approximately one-third of the sample lived in military families while the remainder were from civilian families. The mean age of the sample was 16 years, and 35 percent of the military youth were minorities compared with 36 percent of the civilian youth. Two out of three (67 percent) military youth lived with their parents on the military base and 84 percent of the fathers were in the enlisted grades. These percentages are very similar to those that would be expected from an Air Force–wide sample.

DEVELOPMENTAL NEEDS OF CHILDREN

The family and community environments within which children grow up are very important to their personal and relational well-being. Children readily take on the personalities of their parents, kin, friends, and the social context of their childhood. For example, children reared in disadvantaged homes, where their parents are economically and socially deprived, very often adopt patterns of behavior that make it very difficult for them to change their social situation. Likewise, children whose parents are financially well-to-do tend to subscribe to behaviors that make it easy for them to continue this pattern of success (7).

Recent research has indicated children are unusually malleable. While the social status of their families may vary significantly, the majority of children adapt quite well to their social surroundings. Psychological well-being is not necessarily influenced by the economic well-being of the household. Recent studies of divorce also indicate that most children are initially very upset by this event but they usually return to their previous levels of psychological health within one to two years (26).

Needs for Security

Still, there are major costs that children pay if they do not have some of their basic developmental needs met, and the level of response to some of these needs can be influenced by growing up in an organization family. Perhaps most basic is the developmental need for security. Children, as well as adults, need to know that their environment is safe and free from the risk of personal harm. Erik Erikson (8), the noted psychologist, suggested that trust in one's social environment is the earliest need that children express. Unless this sense of trust is established, children are handicapped in each subsequent stage of development.

Security is one of the individual and family needs that is most influenced by the parents' work environment. While some work organizations provide a measure of security and continuity to their employees, others offer little or no hope that jobs will be available beyond the immediate tasks at hand. Studies of worker satisfaction indicate that security is one of the most valuable job assets that an employer can offer (25). One of the greatest attractions allegedly offered by universities to often underpaid faculties is tenure, the promise that the job is permanent.

The level of security offered by the work organization translates very readily to the family. Children too like to know that they can count on their parents' providing them with regular meals and a roof over their heads. One of the attractions of large work organizations is the job security they offer to their employees. They can spread the risks of their organizations across many people and usually provide some degree of protection for individuals with several years of service. This translates to a more financially secure home environment for children.

However, for children in military families, the security of their parents' jobs can be offset by the insecurity caused by job risks. Many military jobs entail risks, both in training and in wartime. The specter of conflict and combat are inevitable parts of the military family life style. As a consequence, these children may be more concerned than others about the possible loss of their parent, particularly during periods of international tension or when living in overseas environments.

Needs for Stability

Children also need some degree of stability in their lives. Because of all the internal, personal developmental changes that they experience, it is important for children to have a relatively stable external environment within which to grow up. Of course, the parental environment is the most important but it is also important for children to have a network of peer and adult relationships that can serve as resources they can call on in time of need.

One of the most unstable aspects of growing up in an organization family is moving. While some organizations move their people infrequently, most large organizations move large proportions of their labor force very regularly. Some have suggested that the initials of the computer giant IBM stand for "I've Been Moved." Likewise, the military services move almost their entire personnel force every two to four years. Adolescents who have grown up in military families report that they have moved on the average every three years; this compares with civilian youth, who move every six years (21).

On the positive side, moving provides children with new experiences and opportunities to start over again in new places. One writer points out:

There's a lot of talk about how military kids learn to adapt and there's probably a lot of truth in that. . . . One of the things that might make adapting easier is the knowledge that nothing is forever in the military. While you may have to make a major adjustment to accommodate your military life, it's almost certain to change within two or three years. (9, p. 99)

The ability to make these changes successfully, it is suggested, can help with later changes.

On the negative side, moving appears to take a psychological toll on many children. Patricia Nida, author of several books on corporate and military moves, suggests, "From my experience, the more a family thinks that relocation is going to be a piece of cake, the more trouble that family is going to get in" (16). In a recent national study of moving among adolescents, it was found that the youth who had moved the most often were the ones with the poorest psychological profiles, even worse than the youth who had moved most recently (6). Apparently, frequent moving during childhood causes some children to turn inward and fear developing relationships, rather than turning them more comfortably toward others (27).

The reaction of people in the community to children from military families can also create social isolation. One child remarked,

The coaches know that as military kids, we will come and go. He's got to try and build a team that can work together for several years at a time. He can't count on us to be there so he sometimes chooses someone from town who he knows will probably be around. (9, p. 163)

To be sure, research on moving does not find that most children are irreparably harmed by the experience. Moves are temporarily stressful for nearly all children but most adjust quite quickly, especially if they are younger (3, 11). When the age of the mobile child is examined, it is apparent that adolescents are the most likely to be apprehensive about the experience (5). For them, their fathers' or mothers' exciting new job challenges are coupled with major shifts in schools, peers, intimate relationships, and, perhaps, career opportunities. Given all the changes that typically accompany this stage of the life cycle (22), it is not surprising that many youth respond quite unfavorably to moves.

Needs for Socialization

One of the major tasks of parents in rearing children is providing socialization into the social rules and norms that represent appropriate behavior (15). Society demands that parents teach their children how to behave in different circumstances. This gives the child freedom to act within prescribed boundaries and adults the knowledge that they do not need to continuously monitor the behavior of children.

The traditional pattern for socializing children placed most of this burden on mothers (23). Fathers were expected to devote their energies to their employed jobs while mothers gave primary attention to child rearing. Not only did the "organization man" father not view socialization as his responsibility, but according to Bratter (4, p. 585), he was "too physically exhausted or emotionally drained to play an active role in the family." His children viewed him as "passive, uninvolved, disinterested, remote, compliant, and ineffectual."

With the majority of mothers now in the labor force, children are falling into a vacuum in which there may or may not be a primary caregiver. Participation of fathers in primary socialization tasks is increasing (18), but even greater teaching roles are now being transferred to third parties, such as daycare centers, schools, and the media. In his book, *Who Will Raise the Children?*, James A. Levine (12) raises the question of whether future generations will pay a significant price for the abdication by working parents of their socialization roles.

Despite these pervasive concerns, it appears that children growing up in working parent, alternate caregiver households are functioning quite normally (24). If anything, children in organization families are somewhat advantaged by the likelihood that large employers are more likely to have benefits that augment the socialization roles of parents. An increasing number of companies and the military services offer on-site daycare, parental leave policies, maternity benefits, and liberal sick leaves that make it more possible for parents to participate in the life events of their children. In these families, mothers and fathers are more likely to have the resources to find higher-quality alternate caregivers, a critical determinant of whether the child will be emotionally hurt by the child-rearing environment.

Needs for Relationships

As children grow up, they also need an expanding cadre of relationships to further encourage their development in new directions. Parents alone are unlikely to be able to fulfill all the needs that children have for knowledge, recreation, or personal support. Clearly, the parental relationship is the most crucial to children, but other relationships are also increasingly viewed as vital.

One of the common by-products of growing up in a corporate or military family is a reduction in the size of the social relationships around the individual or the family. For example, when adolescents from military and civilian families were compared, it was found that those from military families had fewer close friends and they were less likely to have friends or kin that they felt they could go to in times of need (21). Margolis (14, p. 149), writing about children in corporate families, describes through the words of one of the parents the lack of community bonding that these youths experience:

There are some hard things which go on in moves, which people who don't move don't understand. The emotional problems which kids go through, which you may see and you may not see. And the fact that they suddenly have no friends and have to start all over again.

Likewise, children from military families often report little attachment to their communities or deep attachments to relationships in them. There is a tendency for these children, like their parents, to collect acquaintances but not close friendships (17, 19). The latter cause too much personal pain when they have to be replaced very often. Unfortunately, fathers do not always see this strain because their jobs continue and their work environments at least produce colleagues (1). Mothers and children are often left to their own devices with little support from the organization or its member to assist in the transition.

PSYCHOLOGICAL WELL-BEING AMONG YOUTH

As the above suggests, an important indicator of childhood adjustment is psychological well-being. Not surprisingly, the teen years are a time of major psychological and interpersonal adjustment. Erikson (8) suggests that one major developmental task in adolescence is the establishment of a functional ego identity. This task is prolonged over the span of the teen years and involves the dual tasks of defining a sense of personal identity as well as defining the way in which individuals fit into their overall social system. Success in fulfilling these needs is deemed to be critical for preparation to adulthood.

One compelling aspect of Erikson's model is the notion that teens develop within a broader social context inclusive of a familial environment as well as a broader social environment. In the case of the military and many corporate systems, aspects of the work environment impact quite directly upon the psychological and emotional well-being of teens.

One enlightening element of the *Youth in Transition* study (21) was a focus on the conflict between the emerging developmental needs of teenagers and the demands of the parental workplace. It is apparent that organizations can place stress upon adolescents residing within member families, but it is likewise possible for youths themselves to create stress on their parents and, in turn, on the organization. Within the psychological realm, family conflict, physical, emotional and sexual abuse, gang membership, teenage pregnancy, school failure, alcohol and drug usage, and teen suicide are just a few of the problems that have ramifications for parents as well as for the organization's overall mission or level of productivity.

Self-Esteem

One important component of the development of a healthy identity is the emergence of a sense of self. Based on past experiences, individuals learn to believe in themselves and in their abilities to meet future goals. Within a relatively normal course of growth and development, youth gradually learn to master their environments and acquire confidence in their abilities.

Research suggests a strong relationship between high levels of self-esteem and psychological well-being. Low self-esteem appears to render adolescents vulnerable to a multitude of problems. Of particular interest in the *Youth in Transition* study was an attempt to compare the self-esteem levels of teens who have grown up in a military environment with that of teens who have grown up in civilian environments. Low self-esteem levels were reported by only 23 percent of males from Air Force families and 21 percent of males from civilian families, suggesting similarities between the two groups. Among females, however, there were significant group differences. Approximately two-fifths or 41 percent of the girls from military families reported low levels of self-esteem as compared with 32 percent of civilian females.

Although this pattern of sex differences appeared consistent across the teen years, there were some apparent age differences. For example, Air Force females consistently reflected lower levels of self-esteem than their civilian counterparts for all age groups. Likewise, males from Air Force families tended to maintain high levels of self-esteem across all age groups. The self-esteem of males from civilian families showed an increase with age. Civilian females, however, experienced a drop in self-concept during mid-adolescence (ages 14–15) followed by a subsequent increase in esteem levels at ages 16–18.

The importance of self-esteem is reflected in its relation to other significant factors. Major predictors of self-esteem were found to be high life satisfaction, the ability to confide in parents, the presence of good parental relationships, having a number of friends, and academic success.

The correlation between grades and self-esteem was moderately high for all teenagers in the late adolescent teenage years ($r = .33$). Such a finding in all likelihood reflects the fact that older teens are increasingly forced to make academic and/or vocational choices based in large part on their school performance. The relationship between grades and self-esteem was particularly pronounced for Air Force youth. Even among the youngest group of Air Force teens, the correlation is unusually high (Air Force males: $r = .46$); Air Force females: $r = .64$). Within the military environment, successful personal performance tends to be defined by performance-related external criteria. It seems likely that children and youth within such environments tend to incorporate such a belief system into their behavior and from early ages begin to rely on grades as an outward and visible sign of performance, just as their parents use rank and medals to indicate their performance.

The consistent finding of lower self-esteem in females from Air Force families is interesting in comparison to the consistently high self-esteem levels of their male counterparts as well as the significant differences between the esteem of these young women and their civilian counterparts. This suggests that the military environment may not offer as optimal an environment for its female youth to develop strong self-concepts.

One possible explanation for this finding is the observation that the military, like many large-scale organizations, has been, and in large measure still is, a masculine environment. The rules for success and the culture itself tends to reinforce masculine values and roles. Until recently the place of women in the military organization was limited or they served in an adjunct role as the wives of military members. Despite far-reaching changes in the overall military organization and increasing numbers of female members, it remains largely an organization managed by male career officers. Whereas the organization is clearly supportive of male adolescents, offering clear-cut vocational choices/opportunities as well as well-defined role models, it would appear that the expectations and opportunities for females remain somewhat confusing.

Alienation

Alienation, another indicator of psychological well-being, is related to the sense of personal isolation from others. Alienation involves feelings of loneliness, boredom, fear, and rebellion. These feelings can often lead to apathy and are associated with a lack of connectedness to peers.

The youth in the *Youth in Transition* study demonstrated rather low levels of alienation, with only a small to moderate percentage of this group reporting frequent feelings associated with alienation. For example, chronic loneliness is reported by 13 percent of civilian males, 15 percent of civilian females, and 12 percent of Air Force males. Again, however, a significantly higher percentage of Air Force female youth (23 percent) report frequent feelings of loneliness.

When an overall measure of alienation was examined across the groups, civilian males reported the lowest alienation scores, whereas girls from Air Force families reported the highest scores. Again, over and beyond the expected sex differences between adolescent males and females, the singular pattern of higher alienation scores for Air Force girls is notable. Assuming that alienation refers to a sense of personal isolation or a lack of social connectedness, females within the military system experience these negative feelings more keenly than their peers.

One plausible explanation for this consistent finding is that this expression of alienation reflects a military social system that on the one hand encourages personal achievement while simultaneously denying opportunities to actualize this achievement. In addition, it is apparent from other data in the youth study that females have a much more difficult time with relocation, and therefore may experience greater social isolation as a result of frequent moves. The higher alienation scores may result from the pile-up of lost relationships and their inability to replace these friendships as quickly as boys.

Over the course of adolescence, feelings of alienation tend to increase among teens. However, girls from Air Force families experience a dramatic increase in alienation as they get older. The other three groups exhibited only modest changes over time.

The major predictor in a regression analysis of low levels of alienation was the perceived ability to make new friends easily. For girls particularly, a good relationship with parents was also a significant predictor. Two additional predictors characterizing young women from Air Force families included positive school experiences and achieving good grades. It would appear that a good parental relationship, the development of an adequate social network, and a measure of academic success are crucial to females from a military environment and that the lack of these supports can potentially predispose these girls to increased levels of alienation.

Depression

A third psychological state closely tied to self-esteem and alienation is depression. Frequent and intense levels of depression are indicative of psychological distress among youth. Concerns over adolescent depression have recently risen with increases in teen suicide, even among those from "good" corporate and military families.

An attempt was made to assess the frequency of depressive feelings within both military and civilian teenagers. The youth were asked whether during the previous month they had either felt so sad or had had so many problems that they wondered if life was worthwhile. This line of questioning had previously been used in the national High School and Beyond Study. About two-thirds of the adolescents indicated that they had had such feelings. More females, however, reported these feelings (77 percent) than did males (59 percent). When the data were examined to identify youth who reported feelings of extreme depression at least twice in the last month, females from Air Force families were much more likely to report higher levels of depression (52 percent) than civilian females (41 percent) or males from either group (civilian = 30 percent; Air Force = 29 percent).

Depression does not appear to be significantly influenced by age. Among females, depression was more common in 14- and 15-year-olds than among the other age groups. However, 47 percent of the 12- to 13-year-old girls from Air Force families reported frequent feelings of depression.

The close relationship between stress and depression was confirmed in a regression analysis in which stress was found to be a major predictor of depression. This finding was true for all adolescents. Although depression was the greatest among females, and particularly females who were new to their homes or communities, these feelings tended to decline with increasing years in residence. Academic success was associated with lower levels of depression.

Because of the frequency with which relocation is a part of both the military and corporate life styles, these results are disturbing. Apparently invisible but nevertheless complex social and emotional ties are not to be broken lightly, particularly for teenage girls. Of course, many teens and their families manage multiple relocations quite successfully. For other adolescents, low levels of psychological well-being can result.

It is ironic that as parents succeed in either the military or corporate world, frequent relocation is often the result. As adolescents proceed through their psychological development, however, their resiliency to being uprooted appears to decline, not increase. Balancing these two needs is a perplexing and challenging task for families and for the workplace.

STRESS AND COPING

Stress is a condition of human living for both adults and children. Over time, it is inevitable that events will be confronted that arouse anxiety or apprehension. There are elements of doubt and indecision as circumstances are confronted that are confusing or uncontrollable. For the adult who is an organizational employee, the origin of stress can be the demanding set of work responsibilities, a perception of insecurity in a work position, or personal and family problems. For the spouse of an organizational employee, the stress can be one's own work demands if employed, child-rearing demands, or the prospects of a job transfer and the consequences of a geographical move.

Culture has evolved in such a way as to induce other sources of stress. The pervasive idea that achievement is equated with success and economic well-being with competence can serve to stir up anxiety and doubt. In society there is an incessant demand for productivity. As such, the employee in an organizational family is entered in a contest and, like automobiles, evaluated for efficiency and performance. Since most work in an organization is framed as a competitive endeavor, comparisons between oneself and others are natural. Thus, for many workers the attitude that an employee works until the work is completed is an ambiguous one since expectations by one's superiors are typically higher than actual performance. This dilemma can place substantial strain on the employee who desires to be a responsible spouse and parent.

Young persons in organizational families feel these pressures. Some examples include the effects of a parent's job transfer and the subsequent geographical move, which requires changes in peer relationships, school settings, or church or social organizations; frequently absent parents who are required to travel or work long hours; alcohol problems of a parent who is inefficiently coping with stress; and emphasis on personal image (i.e., stylish clothes, cars, or personal appearance).

Family Interaction

Families are important to the development and well-being of adolescents. While peers become increasingly important to all teens by providing opportunities to test their autonomy from parents and to experience validation and a sense of belonging, families continue to provide a stable, reliable support system. In fact, it might be argued that families bonded to organizations take on special importance because of the relational turnover among peers compared with the consistency in the family.

In the study of Air Force youth, the amount of interaction between parents and their adolescent children was related to the willingness of adolescents to confide in their parents. The context of parent–youth interaction was also measured and whether it typically occurred in casual conversation, joking, school work, or household tasks, it appears to be associated with the young person's willingness to confide in parents his or her personal thoughts and feelings.

One of the major opportunities for youth to spend time together and communicate with their parents is during meals. It seems likely that a family that has meals together regularly provides an opportunity for shared experiences. And most families do engage in mealtime activity together, with approximately 80 percent of both civilian and military youth reporting that they eat meals regularly with their mothers, and approximately 70 percent eat meals regularly with their fathers. It would also seem reasonable to assume that such conversation would provide problem-solving opportunities for the family.

In an examination of the data using factor analysis, having meals together was found to be more associated with expressive interaction than instrumental interaction. In other words, the perceptions that young people have about sharing meals together suggest that the social nature of the activity is more relevant for promoting emotional closeness than simply to carry out the household tasks of preparing, eating, and cleaning up at mealtime. Interestingly, the analysis confirmed that having meals together was important not only because it met physical needs, but it was also a context for carrying on conversation.

The data also suggest that the relationship between a young person and a parent is partially contingent upon the young person's relationship with the other parent. For example, if the mother and adolescent experience higher amounts of interaction, the father's status as a confidant is more likely to be greater than in families in which adolescents and their mothers have lower levels of interaction. The reverse is also significant. High levels of interaction between fathers and their children appear to be associated with the mother's status as a confidant. Thus, it seems very important that in attempting to comprehend the nature of a relationship between a parent and adolescent, one needs to inquire about the spouse of that parent and the relationship between that spouse and the young person.

An interesting related finding in this study is that adolescents who reported problems in academic achievement, drug or alcohol use, or trouble with law enforcement were more likely to rate their parents' marriages lower than adolescents who reported fewer of these problems. While it is conceivable that an adolescent with problems such as school failure, an arrest by the police, or drug and alcohol consumption might stir up conflict between parents, it seems just as conceivable that these young persons may be acting out the hostility or emotional distance of the parents' relationship. Furthermore, these young persons' problems are related to relationships with siblings. Adolescents with problems report poorer relationships with their siblings. Again, these data indicate that a young person's adjustment and ability to cope with stress is related to family factors such as the quality of the parents' marriage and the extent and quality of parent–adolescent interaction.

One important result that has implications for the organization family is the discovery that adolescent females from military families have significantly less interaction with their fathers than adolescent males in the military and civilian adolescent males and females. These females were less likely to perceive their relationships with their fathers as close or to confide in their fathers in time of need. Male adolescents in the military, however, reported close ties with their fathers. They were seen as confidants and there was substantially more interaction of both the expressive and instrumental types. In almost all categories of quality of parent-child relationships, the military female adolescents clearly appeared the most vulnerable.

It would appear from the data that the expectations of male and female roles in the military are clearer, or at least less ambiguous or flexible than in the civilian environment. Adolescent females growing up in military families may have a more difficult time adjusting to the more traditional attitudes, values, and role of males in the military, especially when they go to school and make friends in the civilian community off-base. Even though they may be capable of accommodating to it, the discontinuity between what is observed in their father and his work organization and what is increasingly being suggested as a new set of male and female roles in society may be causing these adolescent females the distress they are reporting. Unfortunately, the fathers may be completely unaware of their adolescent daughter's experiences.

Over time, there is a general tendency for interaction between adolescents and their parents to decline. The activities in which decline has been found to be most common include doing schoolwork together, working around the house, recreating, and having meals together. In contrast, interaction in casual conversation, joking around, and talking about thoughts and problems tends to remain relatively steady over the adolescent years among both boys and girls from Air Force and civilian families. This finding is noteworthy in that it goes against the popular belief that adolescent communication with parents drops significantly as they participate more in peer groups. Instrumental or functional communication does drop off, but expressively based communication tends to be retained. Apparently parents do not lose their importance as vital resources in times of need, but day-to-day task-based interaction becomes a less useful indication of the quality of their relationship.

Adolescent Stress and Coping

The ability to handle stress is largely based on experience and resources. Adolescents are usually short on experience. Many of the negative influences they confront are new, so they have little opportunity to practice means of skillfully adapting to new circumstances.

Without a broad base of experience, the ability of adolescents to manage stress depends upon their inner resources or external support networks. The potentially damaging effects of stress on psychological well-being can be mitigated by effective coping mechanisms or strategies. Psychologists recognize that stress is not inherently bad since it motivates change, often in a positive direction. The negative effects of stress are likely to emerge when stress-coping mechanisms are not adequately developed. The ability to cope with stress, therefore, is an important ingredient in psychological well-being.

The most common sources of stress found in this study of adolescents are geographical moves, making new friends, break-ups of close relationships, conflict with parents, school problems, or personal health problems. In this study, one-fifth of the students reported that in the last year they had failed a grade, one-sixth report drug and alcohol problems in another family member, one-fifth of the youth are having a personal drug or alcohol problem, one out of eight youth experienced divorce or separation of their parents, and one out of ten had a close friend or relative die in the past year.

Girls are more vulnerable to relationship issues and problems. These included problems in dating, pregnancy, new friendships, break-ups, or parent conflicts. Boys were more likely than girls to report specific individual behavior problems, such as failing at school, getting into trouble at school, or being arrested. Interestingly, boys and girls had about the same percentage of drug and alcohol problems.

Youth from Air Force families do not differ significantly from civilian youth on most dimensions of stress. They are, however, twice as likely to have moved in the past year, and this ripples through many of the stress events such as going to new schools and making new friends. Although the percentages are modest, it is interesting to note that Air Force youth are somewhat more likely to be arrested by the police than are civilian youth. This may be caused by their greater exposure to military as well as civilian police forces.

Air Force youth are somewhat less likely to be exposed to several areas of stress. For example, they are less likely to have personal or family drug and alcohol problems, academic problems at school, or to have a parent who has lost their job. Still, it is important to note that serious problems like drug and alcohol are not absent from Air Force youth or their parents. One out of seven Air Force youth indicate that another family member has a drug/alcohol problem and one out of six of these youth have that problem themselves.

Overall Stress Levels

There are no major differences between Air Force and civilian youth in their overall levels of stress. This is certainly a noteworthy finding, given the higher potential for stress in the lives of Air Force youth. There are differences in stress, however, between male and female adolescents. Overall, females report slightly higher levels of stress than males, although these differences are not that substantial.

The highest levels of stress tend to be associated with the mid-adolescent years (14 to 15 years of age) for males and females in Air Force and civilian families. Except for Air Force females, the levels of stress tend to go down in the later adolescent years. Among all the groups studied, male youth from Air Force families tend to report the fewest number of stress events, and this adds additional weight to the earlier findings about relatively high psychological well-being among these adolescents.

The linkage between stress and psychological well-being is strongly confirmed in this study. High values on this stress scale tend to be associated with high levels of depression and alienation and low levels of self-esteem. For example, the correlation between stress and depression is strong and significant for civilian boys ($r = .27$), civilian girls ($r = .31$), and Air Force girls ($r = .37$). Since depression in this study is a fairly strong indicator of feelings of worthlessness and personal failure, high levels of stress should be of some concern to professionals who work with these youth in either military or civilian settings.

Not all stressors have the same impact on psychological or relational well-being. An analysis was conducted to determine the factors that are associated with different types of stress. According to this analysis, feelings of depression are most associated with new moves, dating problems, loss of a job, break-ups of relationships, parental problems, teacher and academic problems, and personal or family drug and alcohol problems. In each of these cases, however, the effects on female adolescents are much more dramatic than they are on male adolescents. Low self-esteem tends to be associated with sibling problems, dating problems, parent and school problems, getting arrested, and personal drug and alcohol difficulties.

The stressors that are most likely to be associated with family problems include sibling difficulties, relational break-ups, parent hassling, teacher and school problems, and drug and alcohol problems. The data suggest that when there is a drug or alcohol problem in another family member, it is more likely to be the father, since relationships between teens and their fathers are the most likely to deteriorate if this problem is reported in the family.

Coping with Stress

Stress is a common part of the life experience of adolescents, no matter what their family background or military affiliation. The ability to cope with stress, however, can vary a great deal, depending upon the internal and external resources that youth can call upon in times of need. In the developmental literature, an increasing amount of attention is given to adolescent coping since stress events cannot always be avoided or anticipated.

There are a variety of ways by which adolescents can cope with and adapt to stress in their lives. Even though the specific strategies that individuals may choose to adapt to stress can vary a great deal, there are three common coping themes that include most of these strategies. First, individuals may choose to cope through maximizing their own personal resources. Second, individuals may use their interpersonal support systems of friends and family as resources in times of stress. Third, outside professionals may be identified and utilized as resources once stressful events occur.

Personal Coping Strategies

Each of the youths in this study were asked about their likelihood to use a variety of different personal resources in times of stress. A factor analysis of these reveals two types of personal resource strategies: (1) active coping strategies, which include believing in their own personal power to solve problems, and (2) passive coping strategies, which include waiting for problems to go away, belief in the power of luck, and trusting in God.

Youth from Air Force and civilian families do not differ significantly in their use of personal coping resources and strategies. The overwhelming majority of youth claim that they bring to bear active personal resources when they are facing a major problem in their lives. Female youth, especially those from Air Force families, are somewhat less positive about their personal strength to respond to stress events. While 82 percent of the males believe that they usually have the power to work out problems, this is true for fewer civilian (74 percent) and Air Force females (63 percent). Air Force males, in contrast, are the most likely to believe in the role of luck and tenacity in solving stressful problems. They are more likely to believe that if they wait long enough problems will simply go away. In a military environment, this is a common euphemism and it may have been internalized more by these male youth who identify more clearly with the military culture.

As youth move through adolescence, there is a tendency for personal coping strategies to change somewhat. Active styles that reflect growing personal confidence tend to increase and are used most frequently by older teenagers. Meanwhile, passive coping strategies tend to decline in prevalence over time and are less likely to be used by older teenagers. Girls, in particular, seem to feel more empowered as they get older. For example, 60 percent of the 12-year-old girls feel that they have the power to solve problems themselves compared with 75 percent of those who are 16 years of age and older.

Interpersonal Coping Strategies

In addition to their own internal resources, youth usually have available to them external resources in the form of family and friend support networks. Indeed, it has often been noted in this study the role that parents and friends play in psychological well-being among adolescents. These close, interpersonal support persons are usually nearby and available to help those youth who are experiencing stressful life events.

One interesting difference between the Air Force youth and the civilian youth was in their interpersonal coping resources. Youth from civilian families were more likely to rely on adult friendships and siblings for support during times of stress. Military youth appear to be somewhat more dependent upon the quality of the parental relationship. Frequent moves may limit the interpersonal support networks for youth in organization families.

One finding of concern is that female adolescents in the Air Force families are less likely to seek help from their fathers as they get older. Among these families, 67 percent of the 12 to 13-year-old group report that they are likely to seek help from their fathers, compared with only 36 percent of the older adolescents. These females may find themselves growing apart from their fathers as they age and perceive the relationship as becoming more distant. Thus, their use of fathers as a resource diminishes, which makes them more vulnerable to problems.

Professional Coping Strategies

The mental health system is a potentially widespread solution to providing interpersonal resources for adolescents. Of all the resources inventoried, youth are the least likely to include professionals as part of their strategies to deal with stress. To a listing of clergy, teachers, physicians, and school and community counselors, only one-fourth or fewer of the youth respond that they are willing to contact one of these resources when they are in need.

There are very few differences between males or females or youth from civilian or Air Force families in their likelihood to contact professional resources for coping with stress. Air Force youth are somewhat more likely to seek help from school counselors, but even these differences are not substantial.

In the area of stress and coping, Air Force youth do not differ that significantly from their civilian counterparts. Each group of youth tends to experience a slightly different pattern of stressors, but the accumulated effects on Air Force and civilian youth are similar. Their coping styles are also similar, although Air Force youth are somewhat more dependent on their parents because their interpersonal support systems are otherwise smaller than those of youth from civilian families. Even though Air Force youth are part of a military community, they are no more likely to take advantage of professional community resources than are civilian youth. This may mean that Air Force youth programs and services are not that effective in reaching adolescents or it may mean that adolescents are resistant to these services, given their developmental needs for independence and peer group support.

CONCLUSIONS

Youth growing up in organization families have special challenges they must face. These youth have the same basic needs for security, stability, socialization, and relationships as other youth, but their ability to fulfill these needs is sometimes handicapped by their parents' work demands.

Children in organization families face the reality that their parents may not be able to predict life circumstances as well as parents who control more of their work situations. In order to garner the security that large work organizations provide, members of the military and large corporations usually sacrifice much of the autonomy they otherwise would have in life-course decisions. Children learn to adapt to this way of life but not without some costs.

Based on the results of a large study comparing youth from military organization families and non-military families in their local communities, there are several major observations that can be made. First, the majority of youth are adjusting quite well on most of the dimensions that were included in this study. Most youth are exhibiting healthy, constructive attitudes and behaviors that reflect personal and relational well-being.

Youth from military and civilian families are much more similar than different. While some differences do emerge in the study, the developmental issues with which youth are dealing are much more significant than the household location or the military-civilian status of their parents.

Military youth growing up in organization families are no better at adapting to change than their civilian counterparts. If anything, the data indicate that military youth are not as resilient to the changes they confront in their lives as are civilian youth. The amount of change they have experienced in their lives, especially moving, does not appear to increase their adaptive skills. The smaller size of their social networks tends to inhibit their skills in reaching out to others in times of need.

Male youth from military families are the most psychologically healthy group in the study. The male youth from these families exhibited stronger psychological patterns than civilian males or either military or civilian females. Since the military culture is dominated by masculine values, it is probably easier for males from these families to identify with this culture and find support for their new personality needs and emerging masculine identities. Their comparatively close relationships with their fathers in comparison to other youth provide further support to this observation.

Female youth from Air Force families seem to have the most problematic psychological profiles in the study. The contrasts between male and female youth from Air Force families are very evident in the data. A very high proportion of these female youth are exhibiting severe emotional problems, which may be caused by identity problems that are the opposite of those of their Air Force brothers. The masculine culture of the military service probably frustrates the maturing feminine identity of adolescent girls, especially if they are living in a military family.

The youth who are doing the best are those who have strong, healthy relationships with their parents. This confirms the importance of family support systems for youth. The stronger the relationship with either parent and the better the overall relationships in the family, the more the youth are able to adapt to the changes they experience in their lives.

Not surprisingly, relocation is the most significant adjustment adolescents routinely make. A very high proportion of adolescents in organization families like the military are asked to move and replace their social networks on a regular basis. These moves are associated with major personal and relational distress in youth, even those from military families. Contrary to expectations, youth who move a great deal are just as likely to experience problematic adjustments as those who move less often.

RECOMMENDATIONS FOR RESEARCH

The information in this chapter represents a significant improvement in our understanding of children growing up in organization families, particularly those in military families. Still, we know comparatively little about the impact of parental work experiences and environments on child and adolescent development. There have been very few studies that have seriously examined the work environments of parents and their impacts on children. We know much more about how childcare circumstances impact on children's development than on how the work demands of parents affect their children, even though it is often employment that creates the childcare need.

More studies are also needed of the impacts of parents' work on the development of younger children. We know somewhat more about the consequences of work for adolescents, because adolescents tend to be more verbal and available for research. Younger children, especially those in the primary school grades, are not as able to fill out questionnaires and may require other research strategies in order to determine how they are being affected by their parents' work. It is also important to examine preschool children, since a greater number of mothers of preschoolers are now in the labor force. In addition, many children are now subject to the demands of their parents' two work organizations, each of which places competing obligations on the family. It is vital that we understand better how children at different ages are coping with this.

Another important research need is the evaluation of youth support programs. It is apparent from the *Youth in Transition* study that many youth do not rely on formal support programs and services, even though younger adolescents tend to trust these support systems more than older adolescents. Nevertheless, it is these types of services that both work organizations and parents are increasingly depending on to provide back-up support for children in organization families. We need to know more about which of these programs are effective in attending to youth needs as well as strategies for improving those services that are not achieving their potential.

IMPLICATIONS FOR POLICY AND PRACTICE

Based upon the results of this study, there are a number of recommendations that can be made to organizations that are responsible for supporting the needs of children from military and other organization families. First of all, it is important that organizations extend their relocation assistance more directly to the children and youth in the families who are moving. The needs of youth are different from those of their parents, and it may be necessary to create targeted orientation and youth sponsorship programs for the children and youth who are going through a major move. Programs that assist adults in making these changes may not always help children understand what is available to them in the new community, nor help them replace the relationships that they are losing as a result of organizational demands on their parents.

Second, there is a need to expand teen programs that increase interaction between adolescents of similar ages. It has become increasingly evident that teen-oriented counseling programs are sometimes more successful in reaching troubled youth than programs run by adults. Youth can be trained to listen to the concerns of other youth and then serve as a bridge to helping individuals or organizations that provide the direct service. Unfortunately, many youth will not cross that bridge alone, but they will with another concerned peer.

It is also important to expand the availability of youth hotlines and information about how youth can get support services they need. Many children do not know where to go to get services, and this is especially true for youth who may be experiencing stress but are new to their communities. They may not be able to express their needs to their parents, and yet they want to talk to someone about how they are feeling. Well-advertised hotlines can be a useful adjunct to the peer counseling recommendation made above.

Another important finding from the study suggests the need for more programs that encourage family activities for youth. Families remain one of the most significant, consistent support systems upon which children and youth in organization families depend. But families need both the opportunities and the encouragement to spend time together in order to promote quality parent–child interaction. All too often, work organizations take time away from families. They also need to learn to give employees sufficient time to be with their families. This will increase family support for the working member and the organization.

Finally, it is important to increase the availability of parent education programs that specifically focus on work- and family-related issues. Many parents are unaware of the effects that their work has on their children and they feel guilt or insecurity about their work roles. These parents need to learn how to articulate their concerns and feelings and to develop dialogue with their children around issues that are work related.

All too often, barriers to parent–child communication develop because each expects the other to be aware of their concerns when this is not the case. Developing healthy interaction with adolescents, in particular, can be especially troublesome, and most parent education programs do not focus on relationships with children at that age. As the research in this chapter has pointed out, children at all ages need healthy relationships with their parents, and service providers should be encouraging opportunities for this interaction. Unfortunately, it does not occur naturally in many homes, and professionals in the workplace may be the best able to recognize this need and stimulate these relationships.

NOTES

1. Ammons, P., Nelson, J., and Wodarski, J. (1982) Surviving corporate moves: Sources of stress and adaptation among corporate executive families. *Family Relations* 31:207–12.

2. Barling, J. (1986) Fathers' work experiences, the father–child relationship and children's behavior. *Journal of Occupational Behavior* 7:61–66.

3. Barret, C. L., and Noble, H. (1973) Mothers' anxieties versus the effects of long-distance moves on children. *Journal of Marriage and the Family* 35:181–88.

4. Bratter, T. E. (1973) Treating alienated, unmotivated, drug-abusing adolescents. *American Journal of Psychotherapy* 27:585–99.

5. Brett, J. M. (1982) Job transfer and well-being. *Journal of Applied Psychology* 67:450–63.

6. Brown, A. C. (1988) The effect of relocation on the personal well-being of adolescents. Masters thesis, University of Georgia, Athens.

7. Coles, R. (1977) The children of affluence. *Atlantic Monthly* (September):52–66.

8. Erikson, E. (1968) *Identity, Youth and Crisis*. New York: Norton.

9. Grubbs, J. (1987) *Growing Up in the Military*. Springfield, IL: Independent Publishing.

10. Gullotta, T. P., Stevens, S. J., Donohue, K. C. and Clark, V. S. (1981) Adolescents in corporate families. *Adolescence* 16:621–28.

11. Jones, S. B. (1973) Geographic mobility as seen by the wife and mother. *Journal of Marriage and the Family* 35:210–18.

12. Levine, J. A. (1976) *Who Will Raise the Children?* New York: Bantam.

13. Mancini, J. A., and Orthner, D. K. (1988) The context and consequences of family change. *Family Relations* 37:363–66.

14. Margolis, D. R. (1979) *The Managers: Corporate Life in America*. New York: William Morrow.

15. Murdock, G. P. (1949) *Social Structure*. New York: Free Press.

16. Nida, P. C., and Heller, W. M. (1985) *The Teenager's Survival Guide to Moving*. New York: Macmillan.

17. Orthner, D. K. (1980) *Families in Blue: A Study of Married and Single Parent Families in the U.S. Air Force*. Washington, D.C.: Department of the U.S. Air Force.

18. Orthner, D. K. (1981) *Intimate Relationships*. Boston, MA: Addison–Wesley.

19. Orthner, D. K., and Bowen, G. L. (1982) *Families in Blue: Phase Two*. Washington, D.C.: Department of the U.S. Air Force.

20. Orthner, D. K., Brody, G., and Covi, R. (1985) *Inside Families in Blue: A Study of Air Force Youth*. Washington, D.C.: Department of the U.S. Air Force.

21. Orthner, D. K., Giddings, M. M., and Quinn, W. H. (1987) *Youth in Transition: A Study of Adolescents from Air Force and Civilian Families*. Washington, D.C.: Department of the U.S. Air Force.

22. Otto, L. B. (1988) America's youth: A changing profile. *Family Relations* 37:385–91.

23. Parsons, T., and Bales, R. (1955) *Family, Socialization, and Interaction Process*. Glencoe, IL.: Free Press.

24. Piotrkowski, C. S., Rapoport, R. N., and Rapoport, R. (1987) Families and work. In M. B. Sussman and S. K. Steinmetz (eds.), *Handbook of Marriage and the Family*. pp. 251–83. New York: Plenum.

25. Pleck, J. H., Staines, G. L., and Lang, L. (1980) Conflicts between work and family life. *Monthly Labor Review* 103:29–32.

26. Wallerstein, J., and Kelly, J. (1980) *Surviving the Breakup: How Children and Parents Cope with Divorce*. New York: Basic Books.

27. Weiss, R. S. (1973) *Loneliness: The Experience of Emotional and Social Isolation*. Cambridge, MA: MIT Press.

III

THE ORGANIZATIONAL RESPONSE

7

Toward Conceptual Refinement of Operational Outcome Variables: The Case of Family Life Satisfaction

Gary L. Bowen

In recent years, both private and public sector employers have shown increasing interest in family well-being and satisfaction of their employees (5, 9). This interest parallels the growing recognition by management leaders of the importance of quality family life to personal and emotional well-being, job satisfaction and productivity, and employee morale and commitment (48, 61). Although no systematic data exist on the extent, coverage, and expenditures, this recognition has resulted in a substantial growth of family-oriented policies and services among employers over the last decade (9).

The military services have been at the forefront among employers in developing personnel policies and support programs that enable its personnel to meet military objectives and requirements and still maintain a viable personal and family life. Today the military services are giving relatively greater attention than in the past to developing formal policies and programs that are supportive of family and community life and building informal and formal support systems that enhance the functioning and well-being of families (8).

Despite the demonstrated commitment of the military services to improv-

Development of the value-based approach for defining and conceptualizing family life satisfaction was supported in part under contract no. MDA903–86–C–0260 with the Department of the Army, Office of Chief of Chaplains (DACH-PPDT). All conclusions are those of the author and are not purported to reflect the position of the Department of the Army or the Department of Defense. This chapter is an expanded and integrated version of two previous discussions of the Value-Behavior Congruency Model of Family Life Satisfaction, which appeared in *Family Therapy* 15(1) (1988):7–21, "The Value-Behavior Congruency Model of Family Life Satisfaction: Implications for Clinical Practice"; and *Family Relations* 37(4) (1988):458–62, "Family Life Satisfaction: A Value-Based Approach."

ing the quality of life for servicemembers and their families, the services have struggled to clearly conceptualize the family-related outcomes to which their efforts are directed. For example, although military leadership frequently emphasizes the importance of a fulfilling and satisfying family life to military preparedness (67), the concept of family life satisfaction suffers from both conceptual and operational ambiguity. The military services have found it especially challenging to define family-related outcomes in such a way that respects the tremendous ethnic and cultural diversity found among families in the military services today (6). Overall this difficulty has hampered the development of a guiding framework for assessing marital and family systems for purposes of planning clinical and community interventions.

This chapter proposes a value-based approach for defining and conceptualizing family life satisfaction. This approach is considered to have high utility for guiding clinical and community practice with families in the military community at both macro and micro levels of intervention. After providing a historical overview and critique of past approaches to the definition and conceptualization of family life satisfaction, key dimensions of the proposed approach are outlined, and its key assumptions are grounded both theoretically and empirically. In addition, implications of the approach are discussed from the perspective of clinical and community practice as well as the need for its empirical specification and testing.

HISTORICAL OVERVIEW AND CRITIQUE

The study of the quality of family relationships has a history dating back to Hamilton's (21) classic study of marital adjustment. Since that time numerous attempts have been made to conceptualize and assess the quality of family relationships, especially the marital union. A variety of terms have been promulgated in the process, the most common being "family life satisfaction," "family functioning," "family environment," "satisfaction with the family system," as well as a number of concepts designed to describe the quality of the marital relationship (e.g., "marital satisfaction," "marital adjustment," "marital happiness," "marital stability") and the quality of parent–child interaction (e.g., "parent–child relationship satisfaction"). While these concepts all represent qualitative dimensions and evaluations of relationships within the family, there is a great deal of ambiguity and overlap in the way these concepts are defined and in the scales designed to measure them. This is particularly the case in the definition and measurement of marital-related outcomes (10, 31, 56, 57). Consequently, past family researchers may have been using identical terms for what were very different constructs, the result being that these constructs had very different connotations to the persons who were the focus of study (19). Not only does this lead to confusion with regard to the operationalization and measurement of these concepts (58), but also restricts the comparability and generalizability of empirical findings (19).

Most measures purporting to assess the qualitative aspects of family relationships are based on summation of items, items across subscales, or subscale scores themselves that are defined as conceptually and empirically related to the concept under investigation. In many cases these correlated items or subscales have been developed through factor-analytic techniques. For example, perhaps the mostly widely used scale to assess marital adjustment, the dyadic adjustment scale, consists of four interrelated dimensions: (a) dyadic consensus, (b) dyadic cohesion, (c) dyadic satisfaction, and (d) affectional expression (59). Olson and McCubbin's (44) measure of family satisfaction assessed family member satisfaction on each of the 14 subscales of the Circumplex Model: emotional bonding, family boundaries, coalitions, time, space, friends, decision-making, interests and recreation, assertiveness, control, discipline, negotiation, roles, and rules.

Such measures of the qualitative aspects of family life have tended to treat their underlying subdimensions as linear (the more of the subdimension, the better) and equal in weight and additive in arriving at a total score on the concept under investigation. In most cases, measures have failed to account for differences in perceptions among family members toward underlying subdimensions or simply averaged the respective scores of family members together into a grand mean, implicitly assuming that each subdimension has equal salience or value for family members. The assumption behind such measures is that there is one desirable way for families to function; the implicit assumption is that other ways are undesirable (26). Such underlying assumptions can promote the use of assessment and intervention strategies by family practitioners that are nomothetic in orientation rather than sensitive to the unique situation and values of individual families.

To date, although the attributes and behaviors associated with family life satisfaction can be conceptualized as having both "value" dimensions (what families prefer) and "behavioral" components (how families actually behave), relatively little attention has been focused on how the level of value congruency between family members toward specified marital and family interactional patterns impacts upon their level of family life satisfaction. For example, it is possible that husbands and wives have different values toward the importance of companionship in marriage, and it is unknown how the extent of these differences on this dimension impacts on self-perceptions toward family life satisfaction. In addition, there has been little discussion in past studies of the consequences for family life when spouses are unable to realize their values for family life in behavior. For example, it is possible that husbands and wives may value ties with the larger community, but lack the personal resources, the relational skills, and/or the opportunities to develop these relationships. It is likely that the effect that the relative presence or absence of specified marital and family interaction patterns (e.g., companionship) have on self-defined family life satisfaction will depend largely on the degree to which the family or family members value these patterns.

There is a need for an explicit framework to guide the definition and conceptualization of family life satisfaction within the military services. Although prior research has suggested the dimensions of marital, parental, and family life satisfaction to overlap empirically (12, 44, 47), following the work of Campbell et al. (12) as well as that of Olson and McCubbin (44), this framework must explicitly distinguish family life satisfaction from other forms of satisfaction (e.g., marital, parent–child). The framework must also be capable of generating explicit propositions for identifying crucial processes that underlie different levels of family life satisfaction. It must also be capable of respecting and capturing the rich diversity of family life styles in the military services. Finally, for purposes of clinical and community intervention and evaluation, the framework must be practice oriented, capable of guiding the development, implementation and evaluation of policies, programs, and practices in support of military families.

FAMILY LIFE SATISFACTION: A VALUE-BASED APPROACH

Given the lack of an underlying framework in the study of family life satisfaction, an alternative approach to its definition is proposed that distinguishes it from other concepts. In this approach, at the core of family life satisfaction is the ability of family members to jointly realize their family-related values in behavior.

A key phrase in this approach to defining family life satisfaction is "jointly realize." The level of family life satisfaction is promoted only when each family member is able to move toward realizing his or her values for family life in behavior. For example, if I strongly value spending time with my family, my ability to realize this value in behavior will be an important aspect of my self-professed level of family life satisfaction. On the other hand, if I do not strongly value a great deal of time together with my family, a lack of time together will have fewer implications for my self-professed level of family life satisfaction. Problems in family life may develop when family members are not able to realize their values for family life in behavior or when they hold conflicting values across family life domains that one or more family members define as important. For purposes of definition, family life satisfaction is conceptualized on a continuum from low to high.

Toward a Definition of Values

Although there is no consensus on the definition of values in the literature (e.g., 10, 40), values are defined broadly as organized sets of preferences for how individuals wish to conduct their lives (14, 36, 60). These preferences are conceptualized as cognitive, serving as a basis for choice and as a guide for action.

In addition, values are assumed to be logically ordered from the most abstract to the most concrete and connected across levels of abstraction (37). Although higher-order values are considered to serve as a general frame of reference for the individual (e.g., the importance of family integration), they are seldom discussed. However, they do provide an overarching structure for ordering and evaluating lower-tier values, which are more open to direct consideration and discussion (e.g., preferences for spending time together as a family).

At each level of abstraction, values are conceptualized as hierarchically arranged from most important to least important. It is this property of values that best distinguishes them from a closely related concept—attitudes (40). All else being equal, individuals are likely to behave in ways that validate their values at the highest level (18, 37).

Although learned primarily from parents and significant others in childhood and adolescence, neither values nor their respective importance within levels of abstraction are considered as fixed. They are defined as variables that may change in response to a variety of familial and extra-familial influences, including normative influences in society. Although some authors attempt to distinguish values from related concepts such as goals, preferences, and ideals, in agreement with Byrne (11), little seems to be gained by drawing such fine distinctions.

Assumptions

This approach to defining family life satisfaction proposes that neither families nor family members necessarily share similar values for family life— "different strokes for different folks." In addition, families or their members may share values that are associated with positive family interaction, but lack the personal resources or relational skills, or have other constraints, such as work obligations or financial restrictions, that hinder their ability to behave in a way that is consistent with their values toward preferred patterns of marital and family interaction. Thus, it is proposed that the realization of family-related values in behavior is influenced by at least three factors: (a) the level of congruity of values among family members, (b) the relative presence or absence of personal resources (e.g., self-esteem), and relational skills (e.g., communication) necessary to act in accordance with stated values, and (c) the nature and magnitude of system-level constraints that serve as obstacles to realizing family-related values, including family- and work-related demands and stressors.

From this perspective, the level of satisfaction in families can be enhanced by (a) reducing value incongruity between family members, or, at a minimum, helping family members to become more aware of their value differences and the consequences of those differences; (b) helping family members to better realize their values in behavior through resource and skill development, including skills in negotiation and problem-solving; and (c) modifying system-level constraints that prevent family members from realizing or behaving in a way that is consistent with their values. Consistent with a rational-emotional approach to family intervention (33), value conflicts between family members or value and behavior discrepancies can be resolved by modifying either values, behaviors, or both.

It is important to underscore that this value-based definition of family life satisfaction contrasts greatly with more static definitions of this concept, which imply a fixed reference point for marital and family interaction patterns. From this perspective, the nature of family life is seen as a dynamic, fluid, interactional process among family members, with members constantly working to achieve desired family-related ends in the context of ever changing and emerging family-related values (32). As such, clinical and community intervention is directed to helping families move toward relational growth and fulfillment.

A SOCIAL EXCHANGE PERSPECTIVE

The importance of using "value" as a contingent variable in defining family life satisfaction is consistent with the tenets of social exchange theory. Although the essentials of this theory have been outlined elsewhere (3, 16, 22, 24, 25, 41, 42, 53, 63, 64), a brief review of its main focus and essential components will provide a framework for discussing its applicability to the current issue.

Social exchange theory assumes that human actors seek to obtain rewards (tangible and intangible) and attempt to avoid costs (tangible and intangible). Thus, human behavior is not random, but purposive and goal-directed. The pursuit of these goals brings people into interdependence with one another. In other words, the realization of a person's preferences depends on the simultaneous reaction of others to these preferences or goals. Based on their exchange, they either perceive their associations as fair (subjective evaluation that Other has reciprocated justly relative to their input) or unfair (Other has imposed a cost/reward ratio that Actor deems inequitable or unjust).

When the interaction between parties is defined as fair, or when the personal profit from interaction is rewarding, Homans (23, 24, 25) and Blau (3) hypothesized that there is a building up of positive sentiments, and the relationship continues to grow and develop. On the other hand, if the exchange is costly, the sentiment tends to be negative, and the relationship is likely to either slow down in growth and development or be terminated.

An implicit proposition in the work of Homans (25) is the influence of "value" on the amount of profit that partners receive from interaction. As elaborated by Burr (10), the value of interaction between partners influences the amount of profit from the interaction and the level of positive sentiment. In other words, the impact of actions in relationships is influenced by the relative value that partners attach to these actions (10). Burr suggests this to be a positive and monotonic relationship.

The influence of values from the exchange perspective on the salience and consequences of actions or lack of actions in relationships is related to the underlying conceptual link between values and goals. Nye (40) distinguished values from goals as a matter of degree: goals are specific outcomes within a broader category of outcomes that are valued by the individual. Thus, one who values family time may set a goal of devoting every Friday night to interaction with the children.

At the most general level, it would be proposed from an exchange-theory perspective that the level of family life satisfaction will be dependent upon the relative perceptions family members have of their ability to realize important family-related values in behavior. In situations where family members are able to consistently realize family-related values that are defined as important in behavior through interaction with other family members, it is predicted that there is a building up of positive sentiments toward the family system. On the other hand, the consistent failure of family members to realize important family-related values in behavior is likely to result in frustration and disappointment, leading to less rewarding interaction and the development of negative sentiments toward the family system. Thus, consistent with the premises of exchange theory, satisfying family relationships may be conceptualized as equitable reciprocal exchanges based on the ability of family members to jointly realize family-related values in behavior (2, 65).

From this perspective, it is important to underscore that the exchange patterns in family relationships are not static; they may change through either implicit or explicit bargaining to permit one or both parties to experience greater rewards and fewer costs (13, 53). For example, Levinger (30) discusses not only the changing nature of values for partners over time, but also how the values of partners can converge over the course of the relationship through a process of accommodation. According to Levinger, such accommodation of partners may result from a long-term convergence over time in the values of one or both partners ("dispositional transformation") or by deliberate actions of one or both partners to adapt to the needs and wishes of the other for a period of time ("motivational transformation").

Moreover, exchange relationships may not have an immediate payoff. Specifically, one Partner may provide the Other with a reward, trusting that the Other will reciprocate in some future transaction, a phenomenon that helps explain actions by family members that are not congruent with their professed values. This indebtedness is interpreted as binding actors together and giving solidarity to their relationship (54).

Last, social exchanges do not occur in a vacuum, but within a larger social network. Prevailing social norms and alternative suppliers of rewards play an important part in the process of social exchange by shaping, defining, and reinforcing definitions of what is preferable and what is fair or just (55).

LITERATURE REVIEW

The nature and impact of family values in marriage and family life have been an important focus of study in family social science, including family life studies in the military. They have been studied in relation to mate selection as well as to various dimensions of family well-being and stability (1, 7, 27, 30, 31, 47, 62). For example, the level of husband-and-wife value consensus has been correlated with various dimensions of marital quality and stability (31).

The pioneering work of Don Byrne (11), George Levinger (29, 30), and others (20) has led to the conclusion that value congruency operates as a reward in relationships; it leads to interpersonal attraction and stability because it provides consensual validation for one's point of view. Levinger (30) recently hypothesized that the greater the fit between the values of partners, the greater their relational involvement as well as their level of compatibility.

As early as 1970, Klemer (28), a noted family life educator, discussed the importance of shared values as a basis for marital life satisfaction:

In order to achieve satisfaction in anything (and especially in marriage), you must first know what you expect, and also what is expected of you. . . . If too much is expected, if what is expected of you is not made clear, or even if not enough is expected, it is not probable that you will get very much satisfaction. (p. 31)

Maxwell (33) later revised Klemer's statement slightly to assert that an important basis for the success of the marital relationship is the harmony of expectations between spouses and their respective capacity to meet their expectations behaviorally. Although both Klemer and Maxwell refer to marital dynamics rather than family dynamics *per se*, Satir (52) maintains that one of the best ways to enhance family life is to strengthen the marital relationships of the mother and father, who are the architects of the family.

In studying how the individual perceptions of family members toward the family unit mediate the impact of family experiences on family-related outcomes, research conducted by Van Der Veen and colleagues in the early 1960s provides important historical support for the proposed conceptualization of family life satisfaction (66). Using small clinical and nonclinical sample groups, the investigators found that the greater the discrepancy between the ideal expectations of parents toward the functioning of the family unit and their actual experiences, the greater the level of family dissatisfaction and family maladjustment. Van Der Veen and colleagues recommended that an important focus of clinical intervention with families is in helping members to recognize their different expectations toward the family unit, and to focus on those areas where family functioning falls short of ideal expectations.

Conceptual and empirical support for the proposed framework of family life satisfaction is also found in more recent literature, including the theoretical and empirical work by McCubbin and Thompson (35), Moos and Moos (38, 39), Olson and associates (43, 45, 46), and Sabatelli (50, 51). Overall, the work of these family practitioners and researchers clearly suggests that both families as well as members within the same family may in fact differ in their preferences toward family life; they may also have differential success in realizing their preferences for family life in behavior.

McCubbin and Thompson

In their innovative construction of family typologies, McCubbin and Thompson (35) explicitly recognized the importance of shared values by family members for the successful management of family tension and strain. In addition, the authors' fourfold typology of rhythmic families (one of the four family typologies discussed by the authors) is operationalized based on the level of balance between valuing family time and routines and the actual efforts of the family to routinize family life into predictable activities. In McCubbin and Thompson's fourfold typology, families that both value family time and routines and embrace these values in behavior were labeled "rhythmic."

In their analysis, McCubbin and Thompson compared families that placed little value on family time and routines and little behavioral emphasis on such practices (i.e., "unpatterned" families) as well as families that evidenced value and behavioral incongruity in respect to family time and routine (i.e., "structured" families and "intentional" families, respectively) to rhythmic families. The authors found that rhythmic families as compared with the other family types evidenced greater family-related outcomes in the following domains: traditions and celebrations, bonding, flexibility, hardiness, coherence, family satisfaction, marital satisfaction, child development satisfaction, community satisfaction, and overall family well-being.

When the category of rhythmic families was compared across the family life cycle (i.e., single, couple, preschool and school-age children, adolescence and launching, and empty nest and retirement), the highest proportion of rhythmic families was found among couples with preschool and school-age children, as well as among couples in the empty nest/retirement period of life. The lowest proportion of rhythmic families was found in the adolescent-through-launching phase of the family life cycle; in this stage, families with low levels of family time and routines and low valuing of these routines and investments in family life (referred to as "unpatterned" families) were the most prevalent.

McCubbin and Thompson's emphasis on the link between family-related values and behavior in their development of family typologies provides an important conceptual and empirical foundation to the proposed conceptualization of family life satisfaction. As in their work, it will be important here to evaluate the ability of the proposed framework to make predictions about family-related outcomes.

An important finding by McCubbin and Thompson is the importance of examining the congruency of family-related values and behaviors in the context of the family life cycle. Their findings suggest that family members may have particular difficulty realizing their values in behavior at certain stages of the family life cycle. For example, families that greatly emphasize the value of family time and routines, but that actually practice these patterns with little frequency (intentional families) were most prevalent among childless couples. In the proposed framework, these families may be particularly likely to face a high number of system-level constraints both from their families of origin as well as from their beginning careers that limit their ability to realize important family-related values.

Olson and Associates

An important empirical foundation of the present conceptualization of family life satisfaction is reflected in the work of Olson and associates. Their integration of normative expectations of family members as an additional design feature of both FACES II and III (modifications of the original Family Adaptability and Family Cohesion Evaluation Scores) explicitly responds to the importance of considering family-related values as a contingent variable in understanding marital and family dynamics (43, 45, 46). Recognizing the tremendous variation in family values across different cultural groups, the researchers have designed the 30-item FACES II and the 20-item FACES III not only to assess how individual family members perceive their family, but also to assess the level of discrepancy between how family members actually see their family (perceived) and how they would like it to be (ideal).

According to Olson and associates, the level of satisfaction with the family system is determined by comparing the "perceived" with the "ideal" across all family members—the less the cumulative discrepancies for family members, the higher the family's level of satisfaction with their current family system (45). Since the perceptions of family members often vary toward how they perceive the family system as well as how they would like it to be, Olson and associates stress the importance of obtaining the perceptions of all family members in determining the level of family life satisfaction (46).

The explicit recognition by Olson et al. of how families may differ in their values for family life underscores the importance of assessing family life satisfaction from the vantage point of family values. In agreement with Olson and associates, it is likely that families will function quite adequately as long as there is a high level of congruence between the family-related wishes and outcomes for all family members (46).

Moos and Moos

The self-administered 90-item family environment scale (FES) by Moos and Moos (38) is composed of ten subscales that assess the perceptions of family members toward the social-environment features of their family. These ten subscales assess three underlying dimensions: the *relationship* dimension (i.e., cohesion, expressiveness, and conflict), the *personal growth* dimension (i.e., independence, achievement orientation, intellectual-cultural orientation, active-recreational orientation, and moral-religious emphasis), and the *system maintenance* dimension (i.e., organization, control).

The Real Form (Form R), which measures the perceptions of family members toward their families of origin or orientation, is most commonly used. However, two special reworded forms of Form R are available to assess both the type of family environment that family members would ideally like (Form I)—to measure the goals and value orientations of family members—as well as the type of family environment that they expect (Form E).

Although Moos and Moos (38, 39) do not explicitly discuss how these forms may be combined to assess the level of family life satisfaction, they do suggest that Form I can be used with Form R to identify discrepancies between what family members prefer and what they actually experience. They contend that such an understanding of discrepancies between the actual and preferred provides important information for guiding clinical intervention. In addition, they suggest that Form E could be used productively in premarital counseling sessions to facilitate discussion between prospective spouses about their expectations for family life.

For each form, it is possible both to calculate scores for each family member and to calculate family averages. These profiles can then be used to compare the perceptions of individual family members as well as to draw comparisons across families.

Sabatelli

Recent conceptual development and empirical research by Sabatelli (50, 51) support the viability of applying a social exchange perspective to understanding and evaluating relationship satisfaction. Based on the "Comparison Level" concept of Thibaut and Kelley (63), Sabatelli (50, 51) proposes that individuals evaluate their relationship experiences based on the expectations they have for those relationships. Sabatelli defines expectations as "a person's subjective impressions of what they feel is realistically obtainable from a relationship" (51, p. 219). In cases where relationship experiences consistently exceed expectations, relationship satisfaction is hypothesized to be enhanced; where relationship experiences consistently fall below expectations, relationship satisfaction is hypothesized to decline.

To assess the degree to which individuals perceive their relationships as meeting their expectations, Sabatelli (50) developed the Marital Comparison Level Index (MCLI). Using this instrument, Sabatelli (50, 51) has not only demonstrated significant differences in the relationship expectations of dating and married couples, but also high correlations between the ability of spouses to realize their expectations in marriage and measures of relational equity and marital commitment.

However, it is important to note that Sabatelli's definition of expectations is clearly different from the definition of values as presented above (i.e., organized sets of preferences for family life irrespective of whether they are viewed as realistically obtainable in the marriage). Sabatelli's definition of expectations also differs from the conceptualization of expectations by Van Der Veen et al. (66) and Olson and associates (43, 45, 46). By incorporating the notion of "ideal" as compared with Sabatelli's notion of "realistically obtainable" as the basis of their definitions of expectations, the use of the term by Van Der Veen et al. and Olson and associates is more conceptually similar to the above definition of values than Sabatelli's definition of expectations.

As an approach to conceptualizing relationship satisfaction, it is argued that the "value-based" definition is more heuristic in continued exploration than Sabatelli's "expectation-based" definition. For one, as defined above, values are conceptualized as hierarchically arranged from most important to least important across levels of abstraction. This definitional property of "values" reflects the potential differential salience of relational attributes and patterns to family members and allows for a richer assessment and understanding of relationship satisfaction than the "expectation-based" approach as outlined by Sabatelli. Unlike Van Der Veen et al. and Olson and associates, Sabatelli's definition of expectations fails to incorporate the notion of differential salience of expectations across relationship domains. As a consequence, all relational attributes and patterns are treated as equally salient in their potential impact on relationship satisfaction—an assumption that the value-based approach is designed to circumvent.

In developing the MCLI, however, Sabatelli (50) did measure the relative importance of each item on the index to sample respondents—a "value" perspective. In fact, he found variation in the importance that respondents assigned to the specified relationship attributes and patterns represented as items on the MCLI (albeit skewed toward high importance). Unfortunately, he downplayed this variance, choosing neither to differentially weight the items by their respective importance ratings, to examine the correlations between weighted and unweighted items, nor to consider the calculation of discrepancy scores between the "importance" and the "expectations" ratings for their potential implications in explaining relational outcomes. In other words, he chose to treat all items on the MCLI as equally salient and additive in determining relational outcomes.

Besides the definitional distinctions between "values" and "realistic expectations" in marriage, values as defined above and expectations as defined by Sabatelli may also differ in their relative stability over time. Although both are subject to change, expectations are considered to be more situationally influenced than values. For example, the failure to realize family-related values in behavior over time is more likely to lead a person to "expect" less from the relationship in question than to modify values per se. However, all else being equal, this lessening of expectations should not promote more relationship satisfaction; it should only help spouses to anticipate the likelihood that they will not have their values for family life met behaviorally. In addition, too low expectations for family relationships may serve as a system-level constraint to realizing important family-related values in behavior—a self-fulfilling prophecy.

Despite the conceptual differences between the "value-based" approach and Sabatelli's "expectation-based" approach to understanding relational outcomes, the work of Sabatelli suggests the potential richness of conceptually distinguishing between "values" and "realistic expectations" in the same model. Such distinctions are consistent with the work of Moos and Moos (38, 39), noted above, who developed separate forms to assess both "value" dimensions and "expectation" dimensions of the family environment. However, Moos and Moos only discussed comparing the "ideal" form with the "real" form; they did not discuss the combined use of the "expectations" form with the "real" form. Further conceptual refinement of the proposed value-based approach to defining and conceptualizing family life satisfaction should explicitly consider how expectations about what is realistically obtainable from the relationship in question may mediate the relationship between value and behavior congruency as well as the relationship between value/behavior congruency and relational outcomes.

IMPLICATIONS FOR CLINICAL AND COMMUNITY PRACTICE

From the perspective of clinical and community practice, the value-based approach to the definition and conceptualization of family life satisfaction is rich in its implications. First, it is important to help family members better understand their values regarding family life. It is particularly important to help family members identify areas where they have value differences or incongruities with one another. For example, the husband and wife have differing views toward the sharing of household tasks and responsibilities. It is likely that value discrepancies between family members that are not recognized or discussed, but where the value in question is more important to one family member than the other, can create an undercurrent of tension and conflict in the family, especially in cases where the discrepancy limits the opportunity of the family member to realize the value in behavior. Such a situation is hypothesized to negatively affect the level of family life satisfaction by decreasing the level of positive sentiment toward the family system. On the other hand, value consensus, or at least value congruity among family members across those value domains that are defined as important, is likely to facilitate the development of family relationships that are defined as equitable and just (4).

Second, it may be valuable to have family members compare their values for family life with their actual patterns of marital and family interaction. Such a focus on gaps between family-related values and behaviors would aid family members in better understanding their current level of satisfaction with the family system as well as in identifying aspects of family life that they would like to promote or change. Such an exercise would be especially valuable if family members were able to share their values and perceptions with one another under the guidance of a trained family specialist.

Third, it is possible that family members may value or expect certain outcomes in their family relationships, but lack the personal resources or relational skills necessary to realize these outcomes. For instance, parents may value positive communication channels between themselves and their adolescent sons or daughters, but lack effective communication skills to realize this value in behavior. Practitioners can work with families to help them develop the skills and resources necessary to realize their values for family life in behavior. Otto (49) has referred to this type of intervention as helping families to achieve their full "family potential."

Fourth, practitioners can serve as community advocates to help develop policies and programs that are more supportive of family life. This implication of the model for clinical and community practice is consistent with the challenge by Curran (15) for institutions to work in concert with families to better realize their values for family life. Of course, practitioners must be careful not to impose their own family paradigms in assuming the role of advocate. Through policy and program development, community programs and services can be structured to better support families in realizing their values and expectations for family life. The aim is to help remove obstacles that may prevent families from achieving their full relational power rather than structuring solutions to family problems. The development and implementation of such policies and practices should help create a sense of partnership between the military and its families in accomplishing their respective missions.

An important feature of the proposed approach is its relatively value-free position. Intervention with families is geared to assisting family members to better understand their own value positions toward family life, helping family members to develop requisite resources and skills to better realize their own defined values in behavior, and working with or advocating on behalf of family members or families to remove or reduce the interference of system-level constraints that hinder their ability to realize family-related values in behavior. As a consequence, practitioners are not required to assume an explicit value position. The practitioner plays a facilitative and enabling role in working with and on behalf of the family—a particularly important role, given the results of recent studies that suggest some disparity between the marital and family goals of families and the intervention objectives of marital and family practitioners (17). In addition, since the elements of the approach fit logically together in an integrated whole, practitioners should be able to help families better understand the dynamics of family life satisfaction.

A NEED FOR CONTINUED DEVELOPMENT

This alternative approach to the definition and conceptualization of family life satisfaction within the military community has several important advantages. First, it defines family life satisfaction as relative to the ability of family members to realize their own values for family life in behavior. This approach leads to an interactional process view of family dynamics that has rich implications for both clinical and community practice. It also anchors the definition and conceptualization of family life satisfaction within than explicit theoretical perspective: social exchange theory.

Second, it explicitly acknowledges that neither families nor members within the same family may necessarily value or want the same things from family life. As a consequence, it is important to focus on the values of individual family members, the levels of value congruency between and among family members, and value differences across families. From this perspective, the family-related values both within families as well as across families are seen as "different from" rather than "better than" or "worse than" those of other members or families. These differing value orientations pose implications for desired family-related outcomes at the level of the individual, the dyad, the family unit, and the military community.

At this point in its development, the suggested approach to the definition and conceptualization of family life satisfaction is offered merely as "grist for the mill." Work needs to continue in further developing the potential of this approach for guiding clinical and community intervention with families in the military community.

A key challenge is to develop an empirical measure that is consistent with the conceptual definition of family life satisfaction as defined above. It will be necessary first to determine the range of family-related values that will be included on the measure. These values should be at least conceptually related to the broad range of characteristics that have been found to be associated with the concept of family life satisfaction and related concepts in the empirical literature; that is, they should meet the criterion of face validity. The list should also be parsimonious in the number of discreet family-related values included for study. Among the range of values that could be considered include those related to marriage and parenthood, social network connections and community, religious/spiritual orientation and participation, the respective roles of men and women, family economics and spouse employment, job/career, health, and life in the military. To determine the criterion validity of the measure, it will be necessary to obtain broad outcome measures of marital and family life satisfaction. Since the level of consensus and congruity between spouses across family-related values is a key component to the suggested approach to family life satisfaction, it will be important to collect information from husbands and wives from the same marriages. In addition, the eventual measure must be capable of discriminating between deeply held convictions and those asserted for normative or emotional reasons. As a consequence, it may be necessary to augment traditional survey techniques with more intensive interview protocols, including the use of Q-sorts.

It will be important in future research to assess the predictive validity of this approach for other marital and family life outcomes (e.g., marital stability, community satisfaction) as well as military-related outcomes (e.g., family satisfaction with military life, retention intentions, readiness). At least three levels of analysis are possible: (1) the effects of values and the level of value congruity among family members on outcomes, (2) the effects of behaviors and the level of behavior congruity among family members on outcomes, and (3) the effects of value/behavior congruity on both individual and family outcomes. An important focus of study will be to examine how family members cope with value incongruities among themselves as well as with situations in which values are not realized in behavior.

It is vital that the utility of this approach to family life satisfaction be examined for families at different stages of the family life cycle, as well as across racial/ethnic and social status/rank groups. Such an analytic strategy will provide important data for guiding clinical and community practice, including information on each of the following: (1) variations in values across different population groups and subgroups, (2) levels of success among various population groups and subgroups in realizing their family-related values in behavior, and (3) the consequences of value similarity and value-behavior congruency among family members on both self-professed family-related outcomes and adaptation to military life.

An important challenge will be to identify those relationship patterns and characteristics in families as well as those interpersonal skills and competencies of family members that maximize the ability of family members to jointly realize family-related values in behavior. Perhaps, more importantly, given that relatively few families are probably able to provide a context where all family members are able to fully realize their family values in behavior, it will be important to identify patterns of family interaction that foster the ability of family members to live together in spite of their differences and to deal constructively with the realities and demands of family life.

NOTES

1. Adams, B. N. (1979) Mate selection in the United States: A theoretical integration. In W. R. Burr, R. Hill, F. I. Nye, and I. L. Reiss (eds.), *Contemporary Theories about the Family*, pp. 259–67. New York: Free Press.

2. Bagorozzi, D. A., and Wodarski, J. S. (1977) A social exchange typology of conjugal relationships and conflict development. *Journal of Marital and Family Counseling* 3 (4):53–60.

3. Blau, P. (1964) *Exchange and Power in Social Life.* New York: Wiley.

4. Bowen, G. L. (1987) Changing gender-role preferences and marital adjustment: Implications for clinical practice. *Family Therapy* 14:17–33.

5. Bowen, G. L. (1988) Corporate supports for the family lives of employees: A conceptual model for program planning and evaluation. *Family Relations* 37:183–88.

6. Bowen, G. L., and Janofsky, B. J. (1988) *Family Strength and Adaptation to Army Life: A Focus on Variations in Family Values and Expectations across Racial/Ethnic Group and Rank.* Washington, D.C.: Department of the Army, Office of the Chief of Chaplains.

7. Bowen, G. L., and Orthner, D. K. (1983) Sex-role congruency and marital quality. *Journal of Marriage and the Family* 45:223–30.

8. Bowen, G. L., and Scheirer, M. A. (1986) The development and evaluation of human service programs in the military: An introduction and overview. *Evaluation and Program Planning* 9 (3):193–98.

9. Bureau of National Affairs (1986) *Work & Family: A Changing Dynamic.* Washington, D.C.: Bureau of National Affairs.

10. Burr, W. R. (1973) *Theory Construction and the Sociology of the Family.* New York: John Wiley & Sons.

11. Byrne, D. (1971) *The Attraction Paradigm.* New York: Academic Press.

12. Campbell, A., Converse, P. E., and Rogers, W. L. (1976) *The Quality of Life: Perceptions, Evaluations and Satisfactions.* New York: Russell Sage Foundation.

13. Chadwick-Jones, J. K. (1976) *Social Exchange Theory: Its Structure and Influence in Social Psychology.* New York: Academic Press.

14. Christensen, H. T. (1964) The intrusion of values. In H. T. Christensen (ed.), *Handbook of Marriage and the Family*, pp. 969–1006. Chicago, IL: Rand McNally.

15. Curran, D. (1983) *Traits of a Healthy Family.* Minneapolis, MN: Winston Press.

16. Edwards, J. (1969) Familial behavior as social exchange. *Journal of Marriage and the Family* 31:518–26.

17. Fisher, B. L., Giblin, P. R., and Hoopes, M. H. (1982) Healthy family functioning: What therapists say and what families want. *Journal of Marital and Family Therapy* 8:273–84.

18. Friedman, D. (1987) Notes on "Toward a theory of value in social exchange." In K. S. Cook (ed.), *Social Exchange Theory* pp. 47–58. Newbury Park, CA: Sage Publications.

19. Gilford, R., and Bengtson, V. (1979) Measuring marital satisfaction in three generations: Positive and negative dimensions. *Journal of Marriage and the Family* 41:381–98.

20. Grush, J. E., and Yehl, J. G. (1979) Marital roles, sex differences, and interpersonal attraction. *Journal of Personality and Social Psychology* 37(1):116–24.

21. Hamilton, G. (1929) *A Research in Marriage.* New York: Boni.

22. Heath, A. (1976) *Rational Choice Theory and Social Exchange.* New York: Cambridge University Press.

23. Homans, G. C. (1950) *The Human Group.* New York: Harcourt, Brace.

24. Homans, G. C. (1958) Social behavior as exchange. *American Journal of Sociology* 63:597–606.

25. Homans, G. C. (1961) *Social Behavior: Its Elementary Forms.* New York: Harcourt, Brace, & World.

26. Karpel, M. A. (1986) Questions, obstacles, contributions. In M. A. Karpel (ed.), *Family Resources: The Hidden Partner in Family Therapy,* pp. 3–61. New York: Guilford Press.

27. Keith, D. V., and Whitaker, C. (1985) C'est la guerre: Military families and family therapy. In F. W. Kaslow and R. I. Ridenour (eds.), *The Military Family,* pp. 147–66. New York: Guilford Press.

28. Klemer, R. H. (1970) *Marriage and Family Relationships.* New York: Harper & Row.

29. Levinger, G. (1965) Marital cohesiveness and dissolution: An integrative review. *Journal of Marriage and the Family* 27:19–28.

30. Levinger, G. (1986) Compatibility in relationships. *Social Science* 71(2/3):173–77.

31. Lewis, R., and Spanier, G. (1979) Theorizing about the quality and stability of marriage. In W. R. Burr, R. Hill, F. I. Nye, and I. L. Reiss (eds.), *Contemporary Theories about the Family,* Vol. 1, pp. 268–94. New York: Free Press.

32. Mace, D. R., and Mace, V. (1978) Measure your marriage potential: A simple test that tells couples where they are. *The Family Coordinator* 27:63–67.

33. Maxwell, J. W. (1979) A rational-emotive approach to strengthening marriage. In N. Stinnett, B. Chesser, and J. Defrain (eds.), *Building Family Strengths: Blueprints for Action,* pp. 107–24. Lincoln, NE: University of Nebraska Press.

34. McCubbin, H. I., and Patterson, J. (1983) *One Thousand Army Families: Strengths, Coping, and Supports.* St. Paul, MN: University of Minnesota.

35. McCubbin, H. I., and Thompson, A. I. (1987) Family typologies and family assessment. In H. I. McCubbin and A. I. Thompson (eds.), *Family Assessment Inventories for Research and Practice,* pp. 35–49. Madison, WI: University of Wisconsin.

36. Mindle, C. H., and Habenstein, R. W. (eds.) (1977) *Ethnic Families in America: Patterns and Variations.* New York: Elsevier.

37. Montgomery, J. (1982) *Family Crisis as Process.* Washington, D.C.: University Press of America.

38. Moos, R. H., and Moos, B. S. (1981) *Family Environment Scale Manual.* Palo Alto, CA: Consulting Psychologists Press.

39. Moos, R. H., and Moos, B. S. (1984) Clinical applications of the family environment scale. In E. E. Filsinger (ed.), *Marriage and Family Assessment: A Sourcebook for Family Therapy,* pp. 253–73. Beverly Hills, CA: Sage.

40. Nye, F. I. (1967) Values, family, and a changing society. *Journal of Marriage and the Family* 27:241–47.

41. Nye, F. I. (1978) Is choice and exchange theory the key? *Journal of Marriage and the Family* 40:219–33.

42. Nye, F. I. (1979) Choice, exchange and the family. In W. R. Burr, R. Hill, F. I. Nye, and Reiss, I. L. (eds.), *Contemporary Theories about the Family*, Vol. 2, pp. 1–41. New York: Free Press.

43. Olson, D. H. (1986) Circumplex model VII: Validation studies and FACES III. *Family Process* 25:337–51.

44. Olson, D., and McCubbin, H. I. (1983) *Families: What Makes Them Work.* Beverly Hills, CA: Sage Publications.

45. Olson, D. H., and Portner, J. (1984) Family adaptability and cohesion evaluation scales. In E. E. Filsinger (ed.), *Marriage and Family Assessment: A Sourcebook for Family Therapy*, pp. 299–315. Beverly Hills, CA: Sage.

46. Olson, D. H., Russell, C. S., and Sprenkle, D. H. (1983) Circumplex model of marital and family assessment: VI. Theoretical update. *Family Process* 22:69–83.

47. Orthner, D. K., and Bowen, G. L. (1982) *Families-in-Blue: Insights from Air Force Families in the Pacific.* Greensboro, NC: Family Development Press.

48. Orthner, D. K., and Pittman, J. F. (1986) Family contributions to work commitments. *Journal of Marriage and the Family* 48:573–81.

49. Otto, H. (1979) Developing human and family potential. In N. Stinnett, B. Chesser, and J. Defrain (eds.), *Building Family Strengths: Blueprints for Action*, pp. 39–50. Lincoln, NE: University of Nebraska Press.

50. Sabatelli, R. M. (1984) A marital comparison level index: A measure for assessing outcomes relative to expectations. *Journal of Marriage and the Family* 46:651–62.

51. Sabatelli, R. M. (1988) Exploring relationship satisfaction: A social exchange perspective on the interdependence between theory, research, and practice. *Family Relations* 37:217–22.

52. Satir, V. (1972) *Peoplemaking.* Palo Alto, CA: Science and Behavior Books.

53. Scanzoni, J. (1978) *Sex roles, Women's Work, and Marital Conflict: A Study of Family Change.* Lexington, MA: Lexington Books.

54. Scanzoni, J. (1979a) Social exchange and behavioral interdependence. In T. L. Huston and R. L. Burgess (eds.), *Social Exchange and Developing Relationships*, pp. 61–98. New York: Academic Press.

55. Scanzoni, J. (1979b) A historical perspective on husband–wife bargaining power and marital dissolution. In G. Levinger and O. C. Moles (eds.), *Divorce and Separation*, pp. 20–36. New York: Basic Books.

56. Spanier, G. B. (1972) Romanticism and marital adjustment. *Journal of Marriage and the Family* 34:481–87.

57. Spanier, G. B. (1976) Measuring dyadic adjustment: New scales for assessing the quality of marriage and similar dyads. *Journal of Marriage and the Family* 38:15–28.

58. Spanier, G. B., and Cole, C. L. (1976) Toward clarification and investigation of marital adjustment. *International Journal of Sociology of the Family* 6:121–46.

59. Spanier, G. B., and Filsinger, E. E. (1984) The dyadic adjustment scale. In E. E. Filsinger (ed.), *Marriage and Family Assessment: A Sourcebook for Family Therapy*, pp. 155–68. Beverly Hills, CA: Sage.

60. Spiegel, J. (1982) An ecological model of ethnic families. In M. McGoldrick, J. K. Pearce, and J. Giordana (eds.), *Ethnicity and Family Therapy: An Overview*, pp. 31–51. New York: Guilford Press.

61. Stillman, F., and Bowen, G. L. (1985) Corporate support mechanisms for families: An exploratory study and agenda for research and evaluation. *Evaluation and Program Planning* 8:309–14.

62. Szoc, R. (1982) *Family Factors Critical to the Retention of Naval Personnel.* Columbia, MD: Westinghouse Public Applied Systems.

63. Thibaut, J. W., and Kelley, H. H. (1959) *The Social Psychology of Groups.* New York: John Wiley & Sons.

64. Turner, J. H. (1978) *The Structure of Sociological Theory.* Homewood, IL: Dorsey.

65. Walster, E., Walster, G. W., and Berscheid, E. (1978) *Equity: Theory and Research.* Boston, MA: Allyn & Bacon.

66. Van Der Veen, F., Huebner, B., Jorgens, B., and Neja, P. (1964) Relationship between the parents' concept of the family and family adjustment. *American Journal of Orthopsychiatry* 34:45–55.

67. Wickham, J. A., Jr. (1983) *The Army White Paper.* Washington, D.C.: Chief of Staff, United States Army.

8

The "Company Town" in Transition: Rebuilding Military Communities

James A. Martin and Dennis K. Orthner

At the turn of the twentieth century, the landscape of America was dotted with company towns. These villages and small cities were controlled by the industries that attracted the workers and their families. The companies bought the land for the towns, built the homes in which the people lived, brought in the stores and shops where the people could purchase goods and services, and allowed families to live there for a modest cost of living as long as the employee was contributing to the profitability of the employer.

The types of company towns were as varied as the industries they represented (6). One of the largest and most attractively planned was created in the Midwest by Pullman, maker of railroad cars. This was a totally planned community with inviting neighborhoods, shops, parks, and schools. Other company towns were located in various parts of the country, often associated with textile industries, mining, and large-scale manufacturing. One exception to this pattern was a type of company town fostered by the government—the military post. These were often isolated and typically had few families. Still, they fell into the same pattern as other company towns, with housing and services being provided by the employing organization, and the soldier and family were expected to conform to organizational demands.

This type of organization and family interdependence represented both

The authors are grateful to the following individuals for their critical review and insightful suggestions: Col. Larry Ingraham, Dr. David Marlowe, Cpt. Paul Bartone, Dr. Joel Teitelbaum, Lt. Col. Robert Schneider, Dr. Mady Segal, Dr. Florence Rosenberg, Dr. Gary Bowen, and Lt. Col. Paul Furakawa. Without the editorial assistance of Ms. Jeannette Ickovics and Anna Robinson this document would never have been completed.

The authors do not purport to reflect the position of the Department of the Army or the Department of Defense (para 4-3, AR 360-5).

the strengths and weaknesses of the Industrial Revolution. On the positive side, families were offered many benefits that they otherwise might not have been able to afford, such as housing, medical care, and less expensive goods. Many of the people attracted to these industries were immigrants, either from overseas or rural areas, and they did not have the resources to successfully provide these living requirements with the meager wages that they earned. The company town employers were attractive because they offered a quality of life that could not easily be purchased by people with limited means. This was believed to be a small price for commitment and loyalty.

Unfortunately, there was also a dark side to the company town—organization family relationship. Not everyone relished the idea of losing their autonomy and their ability to make meaningful life choices. Never being able to get out from under the influence (or the watchful eyes) of the company led to growing unrest. The mournful words of the 1950s song, "I owe my soul to the company store" captured the feeling of entrapment that came from using company-provided services and credit. All of this frustration came to a head by the 1920s. Through strikes and other forms of rebellion, most industries were forced to give their workers more wages and autonomy rather than continue parent-like control over their lives.

The military services, nevertheless, continued their pattern of control. Unlike their civilian counterparts, the company town concept remained firmly in force, in policy and practice. The system of providing housing, medical care, and other lower-cost services remained, even though a growing number of posts and bases were located in or near urban areas. While the company town concept was a practical solution to the problems associated with sending mostly single men to isolated areas, it became somewhat anachronistic when the installations were increasingly surrounded by less hostile communities in which many of the military personnel and their families lived. And, as the number of married soldiers, sailors, and airmen increased, the systems that had been put into place to support isolated single men grew to include more complex support systems that could meet the needs of these diverse personnel and families.

Today each of the military branches still provides a host of services that approximate the company town of yesteryear. While most large employers long ago gave up the belief that it is in the best interests of the company and its employees to control the service delivery system, this notion still remains strong in the military. Nevertheless, the national debt and public concern about defense spending are likely to force the Department of Defense to face a period of significant defense budget cuts expected in the 1990s. Current military community facilities and programs are likely targets for a share of these reductions. With reduced resources for these programs and facilities, there is growing concern among leaders that without adequate resources for our military communities, it will not be possible to provide the quality of life required to keep military units manned and operationally effective.

Given these potential fiscal constraints, it is important to reexamine some of the premises that underlie assumptions about performance and personnel retention. This chapter views community service programs and facilities as necessary but not sufficient contributors to organizational effectiveness. It also challenges the assumption that self-contained military installations, and their array of programs and facilities, adequately promote readiness and retention. In light of the potential move toward reduced spending and the corresponding "civilianization" of existing programs and facilities, this chapter recommends that the military place more emphasis on developing small group associations as the basis for promoting a psychological, rather than a service-focused, sense of community. It argues that the natural building blocks for these associations are small military units.

MILITARY "COMPANY TOWNS"

Our nation's military services include more than 2 million active duty personnel. The spouses, children, and family members of these active duty military personnel number an additional 3 million. Most live on or near military installations operated by the military services. In addition to 870 installations in the United States, the Department of Defense (DoD) operates 370 installations in 21 foreign countries, and 19 in U.S. territories. With a 1988 budget authority of approximately $300 billion (6 percent of our nation's gross national product), the DoD is our nation's largest employer of young adults (2).

Our nation's military leaders are committed to the well-being of the military family (35), and they have actively supported funding for military community facilities and service programs (5). Their arguments for the more than $8 billion worth of "quality of life" items in the 1988 DoD budget reflect two key military concerns: readiness and retention (32). For the generals and admirals who operate our military services, taking care of soldiers, sailors, marines, and airmen as well as their families has become an important aspect of preparing for conflict.

It is assumed that military members will be able to give unrestricted effort to their jobs and the military mission as long as their families are assured of receiving adequate care in time of need (26). In this sense, family programs contribute to the performance of individuals and work units. Likewise, servicemember retention is considered a product of increasing soldier and family satisfaction with military life (10).

Military leaders typically promote the belief that member identification with the military is enhanced when community programs are operated by the services themselves. Many military leaders lament the rapid "civilianizing" of programs on military installations, whereby civilian companies contract for the operation of facilities and community programs that in the past were run by military members and career civil servants. The concern is that turning these programs and services over to the civilian sector will decrease military family trust and identification with the military as an institution.

Most importantly, like their industrial counterparts in the old company towns, military leaders fear that the erosion of the highly structured military community will result in a corresponding decrease in servicemembers' commitments to one another. They see this "caring for our own" as particularly important when families are faced with the various stressors that highlight military family life (e.g., deployments, overseas moves, unaccompanied tours). Like the idealized, mythical small company town, these leaders believe that it is through residents taking care of each other as friends and neighbors that the cohesion, esprit, loyalty, and dedication to duty thought to be required to sustain military family members is built.

These often expressed beliefs are in line with the readiness and retention objectives conveyed by Moskos' (27) notion of military service as a vocation rather than just an occupation. Unfortunately, even with the current array of military community programs and facilities, the concept of military service continues to shift in the direction of an occupation rather than a vocation (23). While there is an intuitive acceptance of the importance of military community programs and facilities, there is only limited evidence of any direct relationship between expenditures for these programs and facilities and any enhancement of readiness and retention (7, 29, 32).

In reality, the majority of military families today live in civilian neighborhoods rather than in government quarters. The availability of installation housing has and will continue to be insufficient, especially for young enlisted families. Many career military families also prefer the economic benefits associated with home ownership, as well as the privacy and independence that off-post living offers (28). Despite living off base, military families are encouraged to use an array of installation programs and facilities. Their use of these military community resources is typically based on economic factors, rather than either convenience or the lack of similar resources in the local civilian community. These military community facilities and programs are a "non-wage" economic benefit of service, very similar to the company facilities often provided to employees of major corporations.

There are a number of negative by-products associated with the current military community model. First, this company town model requires military leaders to function as mayors and social welfare program managers, regardless of their knowledge, interest, or inclination to do so. More critically, it requires work unit commanders to become the "overseers" of those they lead. A common complaint of these small unit commanders is that more of their time is spent on personnel issues than on combat training (9). Further, they make military families dependent on a system of social welfare services and programs that many find intrusive, demeaning, and/or inadequate. In fact, one might argue that our most traditional military communities are reminiscent of the company towns of the late nineteenth and early twentieth centuries, and that they represent the last great vestige of American welfare capitalism (13).

Rather than promoting productivity (in military terms, creating and preparing high-performance units for possible combat), strengthening the bonds between servicemembers and the military, or even encouraging careers, the military version of the "company town" fosters dependence on what some families consider to be a second-class system of benefits and services. At times, this system can rival some of the worst aspects of a socialized society. At the extreme, life in a military community can result in dehumanizing encounters with a bureaucratic environment

where everybody lives in government quarters, stands in line at government hospitals, department stores, restaurants. . . . and universally deplore the type of services rendered . . . [this is] a departure from the free enterprise system upon which this nation was founded [and from the] . . . form of governance we [members of the military] have taken an oath to defend our country against. (15, p. 10)

While it is important not to overstate the extremes, when the employer is also the governor, it is not uncommon to have conflict concerning the boundary between work and private life (31).

Finally, the promulgation of separate and distinct military communities contributes to the isolation of military families from the broader civilian community. This isolation is especially problematic for military families who reside in the local community. For these families, exclusive dependence on installation programs and facilities is counterproductive. It not only creates some degree of inconvenience, but it also serves as a psychological barrier to the development of potentially supportive relationships between military families and members of the local civilian community (17).

AN OPPORTUNITY FOR CHANGE

There are many forces at work, particularly economic ones, that are rapidly moving the military toward a system of community programs and facilities based on a free market "employee benefits" concept rather than on the current "employer-owned and operated" concept. To a large extent, these are the same forces that caused large corporations to abandon the company town concept decades ago. Conference Board researchers have noted that the current competitive labor market for quality workers has accelerated the competition between employers and resulted in an expansion of benefits to employees and their families (33). But these benefits are not typically provided by the companies; they are usually sponsored by the companies and offered through third parties. Thus, the employee retains autonomy and the employer is viewed as supporting the needs of employees and their families.

It is possible to imagine a time when military commands will only directly provide facilities and services out of necessity (i.e., only when and where the private sector will not go and/or state and local facilities are inadequate or nonexistent). The current evolution (or revolution) in the military health care delivery system involving the use of contracts with civilian health care providers is but the precursor to potentially broader changes. As these changes occur, it will also be necessary to change our current tax laws so that the frequently used opportunity for state and local tax avoidance for military members is eliminated (12). In order to share in the benefits, military members will have to contribute a fair share to the operation of local and state government.

Some may believe that this "civilianizing" of military community programs and facilities will destroy the cohesive bonds that bind soldiers and families together in a unique military life style. In reality, there is little current evidence that any protective sense of belonging among most military members and their families exists as a result of the current company town system. The primary and often exclusive source of interpersonal support for most military spouses is their own husband or wife (16, 28). Moreover, it is increasingly argued that one's sense of military identity is most directly related to close associations and identifications at the level of the servicemember's work group, not the larger military community (11).

It is important to emphasize that this chapter is advocating neither the removal of benefits nor increased compensation for military families based on needs created by various military life stressors. What is being suggested is a restructured, far less controlling life style designed to support healthy, maturing military families. Rather than increasing on-base programs and facilities, it is suggested that there may be advantages in limiting military-owned and operated services to only those that cannot be conveniently provided by the civilian sector. This may result in cost savings, more effective services, and a greater appreciation for what the military service is doing to facilitate a positive work and community environment within which the family is living.

Most importantly, it is suggested that building and maintaining company towns is not an effective way to enhance readiness and promote retention. With a volunteer force, it is necessary to provide a work environment that is satisfying, yet not in excessive conflict with personal or family life. For a military that has become a predominately married force, new alternative patterns of community development must be implemented in order to build supportive social networks among families in ways that contribute to military unit cohesion without intruding into the personal and family lives of military members. In the next section, the benefits of belonging to this kind of community are described, followed by a consideration of how best to obtain these benefits.

PROMOTING A SENSE OF COMMUNITY

With the creation of the all-volunteer force and the rapid expansion in the proportion of married servicemembers, the military has paid considerable attention to the development of the military installation (the *Gesellschaft*) but not enough to the development of small group associations (the *Gemeinschaft*) (34). Rather than focusing on "community of residence" (a specific geographical location and a corresponding collection of programs and services), it is alternatively possible to use the workplace and the small military work unit as the key building block for linking military members and their families into a "psychological sense of community" (14). This psychological sense of community is characterized by homogeneity, interdependence, shared responsibility, face-to-face relationships, and commonly shared goals. It fosters a sense of belonging that is a crucial aspect of social existence. The current preoccupation in the scientific literature with the concepts of social networks and social support demonstrates this point. Empirical evidence in medicine, psychology, and sociology suggests that such relationships act as primary sources of well-being and buffer the stressors of modern life (1, 8).

Whether one is talking about military service, membership in a religious order, or employment in a large corporation, one's sense of belonging to a unique group is typically rooted in day-to-day interactions with other members of a small primary work group. Likewise, the benefits, especially the psychological benefits, that derive from membership in any organization are typically conveyed from and through the primary group relationships embedded in the structure of the larger organization. It is in this sense that we must nurture the development of healthy small work groups and use these groups as the building blocks for community development.

This sense of belonging, described as a psychological sense of community, has been directly linked to the overall well-being and life satisfaction of servicemembers and their families, and indirectly linked to the performance of military units. For example, in a study of military spouses living in an overseas military community, Schneider and Gilley (30) found that wives who were low on a measure of psychological sense of community were five times more likely to "return early" to the United States when compared with wives who were high on this measure. The impact of a spouse's decision relates to readiness because such family stress has a negative impact on the soldier's performance and psychological well-being (4).

The well-being of servicemembers and their families who face the stress often associated with overseas living, extensive training separations, and/or the possibility of actual combat has been critically linked to military group identification (18). Families who encounter these demanding experiences are at risk for stress-related difficulties. However, if they are psychologically embedded in a strong unit-based support network, the risk decreases (22).

Since 1981 scientists from the Walter Reed Army Institute of Research (WRAIR) have been involved in evaluating the Army's Unit Manning System (UMS), an effort by the Headquarters, Department of the Army, to change the way the Army forms and deploys its combat units (24). In its simplest form, the UMS is an effort to change the Army's individual replacement system to a group replacement system. Rather than treating soldiers as interchangeable parts on an assembly line, the UMS is designed to keep soldiers together for reasonable periods of time (typically three years) in stable small groups with corresponding stable leadership. The objective is to create high-performance combat units with the kind of cohesive spirit that is believed necessary to psychologically sustain soldiers in the face of the enormous stress of modern combat (4, 22).

UMS data now include more than 2,000 individual and focused group interviews with soldiers and family members in 130 company-sized units, 450 person-days of observations (including observations conducted during field operations), and the administration of more than 26,000 soldier and family member surveys. These data clearly demonstrate a reciprocal family–unit relationship. While it is true that the soldier carries the burden of family stress into his or her duty environment, one of the most consistent observations from these data has been the critical importance of the small unit as a source of satisfaction and/or stress in the life of the soldier. This satisfaction and/or stress is then transmitted through the soldier to family members.

For the families WRAIR is studying, the Army is neither the military leaders in Washington, nor the local officials at the installation where the service-member is assigned. For these families, the real Army—the Army that helps or hinders personal and family life—is the soldier's unit. Small-unit leaders control soldiers' time and dominate their emotional states. Soldiers' peers (including other unit families) provide the sense of belonging, companionship, and support necessary to enjoy and to survive day-to-day unit activities and duty demands. Together, these unit experiences and relationships determine the quality of life for soldiers and their families.

WRAIR scientists have also observed the important influence of small-unit leadership practices on the development of relationships across soldier ranks and among unit families (3). At one extreme are commanders who literally prohibit cross-rank associations (including associations among families) because they fear that "fraternization" will develop, which will undermine authority. These units typically run under a feeling of fear and punishment. When soldiers and families in these units bond together it is out of fear; this is called "defensive bonding."

WRAIR scientists have also encountered units where leaders have created climates of trust and brotherhood among group members (19). In these units, respect and authority are typically based on leader competence and

fore, promote cohesive and highly productive work units that serve the needs of the organization and maintain its profitability. They also stimulate the local community by involving their employees in civic organizations, hiring from the local labor market, utilizing local services and suppliers, and fostering the development of quality support programs for their personnel and families.

The transition from a tightly controlled, company town community model to that of a more diversified community model will not be easy for the military services—but it is probably necessary. It is clear that real-world demands (including severe budget and personnel constraints) require military leaders to focus their attention on the primary military mission and not the personal management of a bewildering array of non-military support programs and facilities. It is also apparent that the military services need to integrate their families into the civilian society and give them more control over the economic and social service aspects of their lives. As other industries have already realized, personnel and family independence, not dependence, is the proper route to success today. Unless this approach is undertaken, military leaders are encouraging a condition where military service becomes a semi-welfare system that is primarily attractive to individuals and families unable and/or unwilling to care for themselves.

IMPLICATIONS AND RECOMMENDATIONS

The rebellions experienced by the company towns nearly a century ago are beginning to be felt within the military communities of today. Whether in family and community forums run by the services themselves or from advocacy groups such as the National Military Family Association, there is growing pressure for military communities to change. Many of the "best and brightest" are leaving the services rather than putting up with inadequate support services. Even single personnel are evaluating their military career options based on what they think their future spouses and children can expect from military community life (29).

From the 1990s on, there will be substantial restraint on the nation's defense budget. To deal with these limited resources, the military services will have to undergo change. Rather than viewing change as a threat, military leaders need to realize that evolving conditions can provide an opportunity to recast traditional notions of military life. Further, change provides the opportunity to create conditions where military families can prosper in ways that will support the quality of military forces and the readiness of its units.

Healthy military services must provide reasonable living and working conditions. Soldiers, sailors, marines, and airmen recognize that the ultimate reason for their presence in uniform is combat. What they and their families need is adequate training and preparation for such a requirement. They also want to know that they have been given the capability (e.g., competent leadership and quality equipment) to succeed in their military roles and missions.

Recent history has demonstrated that survival in combat is partly a function of one's emotional state (4). Stress is cumulative, and the individual who enters combat worried or preoccupied by thoughts and concerns about loved ones at home is at considerable risk for breakdown and/or death. It is critically important that this nation's military personnel feel confident about the health, security, and safety of their family members. This primary sense of trust must come from a belief, developed during peacetime training, that their families are part of a caring collective that will protect and assist one another in time of need (18).

Efforts to build the armed forces for the 1990s must begin by ensuring adequate wages and reasonable benefits, and by providing access to necessary services, programs, and facilities (although not necessarily owned and operated by the military). The income of military personnel must remain sufficiently high so as to allow them to purchase a greater share of their expenses from the local community, including adequate housing. As military budgets are planned for the future, a higher proportion of the budget should be allocated to indirect benefits that are purchased from suppliers, such as health insurers or mental health agencies, rather than direct services from military personnel. This will allow current service agencies to focus more on information and referral or to act as providers of services to people in more remote locations.

Greater attention should be given to building community cohesion at the work-unit level. It is at this level that military personnel and family members should be most closely linked. As policies are put into place to build high-performance military units, it is imperative that these include actions designed to develop feelings of personal competency and a sense of community among family members. Achieving such goals will require changing some current practices. For example, ways must be found to provide more stability to both unit and family life. Continuous personnel turnover diminishes unit performance, and frequent reassignments are a cause of enormous psychological and financial hardship on military families. Such turbulence inhibits the development of cohesion among unit members and prevents the formation of stable, supportive relationships among family members. Increased levels of caring and concern create a sense of belonging to a group that will offer informal support and assistance as unit personnel and families attempt to cope with the demands of military life.

One of the keys to success for this strategy lies in greater stability for military personnel. The number of major moves needs to be reduced so that stable relationships can be developed. A decade ago, the U.S. Air Force introduced a program called "Why not Minot" to attract personnel to a rather isolated North Dakota base. They offered stable, five-year tours and they received an overwhelming number of applicants. The U.S. Navy has experienced very positive personnel and family outcomes from their "home-porting" concept in which ships are assigned to specific home ports where families can stay for relatively long periods of time. The success of these and other such programs suggests that it is possible to keep people in place longer, let them build a stronger sense of community on their own terms, and still meet the objectives of career progression and training necessary for individual and unit performance.

CONCLUSION

Tomorrow's military organization needs to be as open as possible, and not isolated by gates and guards. Military families are not well served when they are kept segregated from the rest of society and dependent on a system of noncompetitive services and programs managed by military leaders who often lack the skill and/or interest to operate these facilities effectively (15). Rather than promoting healthy, satisfied servicemembers and families, this archaic community model more often leads to disenchantment among our most competent military members, who, given the opportunity, move off our installations into civilian housing and take their natural leadership talents with them. Some members and families even leave military service alto-gether.

If we want our military families to thrive and prosper in military service, we must give them the opportunities and support required to enjoy family life and to cope with the unique stressors that occur during the course of a military career. They need a reasonable income and decent benefits. They also need the elimination of unnecessary stressors like the excessive require-ment for relocation. The support they require includes building a "sense of community" among families based on their common association with other military families through small-unit relationships. These small units then be-come the building blocks for the creation of a healthy community. In the creation and operation of these workplace-based support systems, leader-ship issues will always remain the critical component. Leadership is the di-mension of the military environment that will either enhance or extinguish the family's sense of association with their peers, the unit, and military ser-vice.

NOTES

1. Alloway, R., and Bebbington, P. (1987) The buffer theory of social support: A review of the literature. *Psychological Medicine* 17:91–108.

2. American Forces Information Services (1987) *Defense 87 Almanac.* Arling-ton, VA.

3. Bartone, P. (1987) *Boundary crossers: The role of Army family assistance officers in the Gander disaster.* Paper presented at the Biennial Conference of the Inter-University Seminar on Armed Forces and Society, October, Chicago, IL.

4. Belenky, G., Tyner, C., and Sodetz, Fr. (1983) *Israeli Battle Shock Casualties, 1973 and 1982* (report no. 83-4). Washington, D.C.: Walter Reed Army Institute of Research.

5. Bowen G., and Scheirer, M. (1986) The development and evaluation of human service programs in the military. *Evaluation and Program Planning* 9:193–98.

6. Brandes, S. D. (1976) *American Welfare Capitalism: 1880–1940*. Chicago, IL: The University of Chicago Press.

7. Chow, N., and Berheide, C. (1988) The interdependence of family and work: A framework for family life education, policy, and practice. *Family Relations* 37:23–28.

8. Cohen, S., and Syme, S. L. (eds.) (1985) *Social Support and Health*. New York: Academic Press.

9. Croan, J., Janofski, B., and Orthner, D. K. (1987) *The Army Community Service and Youth Activities Program: An Exploratory Evaluation*. Oakton, VA: Caliber Associates.

10. Fletcher, L., and Giesler, K. (1981) *Relating Attitudes toward Navy Life to Reenlistment Decisions*. Alexandria, VA: Center for Naval Analysis.

11. Furukawa, T., Ingraham, L., Kirkland, F., Marlowe, D., Martin, J., and Schneider, R. (1987) *Evaluating the Unit Manning System: Lessons Learned* (report no. WRAIR-NP-87-10). Washington, D.C.: Walter Reed Army Institute of Research.

12. General Accounting Office (1984) *Military and Federal Civilian Disposable Income Comparisons and Extra Pay Received by Military Personnel*. Gaithersburg, MD.

13. Gilbert, N. (1981) The future of welfare capitalism. *Society* 54:28–37.

14. Glynn, T. (1981) Psychological sense of community: Measurement and application. *Human Relations* 7:789–818.

15. Headquarters, Department of the Army (1986) *Military Support Systems*. Washington, D.C.: Office of the Deputy Chief of Staff for Personnel (ODCSPER).

16. Ickovics, J. R. (1988) *Striking a balance after the birth of a child: The effects of multiple role demands and available resources on women's psychological well-being*. Paper presented at the meeting of the Association for Women in Psychology, April, Bethesda, MD.

17. Janowitz, M. (1960) *The Professional Soldier*. New York: Free Press.

18. Johnson, A. (1984) Supporting family members during deployment. *Soldier Support Journal* 11 (4):14–16.

19. Kirkland, F. (1988) Army culture, command climate, and combat potential. In *Proceedings of the 1988 Psychology in the DoD*, April, pp. 241–45. Colorado Springs, CO: U.S. Air Force Academy.

20. Marlowe, D. (ed.) (1986) *Unit Manning System Field Evaluation* (technical report no. 4). Washington, D.C.: Walter Reed Army Institute for Research.

21. Marlowe, D., et al. (1987) *Unit Manning System Field Evaluation* (technical report no. 5). Washington, D.C.: Walter Reed Army Institute of Research.

22. Marlowe, D., and Martin, J. (1988) Human endurance and the modern battlefield. In *Proceedings of the 1988 Psychology in the DoD*, pp. 208–12. Colorado Springs, CO: U.S. Air Force Academy.

23. Martin, J. (1984) *The wives of career enlisted service members: Application of a life stress model*. Doctoral dissertation, University of Pittsburgh, 1983. University Microfilm International, 1416.

24. Martin, J., and Furukawa, T. (1987) The thick and thin of COHORT units. *Soldier Support Journal* (October/December):8–12.

25. Martin, J., and Ickovics, J. (1986) Challenges of military life: The importance of a partnership between the Army and its families. *Military Family* 6:3–5.

26. Military Family Resource Center (1984) *Review of Military Family Research and Literature.* Springfield, VA.

27. Moskos, C. (1980) How an all-volunteer force might be made to survive. *Public Interest* 61:74–89.

28. Orthner, D. (1980) *Families in Blue: Implications of a Study of Married and Single Parent Families in the U.S. Air Force* (USAF contract no. F33600-79-0423). Washington, D.C.: Office of the Department of the Air Force.

29. Orthner, D. K., and Pittman, J. (1986) Family contributions to work commitment. *Journal of Marriage and the Family* 48:573–81.

30. Schneider, R., and Gilley, M. (1984) *Family Adjustment in USAREUR: Final Report.* Heidelberg, West Germany: U.S. Army Medical Research Unit—Europe.

31. Segal, M. (1986) The military and the family as greedy institutions. *Armed Forces and Society* 13:9–38.

32. Vernez, G., and Zellman, H. (1987) *Families and Mission: A Review of the Effects of Family Factors on Army Attrition, Retention, and Readiness* (Rand note: N-2624A). Santa Monica, CA: Rand Corporation.

33. Voydanoff, P. (1987) *Work and Family Life.* Beverly Hills, CA: Sage.

34. Warren, R. (1978) *The Community in America.* Chicago, IL: Rand McNally.

35. Wickham, J. (1983) *The Army Family.* Washington, D.C.: Headquarters, Department of the Army.

Postscript: Toward Further Research

Over the last decade, the Department of the Defense as well as the individual service branches (Army, Air Force, Navy, and Marine Corps) have become increasingly interested in developing personnel policies and support programs that will enable military personnel to meet military requirements and still maintain a viable personal and family life (9, 12, 13, 14). This expanded interest in family well-being and support stems from a convergence of factors, including greater competition with the civilian sector for a declining manpower pool of new recruits (3), a substantial increase in the proportion of servicemembers with family responsibilities (1, 10), and a general societal trend toward revaluing personal and family life (26). It also parallels the expanded recognition by military leadership of the interdependence among quality of life issues, personal and family adaptation, individual readiness and retention, and unit productivity and readiness (9, 22, 24).

This heightened recognition has provided the impetus for the development and expansion of administrative and support programs and services for servicemembers and their families (16). For example, since 1980, each service branch, as well as the Department of Defense, has created family liaison offices, and each service has developed formal mechanisms to better coordinate the delivery of support services and programs to servicemembers and their families (9).

Paralleling and supporting the recent upsurge in policy and program initiatives in support of families, there has been a proliferation of research concerning the support needs of servicemembers and their families and an increase in research designed to evaluate the effectiveness of family-oriented policy and program initiatives (9). For example, there has been a tenfold increase in research on military families alone over the last decade (16).

Without doubt, the military services have entered a new era of involvement in policy and program planning and development, drawing upon their historical respect for behavioral science research to include research on the development and evaluation of policy and program supports for servicemembers and their families.

The leadership shown by the Department of Defense and the individual service branches in responding to the support needs of servicemembers and their families is noteworthy. However, the initiation of policy and program initiatives for families over the last decade has been largely reactive, developed primarily in response to specific problems and their symptoms (e.g., child and spouse abuse). Moreover, there has been a tendency to homogenize the rich variation and diversity among families in the military in the planning, development, and evaluation of policy and program initiatives on their behalf (8). The result has been an ad hoc approach to policy and program planning and development that has lacked a consistent rationale (25), an approach that has also typically failed to account for possible variations in the needs, values, and demands of families, and how these, in turn, may vary over the work and family life cycles.

One reason for this piecemeal approach has been the lack of an over-arching framework to guide the development and evaluation of policy and program initiatives on behalf of families. There is a critical need for an explicit model of work–family linkages in the military (replete with underlying assumptions and operational outcome statements) that not only identifies the factors that promote the level of adaptation to the multiplicity of organizational and family demands faced by servicemembers and their families, but also specifies the direct and the indirect impact that military policies, practices, and programs have on the ability of servicemembers and their families to successfully respond to these demands. This model must reflect the dynamic and interactive quality of work and family life across the work and family life cycles. In addition, it must respect the tremendous age, ethnic, and cultural diversity found among families in the military services today by accounting for personal system-level influences, including the values, needs, and expectations of servicemembers and their families toward both work and family life. Finally, for purposes of clinical and community intervention, the model must be practice based—capable of guiding the development, implementation, and evaluation of policies, programs, and practices in support of families.

EFFORTS TO MODEL WORK–FAMILY LINKAGES

There are several models of work–family linkages in the U.S. military that have been recently conceptualized (5, 6, 11, 23), and other modeling efforts that are currently underway (7, 21) that provide a rich foundation for continued efforts. In each case, these models emphasize the spillover between work and family demands and satisfactions, the importance of person–environment fit to successful adaptation to work and family demands, and the direct and indirect impact that military policies, practices, and programs have in helping servicemembers and their families better balance demands. However, each model requires further delineation and refinement in order to: (a) specify underlying subdimensions of conceptual domains, (b) provide nominal definitions of these conceptual subdimensions to guide their operationalization and measurement, and (c) generate empirically testable hypotheses for guiding research efforts that will lead to model refinement.

Of these modeling efforts, the current work by Orthner and Scanzoni (21) to model the link between work and family outcomes is particularly noteworthy in its attempt to capture the complex dynamic between work and family systems. Understanding the relationship between outcomes at work and at home is especially important to the development of family and community support mechanisms because of the belief among military leadership and service providers that better services will improve the level of family adaptation which, in turn, will enhance job morale and performance (25). Building on assumptions from systems and exchange theory, Orthner and Scanzoni propose that the commitments people make to their work are directly influenced by the adaptation of their families to organizational demands and by the equity or fairness of the work organization.

A key assumption of this model is that individuals and families want to live and work in an environment that best promotes their interests and fullfills their needs. Therefore, people are motivated to behave in ways that maximize their chances of being rewarded and minimize their chances of bearing costs. It is also assumed that they evaluate whether their current situation can be improved by comparing it with other alternatives that may be available to them. If their situation is deemed unfair, in either the family or work environments, they may seek to recover equity by initiating change in one or both environments. The ability of individuals to restore equity in their work and family environments as well as the focus of their efforts to redress the reward/cost imbalances depend in part on the rigidness of expectations in these environments, the relative strength of social controls over work and the family, and the relative costs in each area for nonconformity. If either work or the family is more rigid in its expectations and/or its mechanisms for social control are greater, the available options to restore equity become more limited.

The concept of "family adaptation" is a critical element in the model proposed by Orthner and Scanzoni. The ability of families to fit into the military system has been considered crucial to the ability of the armed services to maintain high levels of preparedness (11, 25). For example, if service personnel have to go into conflict at a moment's notice, the family must be willing to adapt to the demands of the work organization. However, this adaptation is contingent on the level of family agreement with the underlying values and expectations of the military system. If families understand the rationale behind organizational demands and agree with these tenets, it is hypothesized that they are more likely to support these values and expectations when the need arises.

Another important aspect of family adaptation discussed by Orthner and Scanzoni is the ability of families to cope under stressful conditions. Families who are sufficiently flexible and capable of garnering the resources necessary to cope with change are the most likely to accommodate to organizational demands. These families have the necessary internal resources (e.g., good communication, trust, coherence) and/or external resources (e.g., good friends, supportive kinship, community ties) that can be mobilized to help them adapt to new situations. Families with more rigid rules and fewer internal and external resources may find adaptation difficult. They may have particular difficulty shifting roles and priorities when demands are made on the family system.

A second important aspect of the model of commitments proposed by Orthner and Scanzoni is the perceived equity of the work and family environments. It is proposed that servicemembers and their families must view the military organization as fair, in comparison to alternative work organizations, in order for them to work hard to support the mission and to continue their link to the military organization. It is proposed that individuals regularly examine the benefits and costs associated with their situations to determine if they are being treated fairly or equitably. For example, servicemembers and their spouses may interpret as job costs such things as long work hours, frequent family separations because of job demands, physical demands of the job, and the sometimes negative attitudes of job supervisors. These costs may be overcome by rewards that are associated with security, camaraderie, sense of excitement, and positive support from supervisors. The balance between rewards and costs is equity. However, individuals may be quite willing to accept inequitable situations if the prospects for further exchange appear to be promising and to compensate for past inequities. For example, the 20-year retirement option in the military with its unusually high benefits is seen as a reward that helps to compensate for the reward/cost inequities often associated with military service.

Equity in the family domain can be similarly described in terms of the extent that husbands and wives are receiving an appropriate balance of rewards and costs in marriage. For example, the conflicts and difficulties experienced by husbands and wives in marriage may be compensated by their level of companionship and support for one another. When the interaction between family members is defined as fair, it is hypothesized that there is a building up of positive feelings that facilitate relational growth and commitment.

The model goes further to suggest that these perceptions of equity can also be influenced by what are perceived to be the rewards and costs associated with an alternative environment. These perceptions are much more hypothetical than what is actually experienced in the current environment but they are nonetheless likely to influence people's behavior. If the balance of rewards to costs is believed to be more favorable in a civilian job or community, this perception is assumed to positively influence people's decisions to leave the military as well as negatively influence their level of job commitment and performance. On the other hand, if they are either unaware of good alternatives or have a negative view toward alternative jobs in the civilian community, it is hypothesized that they will be less willing to make a change and will perform better in their current work situation.

Models such as the one by Orthner and Scanzoni suggest that the relationship between work and family environments is more ordered than chaotic. This is important because effective community and family interventions depend on the ability of leaders to anticipate the needs for as well as the consequences of policies and programs that are intended to promote a more equitable situation between the military organization and its families. Use of such models by military policy makers and program planners should enable them to: (a) better conceptualize their efforts in support of servicemembers and their families, (b) systematically evaluate the impact of current policies, practices, and programs on behalf of servicemembers and their families on both military- and family-related outcomes, (c) specify the policy and program initiatives that will help maximize the ability of both the military organization as well as servicemembers and their families to successfully meet their respective demands and obligations, and (d) develop an agenda of basic and applied research on the nature and implications of the work–family interface. The modeling effort by Orthner and Scanzoni clearly suggests that both the military and the family system are likely to be winners in an environment that promotes a sense of shared purpose, mutual support and adaptation, cooperation, and commitment between the organization and its members.

RESEARCH NEEDS

How do we determine if our proposed models of work–family linkages are accurate and useful? This takes careful and systematic research and evaluation. Models themselves are always in process, continually being refined and updated, based upon theoretical and empirical discoveries and developments—both an inductive as well as a deductive process.

Over the last decade, there have been significant attempts to gather better information about the needs and concerns of military families. At the beginning of the 1980s we knew comparatively little about these families, including their numbers, their family life patterns, their needs for services and supports, or their role in the retention and readiness of military personnel. Significant strides have been made since the beginning of the decade in our monitoring of these families, with several major studies in each of the services leading the way. Programs to better meet the needs of these families have grown in size and scope, and research efforts have frequently been used to suggest new service directions or to justify policy and program directions.

Still, in the current climate of program accountability and budgetary cutbacks for defense, the military services require better information upon which to base their decisions concerning policies and practices in support of servicemembers and their families. It is only from this perspective that the military services can hope to build toward a coherent and cost-effective set of policies, practices, and programs that will enhance the level of cooperation and equity between the military services and their families, and which ultimately will lead to increased levels of family adaptation and satisfaction and to improvements in retention and military preparedness. Several promising areas for future research and assessment are described briefly below.

Families in Stress

Previous research has indicated that some military families experience more dysfunction in the military environment than others (15, 18). However, only limited research has been conducted that helps to identify those relationship patterns, interpersonal skills and competencies, and social and psychological characteristics that enhance the ability of families to make positive adaptations to the rigors of military life. Moreover, we know relatively little about how stressor events and demands vary in families across the work and family life cycles, and which types of families are most vulnerable to combinations of stressor events and demands. Such information is critical to policy development, especially if programs are to be preventive in orientation rather than just reactive to families in crisis.

Stabilization of Families

Military families move about twice as often as their civilian counterparts (19). Although this rate is beginning to slow down, the overall rate remains high. A number of suggestions have been made to increase the stability of the forces in order to reduce costs and to increase opportunities for families to develop stronger community ties. It has also been suggested that the services consider more "home-basing/porting" as a strategy for improving family stability. This would leave families in one location while units deploy for periods of time. Nevertheless, we know very little about the likely consequences of this proposal or how it compares with the unit-level rotation system that has been tried in the Army. It is difficult to project the possible effects of different strategies for stabilizing families without a better research foundation.

Children and Youth Research

We know surprisingly little about the needs of children growing up in military families. Some of our assumptions about their well-being were shattered in the recent *Youth in Transition* study (19). For example, it was found that adolescent girls are experiencing some major adjustment problems and that moving is a significant hardship on teens. Studies across all the services have found that personnel and their spouses are very concerned about rearing children in the military environment (2, 18). Moreover, these concerns are a very important factor in the retention decisions of married persons (4, 18, 20). With these comments in mind, greater attention should be directed to studies of these children and to the unique challenges they face in growing up in a military family.

Comprehensive Needs Assessments

Effective policy and program development for families is dependent on accurate assessments of family needs and how these vary across structural, compositional, and demographic dimensions (e.g., marital status, stage in the family life cycle, spouse employment status, racial/ethnic group, length of service, military occupational specialty, service branch, and current geographic location). Although the military services regularly survey their personnel across a number of policy and program areas, these assessments are usually quite limited in their foci, and have typically received only limited analysis. Future assessments should have broader and more comprehensive foci, addressing the internal needs of families as well as their needs for external supports. An important product will be the identification of "high-risk" families with marital and family dysfunction with both sensitivity (i.e., the ability to identify dysfunctional families) and specificity (i.e., the ability to discriminate functional from dysfunctional families). An important goal of such needs assessments will be to discern the values and expectations of family members for marriage and family life, and how policies and practices in the military services either facilitate or hinder meeting these values and expectations. In addition, it will be important to determine the expectations of families toward the military in addressing family-level needs and demands. To what extent do families want the military involved in their personal, relational, family, and community life? A related focus is to investigate the perceptions of family members toward military policies, practices, and programs, and to identify individual, family, and community factors associated with positive and negative perceptions. These assessments must not only be more sophisticated in design to ensure a comprehensive focus, but also must be subjected to analysis strategies that respect the complexity of work and family linkages, and the possible buffering and intervening role of military policies, practices, and programs in strengthening family resources and preventing family dysfunction.

A Life Cycle Perspective

Families are dynamic institutions whose membership, function, and needs vary over time. Work careers are similarly dynamic, changing in both form and function over the years (17). Despite this recognition, past research in the military services has often failed to provide a life-course perspective in the study of work–family linkages. Research is required in the military community that traces work–family dynamics over time, exploring the consequences of this interaction for servicemembers as well as for members of their families. It is likely that there are pressure points at certain intersections of work and family careers. For example, many couples attempt to begin their careers and their families simultaneously. The combined responsibilities for the early development needs of children together with the high demands and time requirements of a beginning career, especially if both husband and wife are employed, may present young adults and their families with considerable role demands and pressure for which a special combination of employment policies (e.g., regular work hours) and community supports (e.g., childcare services) are required.

Alternative Service Delivery Systems

Introspection is a critical activity in policy and program development. Despite the tremendous efforts made by the military services over the last decade to increase their supports to servicemembers and their families, a critical question remains: Is the current arrangement of services and programs the best system that can be designed to address the needs of military personnel and families? The issue here is not whether existing systems are doing a good job with available resources, but rather whether some other combination of personnel and service delivery systems could be designed and tested that would perform more effectively and efficiently. Such a system might be more closely tied to military units or perhaps the local civilian community. The possibilities are endless but they should be seriously explored.

In conclusion, efforts toward building supports for servicemembers and their families have moved very quickly since the late 1970s. In charting a course for the 1990s, it is imperative that policy and program decisions be based on the best available information about the situation, needs, and priorities of families, and that research be conducted to better understand the work–family interface and how its nature may vary across the life span and for different population subgroups. Now is the time for reassessing past and current policy and program efforts, to chart a refined and clearly articulated course for building a sense of mutual support between the military organization and its families, and to develop models of work–family linkages through carefully designed and executed research for guiding policy and program efforts that help to create an environment in which both the work organization and the family can fulfill their respective functions and prosper. It is sincerely hoped that the chapters in the volume will stimulate the type of research and dialogue that will promote a high level of cooperation and partnership between the military organization and its families in accomplishing their important missions.

NOTES

1. Armed Service YMCA (1984) *American Military Families: Basic Demographics.* Springfield, VA: Military Family Resource Center.

2. Bowen, G. L. (1985) Families-in-blue: Insights from Air Force families. *Social Casework* 66:459–66.

3. Bowen, G. L. (1986a) Intergenerational occupational inheritance in the military: A reexamination. *Adolescence* 21:623–29.

4. Bowen, G. L. (1986b) Spouse support and the retention intentions of Air Force members: A basis for program development. *Evaluation and Program Planning* 9:209–20.

5. Bowen, G. L. (1987) An ecosystem model of work and family in the U.S. military. In H. G. Lingren et al. (eds.), *Family Strengths 8–9: Pathways to Wellbeing*, pp. 15–26. Lincoln, NE: University of Nebraska Press.

6. Bowen, G. L. (1988a) Work and family linkages in the U.S. military. *Military Family* (February):3–5.

7. Bowen, G. L. (1988b) *The Family Adaptation Model: A Life Course Perspective* (contract no. MDA903-87-C-0540). Alexandria, VA: U.S. Army Research Institute for the Behavioral and Social Sciences.

8. Bowen, G. L., and Janofsky, B. J. (1988) *Family Strength and Adaptation to Army Life: A Focus on Variations in Family Values and Expectations across Racial/Ethnic Group and Rank.* Washington, DC: Department of the Army, Office of the Chief of Chaplains.

9. Bowen, G. L., and Scheirer, M. A. (1986) The development and evaluation of human service programs in the military. *Evaluation and Program Planning* 9:193–98.

10. Carr, R., Orthner, D., and Brown, R. (1980) Living and family patterns in the Air Force. *Air University Review* 31 (2):75–96.

11. Croan, G. M. (ed.) (1985) *Career Decision Making and the Military Family: Toward a Comprehensive Model.* Alexandria, VA: U.S. Army Research Institute for the Social and Behavioral Sciences.

12. Hunter, E. J. (1982) *Families under the Flag.* New York: Praeger.

13. Kaslow, F. W., and Ridenour, R. I. (eds.) (1984) *The Military Family.* New York: Guilford Press.

14. Kohen, J. A. (1984) The military career is a family affair. *Journal of Family Issues* 5:401–18.

15. McCubbin, H. I., and Patterson, J. M. (1983) *One Thousand Army Families: Strengths, Coping and Supports.* St. Paul, MN: University of Minnesota.

16. Military family services and research on the rise (1985) *American Family* (April):2–7.

17. Moen, P. (1983) The two provider family: Problems and potentials. In D. H. Olson and B. C. Miller (eds.), *Family Studies Yearbook*, Vol. 1, pp. 397–427. Beverly Hills, CA: Sage Publications.

18. Orthner, D. K., and Bowen, G. L. (1982) *Families in Blue: Insights from Air Force Families in the Pacific.* Greensboro, NC: Family Development Press.

19. Orthner, D. K., Giddings, M. M., and Quinn, W. H. (1987) *Youth in Transition: A Study of Adolescents from Air Force and Civilian Families* (AFP 30-48). Washington, D.C.: Government Printing Office.

20. Orthner, D. K., and Pittman, J. F. (1986) Family contributions to work commitment. *Journal of Marriage and the Family* 48:573–81.

21. Orthner, D. K., and Scanzoni, J. (1988) *A theoretical framework linking family factors with work commitment.* Paper presented at the Theory Construction and Research Methodology Workshop, National Council on Family Relations Annual Meeting, November, Philadelphia, PA.

22. Segal, M. W. (1986a) The military and the family as greedy institutions. *Armed Forces and Society* 13:9–38.

23. Segal, M. W. (1986b) *Plan for Research on Army Families* (Research Product 86-30). Alexandria, VA: U.S. Army Research Institute for the Behavioral and Social Sciences.

24. Vernez, G., and Zellman, G. L. (1987) Families and mission: A Review of the effects of family factors on Army attrition, retention, and readiness. Santa Monica, CA: Rand Corporation.

25. Wickham, J. A., Jr. (1983) *The Army White Paper.* Washington, D.C.: Chief of Staff, United States Army.

26. Yankelovich, D. (1979) Work, values and the new breed. In C. Kerr and J. Rosow (eds.), *Work in America: The Decade Ahead* pp. 3–26. New York: Van Nostrand Reinhold.

General References

Aldous, J. (ed.) (1982) *Two Paychecks: Life in Dual-Earner Families.* Beverly Hills, CA: Sage Publications.

Axel, H. (1985) *Corporations and Families: Changing Practices and Perspectives.* New York: Conference Board.

Bane, M. J., and Weiss, R. S. (1980) Alone in the world of single parent families. *American Demographics* 2(5):11–14, 48.

Bohen, H., and Viveros-Long, A. (1981) *Balancing Jobs and Family Life.* Philadelphia, PA: Temple University Press.

Bowen, G. L. (1985) Families-in-blue: Insights from Air Force families. *Social Casework* 66:459–66.

Bowen, G. L. (1986) Spouse support and the retention intentions of Air Force members: A basis for program development. *Evaluation and Program Planning* 9:209–20.

Bowen, G. L. (1987) An ecosystem model of work and family linkages in the U.S. Military. In H. G. Lingren, L. Kimmons, P. Lee, G. Rowe, L. Rottman, L. Schwab, and R. Williams (eds.), *Family Strengths: Pathways to Well-being*, Vols. 8–9, pp. 15–26. Lincoln, NE: University of Nebraska Press.

Bowen, G. L. (1988a) Corporate supports for the family lives of employees. A conceptual model for program planning and evaluation. *Family Relations* 37:183–88.

Bowen, G. L. (1988b) Work and family linkages in the U.S. Military. *Military Family* (February):3–5.

Bowen, G. L., and Orthner, D. K. (1986) Single parents in the U.S. Air Force. *Family Relations* 35:45–52.

Bowen, G. L., and Scheirer, M. A. (1986) The development and evaluation of human service programs in the military. *Evaluation and Program Planning* 9:193–98.

Burden, D. S. (1986) Single parents and the work setting. The impact of multiple job and homelife responsibilities. *Family Relations* 35:37–43.

Bureau of National Affairs (BNA) (1986) *Work and Family: A Changing Dynamic.* Washington, D.C.: Bureau of National Affairs, Inc.

Croan, G. M., Katz, R., Fischer, N., and Smith-Osborne, A. (1980) *Roadmap for Navy Family Research.* Arlington, VA: Office of Naval Research.

Crouter, A. C. (1984) Spillover from family to work: The neglected side of the work–family interface. *Human Relations* 37:425–42.

Friedman, D. E. (1983) *Government Initiatives to Encourage Employer-Sponsored Child Care: The State and Local Perspective.* New York: Center for Public Advocacy Research.

Gerstel, N., and Gross, H. E. (eds.) (1987) *Families and Work.* Philadelphia, PA: Temple University Press.

Glynn, T. (1981) Psychological sense of community: Measurement and application. *Human Relations* 7:789–818.

Goldman, N. L., and Segal, D. R. (eds.) (1976) *The Social Psychology of Military Service.* Beverly Hills, CA: Sage Publications.

Greenhaus, J. H., and Beutell, N. J. (1985) Sources of conflict between work and family roles. In B. C. Miller and D. H. Olson (eds.), *Family Studies Review Yearbook,* Vol. 3, pp. 299–319. Beverly Hills, CA: Sage Publications.

Hall, F. S., and Hall, D. T. (1979) *The Two-Career Couple.* Reading, MA: Addison-Wesley.

Hanson, S. M. H. (1986) Healthy single parent families. *Family Relations* 35:125–32.

Harris, L., and Associates, Inc. (1981) *Families at Work.* Minneapolis, MN: General Mills, Inc.

Hertz, R. (1986) *More Equal than Others: Women and Men in Dual-Career Marriages.* Berkeley, CA: University of California Press.

Hill, R. (1949) *Families under Stress.* New York: Harper & Row.

Hiller, D., and Dyehouse, J. (1986) Dual-Career Marriage in the Research Literature. *Journal of Marriage and the Family* 49:787–96.

Hunter, E. J. (1982) *Families under the Flag.* New York: Praeger.

Hunter, E. J., and Nice, D. S. (eds.) (1978a) *Children of Military Families: A Part and Yet Apart.* Washington, D.C.: U.S. Government Printing Office.

Hunter, E. J., and Nice, D. S. (eds.) (1978b) *Military Families: Adaptation to Change.* New York: Praeger.

Janowitz, M. (1960) *The Professional Soldier: A Social and Political Portrait.* New York: Free Press.

Kamerman, S. B., and Hayes, C. D. (eds.) *Families that Work.* Washington, D.C.: National Academy Press.

Kanter, R. M. (1977) *Work and Family in the United States: A Critical Review and Agenda for Research and Policy.* New York: Russell Sage Foundation.

Kaslow, F. W., and Ridenour, R. I. (eds.) (1984) *The Military Family.* New York: Guilford Press.

Kelly, R. F., and Voydanoff, P. (1985) Work/family role strain among employed parents. *Family Relations* 34:367–74.

Kohen, J. A. (1984) The military career is a family affair. *Journal of Family Issues* 5:401–18.

Lavee, Y., McCubbin, H. I., and Patterson, J. M. (1985) The double ABCX model of family stress and adaptation: An empirical test by analysis of structural equations with latent variables. *Journal of Marriage and the Family* 47:811–25.

Louis Harris and Associates, Inc. (1981) *Families at Work: Strengths and Strains.* Minneapolis, MN: General Mills, Inc.

Martin, J., and Ickovics, J. (1986) Challenges of military life: The importance of partnership between the Army and its families. *Military Family* 6:3–5.

McCubbin, H. I., and Patterson, J. M. (1983) *One Thousand Army Families: Strengths, Coping and Supports.* St. Paul, MN: University of Minnesota.

McCubbin, H. I., Dahl, B. B. and Hunter, E. J. (eds.) (1976) *Families in the Military System.* Beverly Hill, CA: Sage Publications.

Military Family Resource Center (1984) *Review of Military Family Research and Literature.* Springfield, VA: Armed Forces YMCA of the USA.

Mortimer, J. T., and London, J. (1984) The varying linkages of work and family. In P. Voydanoff (ed.), *Work and Family: The Changing Roles of Men and Women,* pp. 20–35. Palo Alto, CA: Mayfield Publishing.

Nieva, V. F. (1985) Work and family linkages. In L. Larwood, A. H. Stromberg, and B. A. Gutek (eds.), *Women and Work: An Annual Review,* Vol. 1, pp. 162–90. Beverly Hills, CA: Sage.

Nieva, V. F., and Gutek, B. A. (1981) *Women and Work: A Psychological Perspective.* New York: Praeger.

Orthner, D. K., and Bowen, G. L. (1982) *Families in Blue: Insights from Air Force Families in the Pacific.* Greensboro, NC: Family Development Press.

Orthner, D. K., and Bowen, G. L. (1985) Fathers in the military. In S. M. H. Hansen and F. W. Bozett (eds.), *Dimensions of Fatherhood,* pp. 307–26. Beverly Hills, CA: Sage Publications.

Orthner, D. K., Giddings, M., and Quinn, W. (1987) *Youth in Transition: A Study of Adolescents from Military and Civilian Families.* Washington, D.C.:U.S. Government Printing Office.

Orthner, D. K., and Pittman, J. F. (1986) Family contributions to work commitment. *Journal of Marriage and the Family* 48:573–81.

Piotrkowski, C. S. (1979) *Work and the Family System.* New York: Macmillan.

Piotrkowski, C. S., Rapoport, R. N., and Rapoport, R. (1987) Families and work. In M. B. Sussman and S. K. Steinmetz (eds.), *Handbook of Marriage and the Family,* pp. 251–83. New York: Plenum Press.

Pleck, J. H. (1977) The work–family role system. *Social Problems* 24:417–27.

Raabe, P. H., and Gessner, J. (1988) Employer family-supportive policies: Diverse variations on the theme. *Family Relations* 37:196–202.

Renshaw, J. R. (1976) An exploration of the dynamics of the overlapping worlds of work and family. *Family Process* 15:143–65.

Ridenour, R. I. (1984) The military, service families, and the therapist. In F. W. Kaslow and R. I. Ridenour (eds.), *The Military Family,* pp. 1–17. New York: Guilford Press.

Rodriguez, A. R. (1984) Special treatment needs of children of military families. In F. W. Kaslow and R. I. Ridenour (eds.), *The Military Family,* pp. 46–70. New York: Guilford Press.

Segal, M. W. (1986) The military and the family as greedy institutions. *Armed Forces and Society* 13:9–38.

Sekaran, U. (1986) *Dual-Career Families.* San Francisco, CA: Jossey-Bass.

Statuto, C. M. (1984) *Families in the Eighties: Implications for Employers and Human Services.* Washington, D.C.: Catholic University of America.

Thompson, E.H., and Gongla, P. A. (1983) Single-parent families: In the mainstream of society. In E. Macklin and R. Rubin (eds.), *Contemporary Families and Alternative Lifestyles: A Handbook on Research and Theory,* 97–124. Beverly Hills, CA: Sage Publications.

Vernez, G., and Zellman, H. (1987) *Families and Mission: A Review of the Effects of Family Factors on Army Attrition, Retention, and Readiness* (Rand note: N-2624A). Santa Monica, CA: Rand Corporation.

Voyanoff, P. (ed.) (1984) *Work and Family: Changing Roles of Men and Women.* Palo Alto, CA: Mayfield Publishing.

Voydanoff, P. (1987) *Work and Family Life.* Newbury Park, CA: Sage Publications.

Warren, R. (1978) *The Community in America.* Chicago, IL: Rand McNally.

Whyte, W. H., Jr. (1956) *The Organization Man.* New York: Simon & Schuster.

Index

achievement, stress and, 128
adolescence. *See* youth
age, job satisfaction and, 62, 108, 109
Air Force: assignments away from home, 22, 23, 82; combat risks, 17; drug/alcohol problems and, 131; dual-career couples in, 100, 102–11; job satisfaction and, 64–74; marital quality and, 59–75; retention studies, 42; separation time, 20; single parents in, 84, 86, 90
alcohol problems, 131, 132
alienation, stress levels and, 132
apathy, alienation and, 126
Army: combat risks, 17; dual-career couples in, 99; Family Support Groups, 13; mobility in, 18–19; overseas stations, 22, 23; retention studies, 42; separation time, 20; Unit Manning System, 170–71
Army Family Action Committee, 12–13
Army Family Symposia, 13
The Army Wife, 24
assistance/support programs, 28–29; budget cuts and, 164–65, 173; civilian sector provision of, 165–66, 167–68; dependence on, 166–67; family values and, 156; formal, 4, 12–13; free market concept and, 167–68; research and, 179–80; single parents and, 90

base housing. *See* on-post housing
behavior: constraints on, 7; values realized through, 149
belongingness needs, 168, 169, 171
Benin, M. H., 86
bipolar world, evolution of, 4
Blau, P., 148
bonding, defensive, 170
Bowen, G. L., 40, 41, 84, 85, 86, 87, 90
Bratter, T. E., 122
Burden, D. S., 81, 88
Burr, W. R., 149
Burris, V., 62
Byrne, D., 147, 150

Campbell, A., 145
career commitment: dual-career couples, 102, 105, 107; family influences, 29, 60; motivation of, 9; satisfaction with Air Force and, 108, 110; sense of belonging and, 171; spousal support and, 101; work environment and, 172–73

career cycle: military demands and, 26; retention decisions and, 41; role strain and, 53
childbirth, separation during, 27
childcare: dual-career couples and, 99, 100, 111–12; facilities for, 29; separations and, 27; single parents and, 84, 89–90; working hours and, 21–22
children: acting out, 129; career plans of, 118; coping strategies, 133; developmental needs, 53, 119–23; dual-career couples and, 101; emotional problems of, 133–36; job satisfaction and, 71; marital stages and, 15; military pressures, 117–38; relocations and, 127, 131, 135, 136; research needs, 185; satisfaction with Air Force and, 105, 108, 110, 111–12; self-esteem of, 124–25; separation effects, 20; single parent relationships with, 83–84; social pressures, 24; socialization of, 120, 122–23; stress and, 128–34; time demands, 10. *See also* youth
Coates, C. H., 4
combat risks, 17–18, 174
commitment. *See* career commitment
community: cohesiveness, 171–73; embeddedness, 52, 123; psychological sense of, 169–71
company town, military community as, 7, 163–75
competition, stress and, 128
Coser, L. A., 7, 9, 10, 11
Coser, R. L., 10, 11
Curran, D., 156

date of entry, job satisfaction and, 71
death, risk of, 17
depression, 127, 132
divorce: children's development and, 120; financial problems and, 81; rates of, 5. *See also* single parents
draft system, 5
drug problems: of children, 131; of fathers, 132
dual-career couples: civilian, 98–99;

family influences, 101–2; individual's perceptions of, 107; in military, 11, 30, 97–98, 99–112; socialization of children and, 122–23; work influences, 102
dyadic adjustment scale, 145
Dyehouse, J., 98

education, job satisfaction and, 62, 71
employee assistance programs, 89, 90
enlisted personnel: dual-career couples, 99; marriage of, 4–5; on-post housing and, 5; policymaking for, 29; relocations and, 18, 19, 22–23; as single parents, 82; social pressures, 24
environmental conditions: child development and, 119–20, 121; job satisfaction and, 63
Ericksen, E. P., 102
Ericksen, J. A., 102
Erikson, Erik, 120, 124
exchange theory. *See* social exchange theory

families: adaptation of, 181–82; career advancement and, 24; career commitment and, 29, 60; as dynamic institutions, 53; expectations in, 153–55; individual's perceptions of, 152, 153; interaction in, 14–15, 128–30; intervention with, 155–57; mealtime, communication during, 129; military life style and, 16–26; normative pressures on, 23–24; nuclear, 10; policymaking and, 13–14, 29–30, 144; retention decisions and, 37–55; role definitions, 15; routines in, 151–52; small group associations, 169–71; social environment and, 153; societal changes affecting, 5–6; value consensus, 145–59; well-being, 169–70. *See also* family life satisfaction; work-family linkages
Family Adaptation and Family Cohesion Evaluation Scores, 152
family life satisfaction: conceptualization of, 144; sense of community and, 169–70; social exchange theory and,

148–50, 157; value-based approach, 145–59; variables in, 143–59

Fein, M., 64

Fine, M., 86

foreign countries, duty time in, 22–23

Forgionne, A. F., 86

Gasser, R. D., 87

geographic mobility. *See* relocations

Gilley, M., 169

Goffman, E., 8

Gongla, P. A., 88

grades, self-esteem and, 125

grieving process, 18

group cohesiveness, 171–73

Hall, R. H., 62

Hamilton, G., 144

Hanson, S. M. H., 86

Hertz, R., 98, 99

Herzberg, Frederick, 63

Hiller, D., 98

Homans, G. C., 148

home ownership, relocations and, 19–20

household division of labor: dual-career couples, 101–2, 106, 107; satisfaction with Air Force and, 110, 111

identity: of children, 124; military's provision of, 26; relocations and, 19

income: division of household labor and, 101–2; dual-career couples, 99; military vs. civilian families, 19; purchase of civilian services and, 174; single parents, 81; work–family linkages and, 60

Industrial Revolution, 164

injury, risk of, 17

institutions, greedy, 8, 14, 64–65, 73

isolation: of children, 122, 126; from outside world, 8, 167; of single parents, 87, 90; uniform and, 8

job satisfaction: Air Force and, 64–67, 108, 110–11; civilian vs. military groups, 73–74; demographics and, 62–63, 70–72; dual-career couples,

100–101, 105, 107; extrinsic factors, 63–64, 66, 71, 74; family responsibilities and, 39; gender and, 86; Herzberg's two-factor theory, 63–64; intrinsic factors, 63, 65–66, 71, 74; job-related characteristics, 63–64, 71–72; management policy and, 64, 66–67, 71, 74; marital quality and, 67–69, 72–74; quality of life and, 16, 59; security needs and, 120; spillover from family, 60–61; spousal support and, 52

Kanter, R. M., 59

Kelley, H. H., 153

Keshet, F. H., 81

King, N., 64

Klemer, R. H., 150

Koopman, E. J., 86

language barriers, 23

length of service, 22–23

Levine, James A., 122

Levinger, G., 149, 150

life cycle: career patterns and, 53; military demands and, 26; research needs, 186; retention decisions and, 41

Locke, E. A., 59

London, J., 60

loneliness, girls vs. boys, 126

Loveland-Cherry, Carol J., 86

Lowenstein, J. S., 86

low intensity conflicts, 4

McCubbin, H. I., 145, 146, 151–52

management policy, 64, 66–67, 71, 74. *See also* policymaking

Margolis, D. R., 123

Marine Corps: overseas stations, 22; separation time, 20

marital quality: dual-career couples, 102, 106, 107; family life satisfaction and, 144; job satisfaction and, 60–75, 67–69, 72–74; satisfaction with Air Force and, 108–9, 110, 111, 112; value consensus and, 150–51. *See also* marriage

marriage: affectional expression in, 68; children's rating of, 129; companionship in, 69; consensus in, 68; emotional adjustment to, 10; of enlisted men, 4–5; enrichment training, 112; equity in, 182; expectations in, 154; individual's perception of, 40–41; retention decisions and, 52; satisfaction with, 67–69; stages in, 14–15; tension in, 68–69; transcultural, 23; value consensus in, 150–51. *See also* parents; spouses
Maxwell, J. W., 150
men: family demands on, 10, 11; as principal caregivers, 22; role expectations, 5, 11; support networks of, 108, 111
military: belongingness and, 168; benefits of, 9, 25–26, 166; changing nature of, 4–5; children and, 117–38; cohesive communities in, 171–73; company towns of, 163–75; control patterns, 164; demands on families, 7–8, 11–12, 16–26; dual-career cuples in, 97–98, 99–112; family life satisfaction and, 157; as greedy institution, 14, 64–65, 73; individual volition in, 16; as institution vs. occupation, 9; isolation and, 8, 87; masculine culture in, 24–25, 125, 135–36; normative constraints of, 23–24; personnel policies, 143–44; risks in; 17–18, 120–21; single members' perceptions of, 41; single parents in, 82, 89; small group associations and, 169–71; social changes and, 4–6; women in, 30, 100. *See also* work-family linkages
mobility, geographic. *See* relocations
Mobley, W. H., 42
Moos, B. S., 151, 153, 155
Moos, R. H., 151, 153, 155
Mortimer, J. T., 60, 62
Moskos, C. C., 9, 16, 166
mothers. *See* parents
motivation, institutional mechanisms for, 9–10
Myers, L. J., 86

National Military Family Association, 12
Navy: assignments away from home, 22, 82; retention studies, 42; separation time, 20; social isolation and, 87
Nida, Patricia, 121
Nienstadt, B. C., 86
noncommissioned officers, retention of, 37
norms: socialization process and, 16; work-family linkages and, 7
nuclear families, demands of, 10
nuclear weapons, military changes and, 4
Nye, F. I., 149

occupational status, job satisfaction and, 71
officers: dual-career couples, 99; relocations and, 18, 22–23; retention of, 37; social pressures, 24
off-post housing, junior enlisted personnel and, 5
Olson, D. H., 145, 146, 151, 152–53, 154
on-post housing: availability of, 166; enlisted personnel and, 5; separations and, 27; social pressures and, 24
Orthner, D. K., 42, 82, 84, 85, 86, 87, 90, 124, 126, 181–83
Otto, H., 156

parents: childcare locations and, 84; coping strategies and, 134; daughters' interaction with, 130; drug/alcohol problems of, 132; socialization role, 122; social networks, 86. *See also* men; women
Parents Without Partners, 87
peacetime force, need for, 39
Peeters, V. E., 86
Pellegrin, R. J., 4
Pett, M. A., 86
Pittman, J. F., 42
policymaking: children's needs and, 137; enlisted personnel and, 29; family impacts, 13–14, 29–30, 144; needs assessments and, 185–86; re-

actionary, 180; research and, 179–
80; retention decisions and, 38; single
parents and, 88–89
pregnancy, separation during, 27
Presser, H. B., 22
prestige, job satisfaction and, 62–63

Quinn, R. P., 62

race, job satisfaction and, 62, 71
Raiha, N. K., 100
rank: development of relationships
across, 170; family effects of, 24; satisfaction with Air Force and, 108
readiness: family life satisfaction and,
144; quality of life expenditures and,
165, 166; sense of community and,
169; single parents and, 82; turnover
and, 37
reenlistment. *See* retention
relational skills, realization of values
and, 147, 148
relocations: adjustments to, 127, 135;
assistance in, 12; children and, 127,
131, 135, 136; depression and, 127;
dual-career couples, 99, 102; effects
of, 18–20; gender adjustment differences, 126; group cohesiveness and,
174; life cycle and, 26–27; positive
implications, 121; research needs,
184; satisfaction with Air Force and,
109, 111, 112; single parents and, 82
Repetti, R., 98
residence, combined with workplace, 9
retention decisions: career cycle and,
41; dual-career couples, 100; family
factors, 5, 37–55; life cycle and, 41;
literature on, 39–42; marital status
and, 52; quality of life expenditures
and, 165, 166; single persons and,
41; spousal support and, 39, 40–41,
43, 52
retirees, military-civilian links and, 172
retirement benefits, 25
rewards, social exchange theory and,
148
role cycling, 53

role expectations: adolescent females,
130; division of household labor and,
102; dual-career couples, 98–99,
101, 106; gender-based, 5–6, 11;
learning and, 14; military norms, 9,
25; single parents, 79, 80–83, 88;
time demands and, 81; women and,
83
role-strain theory, 53
Rosenthal, K. M., 81

Sabatelli, R. M., 151, 153–55
Santrock, J. W., 87
Satir, V., 150
Scanzoni, J., 181–83
Schneider, R., 169
Schwebel, A. I., 86
security needs, 25, 120–21
Segal, M., 100
self-esteem: gender differences, 124–
25; single parents, 86; stress levels
and, 132; youth, 124–26
separations: civilian, 7; effects of, 20–
21; life-cycle and, 27; overseas duty
and, 23; peacetime, 20; single parents and, 84; wartime, 18, 20–21
sexual behavior, standards of, 5
shift work, 7, 21–22
single parents, 79–92; active-duty, 11,
82; childcare needs, 84, 89–90; children's relationship with, 83–84; co-
parenting relationships, 84–85; discretionary time, 81–82; as employees, 88; enlistment policies and, 89;
income, 81; personal well-being of,
85–88; policymaking and, 88–89;
productivity of, 80; responsibilities of,
88, 91–92; role strain, 79, 80–83;
societal changes and, 6; support programs for, 90. *See also* divorce
social change: institutional adaptation
to, 9–10; military families and, 5–6
social exchange theory, 148–50, 157,
181
social identity. *See* identity
socialization: children, 120, 122–23;
norms and, 16; wives, 24; work influences, 60

social status, work-family linkages and, 60

Spanier, G. B., 67

Spillover model, of work-family linkages, 3–4, 6, 59–75

spouses: civilian vs. military, 100–101; employment of; foreign-born, 23; interpersonal support for, 168; job satisfaction and, 52; relocations and, 19, 23; retention decisions and, 39, 40–41, 52; role obligations, 11, 24; separation effects, 20; social pressures, 24, *See also* dual-career couples

stability, children's need for, 121–22

stress: children and, 124, 128–34; coping strategies, 131, 132–34, 182; depression and, 127; family problems and, 132; predictable, 28; realization of values and, 147; relocation and, 131; research needs, 184; role conflicts and, 16; sense of community and, 169–70

supervisors: family needs and, 15; socialization of, 16

support networks: dual-career couples, 105; children, 121, 123; families as, 128; informal vs. formal, 25; primary group ties, 171–72; relocations and, 19; satisfaction with Air Force and, 108, 111; separations and, 27; single parents, 86–87; stress management and, 131, 133–34

support programs. *See* assistance/support programs

systems theory, 181

Taylor, C. M., 87

technology, training needed for, 4–5

terrorist attacks, 23

Thibaut, J. W., 153

Thompson, A. I., 151–52

Thompson, E. H., 88

training, costs of, 37, 80

turnover: civilian workplace, 38; positive implications, 40; quality of basic services and, 172; training costs and, 37; voluntary, 38

unemployment, military vs. civilian spouses, 19

uniform, isolation using, 8

values: congruity among family members, 147–48; defined, 146–47; expectations and, 155; family life satisfaction and, 145–59; social exchange theory and, 149

Van Der Veen, F., 150, 154

violence: advocacy programs and, 12; military culture and, 24–25

Voydanoff, P., 60, 73

Walter Reed Army Institute of Research (WRAIR), 170

Warshak, R. A., 87

Weiss, R. S., 87

welfare capitalism, 167

well-being: alienation and, 126; self-esteem and, 124; stress and, 131, 132

Who Will Raise the Children? (Levine), 122

women: employment of, 5, 97–112; family demands, 10–11; in military, 30, 100; role strain and, 83; social changes and, 11. *See also* spouses

work: hours of, 7, 21–22; satisfaction with (*See* job satisfaction) socially constructed reality at, 15

work-family linkages: bureaucratic environment and, 167; career-family life cycles and, 26–27; hierarchical structure and, 25; individual approaches, 15–16; institutional approaches, 6–12; interpersonal approaches, 14–15; models of, 3, 6, 60–61, 180–83; organizational approaches, 12–14; research needs, 183–87; retention decisions and, 37–55; role expectations and, 16, 53; single parents and, 79–92; societal changes and, 6; spillover model, 3–4, 6, 59–75; structural approaches, 12–14. *See also* families

Yancey, W. L., 102
youth: alienation of, 126; coping strategies, 132–34; psychological well-
being, 124–27; relocations and, 26;
research needs, 185. *See also* children
Youth in Transition (Orthner et al.),
124, 126

About the Editors and Contributors

GARY L. BOWEN, Ph.D., ACSW, is an Associate Professor and Chairperson, Services to Families and Children Specialization, School of Social Work, the University of North Carolina at Chapel Hill. He has worked extensively over the last decade with the various service branches in the Department of Defense, and has published extensively on the nature of work and family demands in the U.S. military. Under contract with the Department of the Army, he is currently exploring the nature of the interdependencies between work and family life in the military, and the impact of military policies and practices on the nature of the work–family interface.

DENNIS K. ORTHNER, Ph.D., is Professor and Director of the Human Services Research and Design Laboratory, School of Social Work, the University of North Carolina at Chapel Hill. He has been studying work and family issues in the military services and in corporations for many years. He is on the advisory board of the National Military Family Association and has conducted significant studies of servicemembers and their families for all branches of the armed services. Dr. Orthner also works with U.S. government agencies and corporate policy groups to develop better ways of meeting the needs of organizations and families.

MARTHA M. GIDDINGS, Ph.D., is a Developmental Psychologist at the University of Georgia, and maintains a private practice focusing on the problems of children.

BARBARA J. JANOFSKY, Ph.D., is an Associate, Caliber Associates, Fairfax, Virginia.

JAMES A. MARTIN, Ph.D., is a Lieutenant Colonel in the Army Medical Service Corps and currently the Deputy Chief, Department of Military Psychiatry, Walter Reed Army Institute of Research, Washington, D.C.

PETER A. NEENAN, Ph.D., is a Research Associate, School of Social Work, the University of North Carolina at Chapel Hill.

WILLIAM H. QUINN, Ph.D., is an Associate Professor of Child and Family Development and Clinical Director of the Marriage and Family Therapy Clinic at the University of Georgia.

MADY WECHSLER SEGAL, Ph.D., is an Associate Professor of Sociology at the University of Maryland, Guest Scientist at the Walter Reed Army Institute of Research, and Visiting Professor at the United States Military Academy (1988–89).

DAVID W. WRIGHT, Ph.D., is an Assistant Professor, Department of Human Development and Family Studies, Kansas State University.